Alexander Balloch Grosart, Sir Richard Baker

Meditations and Disquisitions Upon the First Psalm

Alexander Balloch Grosart, Sir Richard Baker

Meditations and Disquisitions Upon the First Psalm

ISBN/EAN: 9783744660594

Printed in Europe, USA, Canada, Australia, Japan

Cover: Foto ©Lupo / pixelio.de

More available books at **www.hansebooks.com**

MEDITATIONS AND DISQUISITIONS

UPON

THE FIRST PSALM;

THE PENITENTIAL PSALMS;

AND

SEVEN CONSOLATORY PSALMS.

BY

SIR RICHARD BAKER, *KNIGHT*.

Author of "A Chronicle of the Kings of England," etc., etc.

(FIRST PRINTED, 1639—1640.)

A NEW EDITION.

WITH BRIEF EXPLANATORY NOTES, AND A TEXTUAL INDEX.

With a Memorial-Introduction by the Rev. A. B. Grosart, LL.D., F.S.A., Editor of the Works, and Biographer, of Sibbes, Brooks, and Gilpin, in "Nichol's Puritan Divines."

LONDON:
CHARLES HIGHAM, 27A, FARRINGDON STREET.
1882.

CONTENTS.

	PAGE
MEMORIAL-INTRODUCTION	ix
MEDITATIONS AND DISQUISITIONS UPON THE FIRST PSALM OF DAVID	1
MEDITATIONS AND DISQUISITIONS UPON THE SEVEN PSALMS OF DAVID, COMMONLY CALLED THE PENITENTIAL PSALMS— . . .	95

    NAMELY, PSALM VI. . . . 99
        " XXXII. . . . 127
        " XXXVIII. . . . 149
        " LI. . . . 171
        " CII. . . . 227
        " CXXX. . . . 257
        " CXLIII. . . . 273

MEDITATIONS AND DISQUISITIONS UPON SEVEN CONSOLATORY PSALMS OF DAVID— . . 301

    NAMELY, PSALM XXIII. . . . 305
        " XXVII. . . . 321
        " XXX. . . . 343
        " XXXIV. . . . 359
        " LXXXIV. . . . 379
        " CIII. . . . 395
        " CXVI. . . . 411

TEXTUAL INDEX 433

MEMORIAL-INTRODUCTION.

THERE have been so many Worthies in Church and State, earlier and later, who have borne the name of SMITH—from sage and grave Sir THOMAS SMITH (or Smyth) to "silver-tongued" HENRY SMITH,—whose sermons are as *quick* to-day as when first preached to vast crowds of "gentle and simple;" and from JOHN SMITH of Cambridge, to JOHN SMITH, "the Essex Dove," and SAMUEL SMITH, of Prittlewell, —richest, rarest, memorablest of our minor Puritan divines— JOHN SHEFFIELD alone excepted; and from ADAM SMITH to SYDNEY SMITH and ALEXANDER SMITH, and present-day GEORGE SMITH, of Coalville,—man of the big brave heart for the helpless, whether in brick-field, canal-boat, or gipsy camp,—leaving out of account many and many others of the multitudinous clan,—that I, for one, shrink from harsh or blaming word of any SMITH. And yet in the knowledge and recollection that Sir RICHARD BAKER—whose books on some of the "Psalms" after so long a time are herein reproduced— left an Autobiography which his son-in-law, "one SMITH," destroyed, it is difficult to repress an objurgation. Covering as his life did so much of the brilliant Elizabethan-Jacobean period, it gives one a heartache to think of how much perished when this ignoble SMITH turned to basest use the Autobiography of such a man. Now, we can but sorrowfully indulge the "Pleasures of Imagination" over it.*

---

* "Wood's Athenæ" (*s. n.*) is our authority for the destruction of this MS., and as his informant was Sir Richard's own daughter, there can be no doubt about it. The passage is as follows: "He also wrote his own life, which he left in MS. behind him; burnt or made waste paper by one Smith, of Paternoster Row, who married one of his daughters."

Perchance it had lacked the zest of SAMUEL PEPYS' immortal "Diary," but it could hardly have failed to illumine names and events and circumstances of a grand period, that should have been right welcome.

The BAKERS are a very old English family. Limiting ourselves to our Worthy's line of Cranbrook and Sissinghurst in Kent, I bring together here various scattered notices of the name and family—helped therein by the fine enthusiasm of a son of Cranbrook.*

1. ADAM BAKER, de Cranebrook, co. Kent, was living temp. King John.
2. JOHN, fil. ADAM BAKER, de Cranebrook, was plaintiff in a plea concerning lands 55th of Henry III., A.D. 1271.
3. THOMAS BAKER, de Cranebrook, paid the subsidy A.D. 1273.
4. NICHOLAS BAKER, of Cranbrook, was living temp. Edward II.; died before the 1st of Edward III.; was defendant in a plea concerning land; paid the various subsidies temp. Edward II.; married Matilda, a widow, in the 12th year of Edward II., in which year she paid 11s. subsidy.
5. HENRY BAKER, of Smithside in Cranbrook, paid 2s. subsidy, 1st Edward III.; died before the 20th of Edward III.
6. THOMAS BAKER, of Cranbrook, paid the subsidies; lived in or about the year A.D. 1347 to 1396; is mentioned in a suit "coram regi," 1371.
7. HENRY BAKER, of Cranbrook, paid the subsidy 1417; was defendant in a plea concerning land in the same year; and had (at least) two sons, viz., Thomas and Henry.
8. THOMAS BAKER, of Cranbrook, paid 14s. subsidy in 1419, and again in 1431.
9. HENRY BAKER, brother of last—Thomas,—paid the subsidy 1431; his will was proved at Canterbury 1477; mentions two daughters.
10. THOMAS BAKER, of Cranbrook; will dated 3rd February, 1493; proved at Canterbury 1497; married Benet, daughter of ——, who was living 1504.
11. RICHARD BAKER, of Cranbrook, is mentioned in the will of his uncle (Thomas, No. 10), 1493; also Henry Baker is similarly mentioned.
12. RICHARD BAKER, of Cranbrook; will dated 7th August, 1504; proved at Canterbury 15th November, 1504.
    James Baker died before his father, 1493; mentioned in will of his father, 1504.
13. RICHARD BAKER (No. 12) had two more sons, viz., Thomas

---

* Viz., Mr. W. Tarbutt, of Cranbrook, whose unpretending tractates on his native place's memorables, I place far above your huge and too often empty "County Histories." See also Appendix to this Introduction.

Baker, who inherited lands at Barwash, in Sussex, mentioned under the will of his grandfather (No. 10), A.D. 1493; was ancestor of the mother of JOHN SELDEN: and Robert Baker, mentioned in his father's will (No. 11), 1504; also Joane, married ——, mentioned in the will of her brother, Sir John (of famous memory, as below); Elizabeth, mentioned in her grandfather's will (No. 10), 1493; and Catharine.*

These BAKERS, though thus leaving traces of being above the "commonalty" by their payment of "subsidies," and by their "lands and goods" distributed in their quaint-languaged Wills, have no place in history, except in so far as the Baker motherhood of JOHN SELDEN imparts lustre to them all. But we have now reached one of the name and line who filled, and nobly, a large space in his long-drawn generation, viz., SIR JOHN BAKER, son of Richard Baker (No. 12). This Sir John Baker was successively Recorder of London, Chancellor of the Exchequer to Henry VIII., Attorney-General (1539), and Speaker to the House of Commons. LLOYD in his "State Worthies" (*s.n.*) grows almost eloquent in his memoir of him. Thus :—

"There is one of this name remarkable in every king's reign since the conquest. There is one now renowned in this: 1. For integrity, to be neither awed nor corrupted. 2. For a spirit public as nature, neither moved with particular respect, nor terminated in a private design."

Then he tells an incident wherein the "stout Knight" figured :—

"The French were so insolent in London, the 8th year of Henry 8th, that when one Williamson, a carpenter, was about to pay for two pigeons he bought, a Frenchman takes them out of his hand, saying, *They were no meat for carpenters*, but for my Lord Embassadour; who concerned himself so much in the case that he had Williamson imprisoned. SIR JOHN BAKER sued the Embassadour for the man; who answered, *That the English knave deserved to be hanged for denying anything to a Frenchman.* Whereupon Sir John replied, *You know not that you are in London:* a notable reply, considering that the city was up next day against strangers in so desperate a tumult, that none could suppress but Sir Thomas More, and none could rebuke but Sir William Kingston and Sir John Baker."

---

* Manning in his "Lives of the Speakers of the House of Commons" (1850), pp. 196-9, has a full but poor memoir of Sir John Baker. Incidentally he states that "a junior branch of Richard Baker, of Rushington, left an only child, Margaret, who was the mother of the learned John Seldon." *Sic*—not even so great a name spelled accurately.

Again:

"Judge Montague was the only person that durst dispute King Edward's will; Judge Hales and Sir John Baker, the only Counsellors that durst refuse it."

Finally:

"This constant and firm resolution to stick to his duty and loyalty brought him to his grave in peace and honour; having been a faithful counsellor and servant to Henry 8th, Edward 6th, Queen Mary, and Queen Elizabeth."

The last an inaccuracy, as he died in a few days after Elizabeth's accession.

Sir John Baker had "large possessions," but his "seat" was at Sissinghurst, near Cranbrook. He erected the now long ruinous mansion-house of Sissinghurst. He married (1) Catherine, daughter of Richard Sackville, Esq., before the year 1524, in which year she is mentioned in the will of her father. Her mother was aunt of Anne Boleyn. He married (2) Elizabeth, daughter and coheir of Thomas Dynely, relict of George Barrett. Her son, Edward Barrett, was left a silver cup, with arms, by Sir John Baker, his step father.

Sir John Baker had issue two sons and four daughters, viz.:—

| JOHN, RICHARD. | CATHARINE, MARY, CECILIA, ELIZABETH. |

From reasons that have not come down, the eldest son—father of our Sir Richard—was disinherited by his father. Certes, Richard his brother, the second son, was in possession of Sissinghurst in 1573, in which year he was knighted by Elizabeth on occasion of a State visit and "Progress" to Sissinghurst—as told in the "Progresses" of the great Queen. Be this as it may, John Baker, eldest son of the eminent Sir John Baker, being then of London, married Catharine, daughter of REGINALD SCOTT OF SCOTT'S HALL, about twenty miles from Cranbrook, not far from Ashford. He had issue two sons and three daughters, according to Harleian MS. 840, f. 42 b:—

```
         JOHN BAKER = CATHERINA, d.
                  |    Reginald Scott,
                  |    and d. of William
                  |    Kemp his wife.
   ┌──────────┬───────┴───┬─────────┬──────────┐
 JOCOSA (or  MARIA   RICHARDUS  THOMAS   ELIZABETH
 JOESSA).
```

The "Richardus" was our Sir RICHARD BAKER. On the authority of ANTHONY-A-WOOD (from one of his daughters), RICHARD was born at the great mansion-house of Sissinghurst. The words are specific enough: "he was born in Kent, particularly [as I have been informed by his daughter [the wife of —— Bury [a Scotchman], a seedsman living at the Frying Pan in Newgate Market in London], at Sissinghurst before mentioned." This seems open to doubt, unless we conclude that its possessor (RICHARD, second son, *ut supra*) was on friendly terms with his disinherited elder brother, and that the parents were on a visit at the time. His grandfather had died in 1558. He was born in 1568. Whatever lessening of estate the disinheritance of his father involved, all the circumstances seem to warrant us in assuming that Master Richard was well-born. His mother's parentage reminds us that he was allied through her to keen-visioned, strong-brained Reginald Scot, of "Witchcraft" scepticism renown—whose book is being revived as this is written.*
Our first definite glimpse of him is that he was "entered a commoner of Hart Hall, Oxford, in 1584, and matriculated in Michaelmas term that year as a "Kentish man born and the son of a gentleman, being then in the 16th year of his age" (= birth 1568, as before). At the time "several of the family of the Scots" were in the said Hall. So writeth Anthony-a-Wood and all the authorities. One famous chamber-fellow he had in (afterwards Sir) HENRY WOTTON. He remained for three years at the University, mainly occupied, it would seem, with logic and philosophy. So again Anthony-a-Wood. But either he remained longer than the

---

* Prospectus and proposals of a careful reprint of this remarkable treatise reach me from my bookish friend Dr. Brinsley Nicholson, of London. May the pious scheme succeed!

alleged "three years," or he subsequently returned, inasmuch as in the FASTI there is this entry:—

Creations.

1594. On the ninth of July, being the day after the act had been finished, these following persons were actually created Master of Arts.
Rich. Baker, Esq.*

He proceeded on leaving Oxford to "one of the Inns of Court." Apparently his tarrying or "residence" there was brief; for speedily he is found "beyond the seas," and "nothing omitted by his parents to make him an accomplished person." This "travelling" and becoming a travelled gentleman (eheu! most are merely travelling, only an elect few travelled) was the *mode* of the time and onward, as WILLIAM COWPER in England and ROBERT BURNS in Scotland pungently satirized.

On his return he must have again "resided" in the Inns of Court. There followed admittance to the Court (of James). On May 17th, 1603, he was knighted at Theobalds, "at which time," the Athenæ informs us, "he lived at Highgate, near London, and was esteemed a most compleat and learned person,"—adding, by inevitable prolepsis, "the benefit of which he reaped in his old age, when his considerable estate was, thro' suretyship, very much impaired." This "suretyship" was *the* master-sorrow of his life. The thing is obscure, and probably never now will be elucidated; but the matter-of-fact seems to have been that, having married Margaret, a daughter of SIR GEORGE MAINWARING, of Ightfield, in Shropshire, he became "surety" for certain members of this family. The date of the marriage has not been ascertained; but the "suretyship" in all probability came some years subsequent. In 1620 he was High Sheriff of Oxfordshire, being then Lord of Middle Aston and of other lands therein; and, continues Wood, "if I mistake not, a justice of the peace." He had issue three sons and three daughters, viz., Thomas (who was knighted before 1638), Mainwaring, and Arthur, Cecilia, Ann, and Margaret.

---

* Wood also mentions this *in loco* in Athenæ (*s.n.*)

By 1635, at latest, he was in trouble. JOSEPH HUNTER, in his *Chorus Votum* (s.n.), cites an original letter preserved in the Exchequer from Sir Francis Cottington to the Remembrancer (17th October, 1635), desiring him to send a "Particular" of the "lands and tenements of Sir Richard Baker in co. of Oxford, as they stand seised in the King's hands for the several debts of JOHN TEMPLE, Esq., SIR RICHARD BROOK, and DANIEL GROOME, Esq., and returned to his office." In our dim light it looks extraordinary that our good Knight should have become "surety" for so many. Whether these belonged to the Mainwaring house I cannot say. From 1635 onward to his death he lay in the Fleet Prison. Contemporary and later accounts give terrible revelations of the state of this and other prisons. I like to believe that in some way or other the confinement was mitigated, and that, though held in bondage, he was able to secure certain indulgences. Thus the whole of his books must have been written in the Fleet Prison; so that he must have been allowed writing materials. Contrasting him with SIR JOHN ELIOT in the Tower, I suppose a distinction was drawn between treatment of a State prisoner and a simple debtor. I suspect that, in addition to the "surety" obligations, Sir Richard was himself in debt, perhaps in strenuous efforts to meet the former, *e.g.*, in the Epistle-dedicatory of his "Meditations and Disquisitions" on "Seven Consolatorie Psalmes," he gratefully acknowledges the forgiveness of a "great debt" by Lord Craven. "I shall," he says, "perhaps move envy to say, Quæ te tam læta tulerunt sæcula? but for myself, I am bound to say it, who have received from your Lordship indeed a great favour, *the remission of a great debt.*"* Other epistles-dedicatory to

---

* William, 1st Baron and Earl of Craven, was eldest son of Sir William Craven, Lord Mayor of London. He was "much affected with military exercises from his youth, and signalized himself in Germany and the Netherlands under Henry Prince of Orange." Having gained much honour, he was on his return knighted at Newmarket, March 4th, 1626, and on the 12th of the same month raised to the degree and dignity of a Baron of the realm, by the title of Lord Craven of Hampstead-Marshall in co. Berks. In 1631 he was commander of forces sent to aid Gustavus, King of Sweden, then in arms in Germany in defence of the Protestants; and when that monarch, with Frederick, Elector-Palatine and titular King of Bohemia, marched out of Bavaria in February 1632, and came before the strong castle of Crutzenack, the English volunteers by their bravery in three assaults obliged the garrison to surrender,

those of his own house—as we shall see—and to the all-potent Earl of Dorset and Mary Countess of Dorset, brought, it is to be feared, slender alleviation of either his poverty or his sorrows.*

The remainder of his life from 1635 has for landmarks only the composition and publication of his several books, as follows:—

(*a*) Cato Variegatus, or Catoes Morall Distichs: Translated and Paraphras'd, with variations of Expressing, in English verse. By Sr. Richard Baker, Knight. 1636. (4to.)

(*b*) Meditations and Disquisitions upon the Lord's Prayer. 1637. 3rd edit., 1638 ; 4th edit., 1640. (4to.)

(*c*) Translation of Letters of M. Balsac : 4 Pts. 1638. (8vo.)

(*d*) Meditations and Disquisitions upon the Seven Psalmes of David, commonly called the Penitentiall Psalmes. 1639. (4to.)

(*e*) Meditations and Disquisitions upon Seven Consolatorie Psalmes of David. 1640. (4to.)

(*f*) Meditations and Disquisitions upon the First Psalme of David. 1640. (4to.)

(*g*) An Apologie for Lay-Mens Writing on Divinity. With a short Meditation upon the Fall of Lucifer. 1641. (18mo.)

(*h*) Meditations and Motives for Prayer upon the Seaven dayes of the Week. 1641-2. (18mo.)

(*i*) His "Chronicle:" 1st edit., 1641 ; 2nd, 1653; 3rd, 1660; 4th, 1665; 5th, 1670; 6th, 1674 ; 7th, 1679; 8th, 1684 ; 9th, 1696 ; 10th, 1730; 11th, 1733. (folios.)

---

and the capitulation was signed by Lord Craven and Boulin, Quarter-master General of the King of Sweden's army. Lord Craven was wounded in the assaults, and coming into the King of Sweden's presence, was told by him, "He adventured so desperately, he bid his younger brother fair play for his estates." Afterwards he was sent to aid the Elector-Palatine, who having besieged Linaegea in 1637, a battle ensued, wherein the Emperor's army being victorious, the Elector with difficulty escaped by flight, and his helpers, Prince Rupert and Lord Craven, were taken prisoners. Obtaining his liberty, he went into the service of the States of Holland, under the Prince of Orange, where he remained until the restoration of Charles II. Though he did not personally serve Charles I., he sent him "considerable supplies," as Charles II. admitted by advancing him to the higher degree of Viscount Craven of Uffington in the same co. of Berks, and Earl Craven of Craven in Yorkshire. The "Parliament" pronounced inevitably his estates forfeited, though it was hesitatingly done. All were "restored" at the Restoration. To the last he was a soldier. He lived to so long as April 9th, 1697, dying then aged 88 years and 10 months. These old warriors had the "fear of God" before them, and so the Epistle-dedicatory of Sir Richard Baker was quite in keeping.

* The Earl of Dorset needs no annotation. He was *the* Dorset of History and of Clarendon. His wife Mary, daughter and heiress of Sir George Curzon, of Croxhall, in co. Derby, Knight, is also historical. By universal testimony she was a lady "accomplished in all virtues, and of excellent judgment." She had the educational custody of the royal children. I suppose she stands alone as the only woman ever decreed by the Houses of Lords and Commons, a public funeral. This took place on 3rd September, 1645.

(*j*) Translation of "Discourses upon Corn. Tacitus." By Malvezzi. 1642. (folio.)

Posthumously published.

(*k*) *Theatrum Redivivum*, or The Theatre Vindicated by Sir Richard Baker, in answer to Mr. Pryn's Historio-Mastix. Wherein his groundless Assertions against Stage-Plays are discovered, his mistaken Allegations of the *Fathers* manifested, as also what he calls his *Reasons*, to be nothing but his Passions. 1662. (12mo.)

This is the same book that was re-issued with a new title-page in 1670, entitled, "*Theatrum Triumphans*," though Allibone and the Bibliographers describe them as distinct works.*

(*l*) Besides these his published works, there is preserved in Sloane MSS., No. 881, an unpublished MS. by him. It is lettered on the back

Baker
on
Honour.

Its title-page thus runs:—Honour | Discours'd of | in the | Theory | of it, and the | Practice | with | Directions | for a | Prudent Conduct; | on Occurrences of | Incivility ; | and | Civility.

There is a brief epistle-dedicatory, the autograph signature to which has been facsimiled beneath the portrait for us:—

To the Right Reverend Father in God, Henry
Lord Bishop of London.

My Lord !

In regard this Discourse Treats of the Gentleman, and the Christian ; of the Humanity, Sweetnesse, and Generosity, inseparable from great and exalted Minds; the Presumption of sending it abrode under your Lordship's Patronage may (possibly) appear the more excusable in My Lord

Yor Lo^{pp's} most Dutyfull, and
Obedient Servant
RICHARD BAKER.†

Of these, *d*, *e*, *f* form the present Reprint, being the whole of his "Meditations and Disquisitions" on the Psalms. Before noticing them, it may be acceptable to pause for a

---

* Allibone's huge "Dictionary of British and American Authors" is an extremely illiterate and unworthy book, mainly made up from Library and booksellers' catalogues and the like, rarely *from actual knowledge of the books*. It is useful in a way, but scarcely ever to be trusted : full where not required, and empty where it ought to be full. He blunders over Baker's Psalm books, misreading special title-pages prefixed to "Psalme li." and "The Three last Psalmes," in the treatise on "The Penitentiall Psalmes ;" *vide* pp. 167 and 225 of this reprint. The present volume includes all he wrote and published on Psalms.

† I hope to utilize this MS. in annotating Hoby's "Courtier." It is not impossible that the Publisher of the present volume may print it in whole or part for special lovers of our elder worthies.

b

little over the others. The first, "*Cato Variegatus*" (*a*), is in my judgment a delightful and suggestive book. It has fallen out of sight, and on its rare chance-occurrences fetches a large price. It combines all the venerable Author's characteristics of ripe learning, fine thinking, gleaming wit, and quaint speech. I think I do not err in believing that selected specimens of these "Distichs," or couplets, will be welcome to all who care for his "Psalmes." Accordingly I shall give a good century of them. They will reward study. They are not to be merely glanced at and done with.

In his Epistle to the Reader in apologizing for his "Periphrases" (Quarles's word also, contemporaneously,) and "Paraphrases" he maintains his liberty in that, while he may be censured to have used it too liberally, "yet so long as *Sensus est in tuto*, and nothing is said but what is drawn *E potentia verborum*," he expects "to be excused at least if not commended." Sooth to say, the more literal translations are "bare grain," while the "paraphrases or collateral conceits" are in not a few instances memorable and weighty. He thus pleasantly explains his rule: "all tend to the same sence; and the direct translations are sent before, as set alwayes next the Latine," and then "they are but after the fashion of young men; who weare thin cloaths in cold winter, but have good warm waste-cotes vnder them, and some men, may bee of that disposition, to take as much delight in the conceit of the Expressing as in the expressing of the conceit." Finally: "Some men will perhaps say; Here is variety indeed, but one well done were better than all: what good doth choice where All is Refuse stuffe? It is true; but let this man bring better stuffes out of his warehouse, and then, let these be thrown away: till then, he may content himselfe with these: they may keepe him warme though not make him fine. And seeing there is variety of Iudgements, it is not vnfit to tender them variety of expressings: some may take better with one Iudgement, some with another, and oftentimes one expressing gives lustre to another, and makes the reason which lay hid before, to looke abroad; which is not yet another thing but the same thing in another light: and lastly, being Precepts of Morality, they cannot have too many allurements. Howsoever it be, the worke I am sure is such as need not repent me of one moneth spent in writing it; nor thee, whosoever thou art, of one houre spent in reading it." These modest apologies (in the old sense) fittingly introduce our String of Pearls from the book. The headings are ours.

1.   *Public Worship.*
God's outward worship, must not be neglected;
But 'tis the inward that is most respected.

2.   *Sleep.*
Sleepe not too much: vices will soone be dead
If with the milke of slothe they be not fed.

Not sleepe, but sleeping much, must be withstood:
Much resting makes men restie to all good.

Sleepe's entertainment, must be order'd thus:
Not we to sleepe goe, but sleepe come to us.

Sleepe is both Prodigal's and Miser's crime:
It hoords yet wasts, the chiefest treasure, Time.

Much Sleepe is a betraying Vertue's ward:
It tyes the Senses' hands which are her guard.

Much Opium doth the Senses overcome:
And what is sleepe but Nature's opium?

Sleeping is as the oyle of our Life's lampe:
Little refreshes; too much, makes a dampe.

3.   *The Tongue.*
The Tongue hath this one rare yet common notion:
It Vertue shewes no lesse in Rest than Motion.

The stronger the Tongue is, the man's the weaker:
Hee that can hold his tongue, is the best speaker.

The Tongue, both stirres Debate and makes it cease:
He holds peace best that best can hold his peace.

The Tongue may thus be encreast or decreast;
Rul'de well, it makes an angell; ill, a beast.

4.   *Luxury.*
Forbeare things hurtfull, though thou hold them deere;
Better hard fare than surfet with good cheere.

Not Gold if over weight worth keeping thinke:
Better goe empty, safe, than laden, sinke.

5.   *Case being altered, alters the case.*
Be gentle or severe, as cause may be:
To change with time is wise men's constancy.

To be now sharpe, now gentle, is no crime :
Wisdome makes men chamelions of time.

6. *Word-combats.*
Words against wordy men, thou must not vse :
That's their owne weapon ; thou must wisdom chuse.

Strive not of talking men, the day to get :
Least it be said, Two parrats are well met.

To strive to put downe men of words, is vaine :
For most have tongue at will, but few have braine.

7. *Spendthrift Kindness.*
Th' account betweene thy friends and thee, so cast :
Thou feast not them, and bring thyselfe to fast.

Be friend to others, but thy owne friend, first :
The kinde foole, of all kindes of fooles, is worst.

8. *Gossips.*
Spread no reports, whatever thy words are :
No text so cleare but that a glosse may marre.

9. *Self-estimate.*
When thou art prais'd, be Iudge thyselfe thereto :
Thou better knowst thyselfe than others doe.

When men praise thee, doe thou judge them, and show
Whether they thee, or thou them, better know.

10. *Conscience.*
Whether men talke aloud, or soft and still :
What is't to thee, if thou have done no ill?

Who doubts men's whispering talk, shew themselves vicious :
'Tis guiltinesse of minde makes men suspitious.

Care not what men betweene them whispering be,
So long as Conscience whispers not to thee.

11. *Fore-think.*
When skies are cleere, take heed of overcast :
Our life, like wine, hath all the lees at last.

12. *Life's uncertainty.*
Since all are mortall, what more vaine can be
Than hope to bury them may bury thee?

What contract canst thou make with Death, that he
Should serve his writs on others, and spare thee?

It is not Hope, but wan hope, to surmize
That thou shalt live to close another's eyes.

Since all our lives are brittle glass and weake,
What reason thine should hold, and others breake?

Thinke not thyself from Death the more at rest
For being young; 'tis greene fruit Death loves best.

The lives of men seeme in two seas to swimme:
Death comes to young folkes, and old goe to him.

Which may we count to Death the greater haster,
The old hath lesse to goe, the young runne faster.

Old folkes so gastly are, and looke so grimme,
That Death fears them as much as they feare him.

13. *Humble Gift.*
When a poore friend for some small thing makes shift,
Looke on the giver's minde, not on the gift.

14. *Naked at both ends of life.*
We came into the world without a clout,
And in as poore a pickle we goe out.

Where life's both ends are in so meane degree,
What matter is't, how meane the middle be?

15. *Fear not dying.*
Betimes thinke on thy last end, and be steady;
He that feares dying is halfe dead allready.

Feare not life's last; each day Death cuts our skore;
And yet not felt: the last will doe no more.

16. *Promise-breaking.*
Thy Promise breaking is the Truth's denying;
And is but a more solid kinde of lying.

17. *Biter bitten.*
When one pretends love that hath no such thought,
Doe thou the like: so Dottrels must be caught.

18. *Flatteries.*
In fawning words, think not true meaning straight:
What good doe trapps vnlesse they have a baite?

19. *Thrift and Cost.*
Account no oddes between things base and deere:
A gilt or wooden dish, make both no cheere.

20. *Life's frailty.*
So fraile is life, dangers so manifold,
That new dayes are but scape-goats of the old.

What's life, or health? what's beauty, strength, or breath?
All is but interest of our debt to death.

Each day that's liv'd is gaind: poore gaine, God wot,
That makes one so much poorer as is got.

If we count that day gayn'd which we have past,
That's lost that's past; and so that's gain'd that's lost.

21.   *Strife.*
Not always strive with friends, thy force to show :
'Tis victory sometimes to take a blow.

'Tis Mastery sometimes to take a Fall :
Hee knowes no manners that still takes the wall:

22.   *Part for Whole.*
Hee's no good Husbandman that will mislike
To sowe a pynte where he may reape a strike.

23.   *Economy.*
As one hand brings in, th' other must lay up ;
Else thou mayst have to dyne, but not to sup.

24.   *Ostentation.*
In keeping Christmas something may be spent,
But not to make the whole year after, Lent.

Thy bounty may have leave sometimes to roame,
But still remember, Love beginnes at home.

25.   *Charities.*
Let Vertue's lustre even to strangers show thee :
Is't not a glory that more love than know thee?

26.   *Foreboding.*
Leave feare of Death ; who can have merry heart,
As long as Feare stands brandishing Death's dart ?

27.   *Ambition.*
Be not aspiring, nor too lofty flie ;
No falls so dangerous as those from high.

Seeke not extremes ; 'tis the conceit of Pride
To thinke it never Flud without Spring-tide.

28.   *Confidences.*
Why shouldst thou make that knowne, which 'tis too much
Thou knowst thyselfe ? sores are not fit to touch.

Blaze not abroad to others thine owne evill :
This were to light a candle to the Devill.

29.   *Reckoning.*
Thinke not that sinnes once done are gone and past :
Time is a Blab, and will tell all at last.

30.   *Little Men.*
Skorne not the strength of men of little size ;
Whom Nature makes lesse strong, she make more wise.

Slight not small statures ; 'tis not said in vaine,
The lesser head, the better is the braine.

Marke Nature's course, and you shall finde she puts
Her choicest wine in runlets, not in buts.

Despise not little men ; 'tis Nature's guise
To give the greater sight to lesser eyes.

Nature is wise, and gives not all to one ;
To some more braine, to others greater bone.

Marke inward worth, and you shall find it then
That lesser bodies make not lesser men.

31. *Retreat not Defeat.* ("Hudibras" in the second anticipated.)
Finding thyselfe too weak, sound a retreat :
We see the conquer'd oft the conquerors beat.

To give ground when there's ods, never disdaine :
He that yeelds now may fight againe, and gaine.

Who yeeld, though loose the day, yet winne the time,
Flee but to fight againe ; fall but to climbe.

32. *Forgotten Words.*
He erres that words of brabbles past, remembers ;
This is to stirre old coales, rak'd up in embers.

33. *Simple Living.*
Vse sparingly thy goods : goods are as oakes ;
Long time in growing, cut down with few strokes.

Spend sparingly : let something be preservd :
No means can serve where no mean is observd.

34. *Wise Folly.*
To be a Foole sometimes, doe not despise :
A folly counterfeit is oft most wise.

Folly sometimes comes out of Wisdome's schoole :
None but wise men can counterfeit a foole.

Wisdome is like the sunne, shines when she list ;
And when she pleases, hides her in a mist.

This we may learne in Observation's schooles :
Fooles cannot be wise men, wise men can fooles.

In stinting wisdome greatest wisdome lies :
No man is ever wise that's over-wise.

If time and place be not before his eyes,
There may be wisdome, yet the man not wise.

He onely wisdome may be said to have,
That holds it as a lord, not as a slave.

I bid not be a foole, but seem to be,
When cause requires it : else thou art not free.

35. *Chatterers.*
Credit not alwayes him tels this or that :
His credit might be more if less his chat.

Credit not alwayes them that talk a vye :
How can their tongues but lye that never lye?

36.   *Drunkard.*
What is much drinke but the Braine's inundation?
Are not men mad that mak't a recreation?

37.   *Opportunity.*
To let time slip is a reverseless crime :
You may have time againe, but not the time.

38.   *Knowledge.*
To fill thy mind with precepts, labour most ;
For without learning, life is but Death's ghost.

39.   *Reality.*
Care what thou dost ; care not what's said of thee :
Virtue itself is not from slander free.

40.   *Sloth.*
Fly Sloth, which is a calme worse than a storme ;
And doth our leaking ship of life more harme.

Fly Sloth, which is to life an irksome guest :
It takes so much rest that it takes no rest.

Fly Sloth, which body fires and mind benumnes :
It is a taste of death before Death comes.

41.   *Bounty during Life.*
When Death now threats to take thy goods from thee,
Doe thou take them from Death, and bounteous be.

"What I gave that I have : " one wrote on's grave :
Then old and rich, give, that thou still mayst have.

42.   *Changed Circumstances.*
If Fortune give thee lesse than she hath done ;
Then make lesse fire, and walk more in the sunne.

If Fortune poure upon thee all her gall,
Yet Patience hath a spleene will hold it all.

Why should the change of fortune make thee pale?
Thou dost but leave the hill to walk i' th' vale.

If Fortune of her anker have thee ridde,
Patience can make an anker of a thridde.

43.   *Witnessing.*
If thou a theft know, let it be reveal'd :
A theefe's concealour is a theefe conceal'd.

44.   *Death.*
Soule brought a bed of body, and deliver'd
Is death : Is not hee that feares thee white-liver'd?

45.   *Rich Beggars.*
It need not riddle be whereat to stagger :
A man may be a rich man, yet a beggar.

46.   *Intellectual Wealth.*
If Nature's treasures thou desire to finde,
Search not the mines of India, but the mind.

47.   *Health.*
To gather riches doe not hazard health ;
For truth to say, Health is the wealth of wealth.

48.   *Choosing Friends.*
In choosing of a friend, observe but this :
Regard not what hee hath, but what hee is.

Thou must to goodnesse, not to goods, attend ;
Or else thou mayst have friends, but not a friend.

A faithfull friende is best known by this marke :
He's lesse discern'd in th' light than in th' darke.

When thou would'st finde a friend to stick unto,
Not mannours make the man, but mannours do.

To know a friend that's more in heart than lips,
Marke him not in the sunne, but in th' eclips.

Friendship and wealth have severall works to do ;
Friendship makes two one, and wealth makes one two.

A reall friend a cannon cannot batter ;
With nom'nall friends, a squib's a per'lous matter.

49.   *Use, not Hoard.*
Use that thou hast ; be not thy monie's slave :
What use to have, if not use what you have?

Use that thou hast, and long not after more :
What good doth store, if only kept in store?

50.   *Self-indulgence in Drinking.*
Drinke but in temper : pleasure without measure
Brings thee at last to measure without pleasure.

Drinke not too much : what man that were not vaine
Would broach his mouth to set a-tylt his braine?

Drinke not too much : such drinking will in fyne
Have a worse skore than paying for the wine.

51.   *Envy.*
What needs the moone with envy looke so pale ?
Shee's great to stars, though to the sunne she's small.

All Fortune's oddes is by Comparison's eye :
Looke up or downe, and thou art low or high.

      Climbe not too high, least thou endanger'd be:
      Low boughes are strong, but weake at top o' th' tree.

52.   *Comparative Loves.*
      The love is great, when all away is swept;
      Yet there are some things better lost than kept.

      It needs must greue to be with losses crost;
      Yet what is lost for friends, is never lost.

53.   *Long-life: life-long.*
      While men their daies of life are multiplying,
      They live not longer, but are longer dying.

      How can we reckon upon life's extent
      That know not what we have till all be spent?

54.   *Not slaves, but men.*
      When for thy use thou buyest servants, then
      Though slaves thou call them, yet know they are men.

In all likelihood, other readers of "Cato Variegatus" would have made other selections, but these are fairly representative of the whole. I very much mistake if many of these "picked and packed" words and sentences do not get into some elect memories. I have the more readily quoted fully, because these books on the "Psalms," now reprinted, furnish kindred condensed and felicitous things (especially on the First Psalm), though not versified.

The "Apologie for Lay-Mens Writing on Divinity" well deserves republication in these days of revived sacerdotal-clericalism, whereby the (so-called) "laity" are marked off with a no less offensive than unscriptural echoing of the old utterance, "Stand by thyself, come not near to me; for I am holier than thou" (Isa. lxv. 5). Evidently his "Meditations and Disquisitions" had been challenged as an intrusion.

The "Apologie" is dedicated "To my worthy much honored cosen Sr John Baker of Sissingherst in the co. of Kent." He is very meek and lowly in his address—*e.g.*, "Sir, I cannot but very much honour you, as being a flourishing branch of that tree of which I am but a withered bough" ... "whereof I have resentment in a very great degree"—resentment having then the sense of "grateful feeling" (as in Barrow, "That thanksgiving whereby we should express an affectionate *resentment* of our obligation to him"—Sermon 6, on Prayer).

The treatise thus effectively opens: "I am very tender to speak on an argument that may any way be drawne to trench upon the cleargie, whose calling I reverence and whose person I respect *tanquam angelos Dei;* but who can bee patient to heare the ignorant murmuring of some men, who as though they would cloyster up God's Spirit and not suffer it *spirare ubi vult*, to breathe where it listeth, prohibeteth laymen wholly from handling matters of divinity, and as if they reckoned them in the number of those of whom God said, 'What hast thou to doe to take mine ordinances in thy mouth?'" Having marshalled facts and arguments, he thus expostulates: "For men that allow laymen to read, and yet deny them to write, what can be conceaved more incongruous? much like as if they would allow men to marry, and not allow them to have children; or if to have children, yet not to be legitimate: for what is this writing but as it were the issue and offspring of their reading? Not that every one that reads must presently be a writer, no more than any one that marries of necessity hath children; but that where the one is lawfully permitted, the other cannot reasonably be denied."

There is very considerable learning and acumen in the "Apologie," and jets of humour reveal that "stone walls," in the author's case, did "no prison make,"—did not even begloom his spirit.

His "Chronicle of the Kings of England" with every deduction supplied a *desideratum*. Granted that the boast of its Epistle to the Reader, that it had been "collected with so great care and diligence that if all other of our chronicles were lost, this only would be sufficient to inform posterity of all passages memorable or worthy to be known," must be read with a good many grains of salt. Nevertheless, it is substantially a good, sound, manly, historical book. All honour to JOSEPH ADDISON that he made the "Chronicle" beloved of Sir Roger de Coverley, and the source of his "many observations." Thumbed and dog-eared copies of the old folios are still to be met with in old manor-houses, and well-preserved ones in "the stately homes of England." *Pace* BLOUNT and BISHOP NICHOLSON—both dry as any "remainder biscuit," I promise the student-reader reward if he turn to the "Chronicle." I do not know that I care to recommend the later editions, with continuations by SIR THOMAS CLARGES and Phillips (Milton's nephew).

The posthumously-published "*Theatrum Redivivum*" is incomparably the most scholarly and best-reasoned "Apology" for the "Theatre" extant. It goes without saying that Prynne's pseudo-learning is scattered as so much chaff. The touch is light, occasionally half-playful, but drawing blood every time. It must, however, be conceded that while unanswerable logically and theoretically, it still remains true that it demands an ideal, not the actual "Theatre," to win our assent or acceptance. One *bit* alone—for it were idle to traverse the argument *pro* and *con*—strikes me as demanding quotation, viz., an incidental vindication of two great Shakespearean actors, and one of them—Burbage—in all probability the painter of the Chandos portrait of Shakespeare. He thus writes of scurrility: " He [Prynne] would make us believe that all the attractive power of Plays, to draw Beholders, is meerly for scurrility: as if it were no Play, at least no pleasing Play, without it. Whereas besides his prejudice, he may be made to confess his ignorance; for let him try it when he will, and come himself upon the stage, with all the scurrility of the *Wife of Bath*, with all the ribaldry of Poggius or Boccace, yet I dare affirm he shall never give that content to Beholders as honest Tarlton did, though he said never a word. And what scurrility was ever heard to come from the mouth of the two actors of our time, Allen [Alleyne] and Burbadge? yet what Plays were ever so pleasing as where these parts had the great part? For it is not the scurrility and ribaldry that gives the contentment, as he foolishly imagines and falsely suggests, but it is the Ingeniousness of the Speech when it is fitted to the person, and the gracefulness of the action when it is fitted to the speech; and therefore a Play read hath not half the pleasure of a Play acted; for though it have the pleasure of ingenious speeches, yet it wants the pleasure of graceful action; and we may well acknowledge that graceful action is the greatest pleasure of a Play, seeing it is the greatest pleasure of the art of pleasure, Rhetorick" (pp. 34-5).

The translations of Balsac (*c*) and of Malvezzi (*j*) were mere hack-work.

Turning now to the "Meditations and Disquisitions" on various of the Psalms, and associating therewith his similar "Meditations and Disquisitions on the Lord's Prayer," and "Meditations and Motives for Prayer upon the Seaven dayes of the Week" (*i*)—the last, I think, having been earlier issued, judging by a reference in the Epistle of the "Meditions and Motives"—as onward—as "Soliloquy of the Soul, or a Pillar of Thoughts," 1641, (12mo), recorded by Wood, but which I have not been fortunate enough to meet with—I must remark, in the outset, that the chief value of all these books lies in their goodness or spirituality. There is learning well in hand ; there is evidence of varied culture ; there is now and again weighty thought ; there is oftener still vivid illumination of a divine sentence flashing into its very heart ; there is quaint playing with words and deft phrasing ; but *the* distinctive signet of the whole of these "Meditations and Disquisitions" is their savour of godliness, their fragrance of prayerfulness, their music of thankfulness, their pathetic yearning and aspiration. For mass of thought, for unexpected things, for striking suggestiveness, for occasional beauty of style, I would not compare any of the present books with another layman and knight's, SIR JOHN HAYWARD. It has always been a mystery to me that *his* matterful and gracious religious books have never been reprinted modernly. But without proverbially "odious comparisons," there need be no reserve in commending these "Meditations and Disquisitions" to the like-minded and like-hearted. I cannot suppose any reading them without spiritual excitement and incitement.

Specifically, I place the "Meditations and Disquisitions on the First Psalm" in the fore-front. The thought is weightier, the exposition closer, the style sinewer, the *memorabilia* plentier in this than in any of the others.

It seems only right to give my readers the benefit of my familiarity with this particular portion of these "Meditations and Disquisitions." Take, then, these few inevitably-marked things, from the commencement forward :—

1. *Negatives.*

"The first godliness that ever was,—that is, the first commandment of God,—was delivered to our first parents in a negative: 'Of the tree of good and evil ye shall not eat;' and if they had well observed this negative, they should never have sinned in any affirmative." ....
"Justly, therefore, the Prophet begins his godliness here with negatives, seeing negatives at first began all godliness" (p. 6).

2. *Choice by rejecting.*

"Thus as God directed Samuel to elect by rejecting, so David directs us here to choose by refusing; and this is a cause, also, that makes negatives, in many cases, so much in request" (p. 8).

3. "*Strange marks.*"

"Are not there, in this case, strange marks? As though we should know a godly man by the posture of his body; or as if a godly man should neither walk, nor stand, nor sit." .... "But they are not the postures that are here blamed, but the impostures" (pp. 9, 10).

4. *The three stages.*

"To *walk* in the counsel of the ungodly, what is it but the act of sin? and to *stand* in the way of sinners, what is it but the custom of sin? and to *sit* in the chair of scorners, what is it but to take a pride in sin?" (p. 15).

5. *Encrease.*

"Whilst nearness works by addition, and continuance by multiplication, the standing in the way of sinners, as gathering heat by both, must needs break forth at last into violent flames of sinning" (p. 17).

6. *Woman is Man.*

"But why would the Prophet say, 'Blessed is the man,' as though blessedness was entailed to heirs male, or as though the law of God were like the law Salic of France, excluding women from the kingdom of heaven? for else he should rather have said, 'Blessed is every man or woman,' and not only say, 'Blessed is the man.' But is it not that David knew better the extent of his words than to be so superfluous; for ever since the time of which Moses saith, 'God made man; male and female, created he them,' women have had as good right to the word as men, though it pass in their name" (p. 19).

7. *Proper Marks.*

"The Prophet therefore stays not here, but proceeds and hastens to the affirmative marks; for they indeed are the proper characters of a godly man; they are never found but in him, and in him they are ever found" (p. 20).

8. *Delight.*

"The Prophet requires not a godliness that bars us of delight; he requires only a godliness that rectifies our delight" (p. 21).

9. *Delight in God.*

"In presence of this, all other delights do lose their light; in balance with this, all other delights are found to be light" (p. 24).

10. *God's Law.*

"This is not a law where the weakest goes to the wall, but the law is a wall to the weakest; the delighting in this law is not a going to law, but a law to our going; . . . . and it is so far from making us to become enemies to our neighbours, that it makes us neighbours to our enemies" (p. 26).

11. *Preparative.*

"A good preparative, and but a preparative, to Divine contemplation; it might serve to strew branches in the way, but not to cry Hosanna" (p. 27).

12. *Believers compared to a Tree.*

"Will the Prophet serve us thus,—make us take such pains for godliness, and keep us all this while in hand, that by being godly we shall be happy, and now bring us to no better a happiness than to be like a tree?" . . . . "Of such good qualities we shall find so many in a tree, that happiness may think itself happy to be compared to it; for was it not a tree that bore the fruit of life in the Garden of Eden? was it not a tree that bore the Lord of life in the field of Golgotha?" (p. 37).

13. *Happiness of Heaven.*

"Seeing it consists of parts in number innumerable, in magnitude infinite, in continuance eternal, what man of art, what art of man, can now come near it?" (p. 43).

14. *Eternal Happiness.*

"What by the time? when time is no more; for time is but the measure of motion and mutation, but happiness hath nothing to do with these, and therefore nothing to do with time; her time is eternity" (p. 44).

15. *Blessings and being blessed.*

"There is great difference between having blessings and being blessed." . . . . "Such things may entitle man *benedicti*, perhaps, but not *beati*" (p. 48).

16. *Temporary Prosperity.*

"What is their present possession but possession of the present?" (p. 63).

17. *Chaff.*

"The wind hath no such meaning towards the chaff: it comes not to exercise it, but to vex it; it makes it not a traveller, but a vagabond; for if it but happen to light anywhere, the least air that moves removes it again: the east wind drives it forward, the west wind turns it backward, the north wind crosseth them both, that the poor chaff hath no standing' but to stand amazed ; it is held up but by contrary motions ; it is of all hands, under the hand of violence ; it hath no natural rest but as it is natural to it never to rest ; it must be somewhere, yet it can be nowhere ; it hath a place, but no mansion ; a being, but no abiding ; no reposing but while the wind is weary ; no resting but till the air be up and ready ; for as long as the air is an element, and hath to do in the world, there is no hope for the misearble chaff to be ever quiet" (p. 72).

18. *Gracious Alms.*

"The giving of a small mite will have no small might in it" (p. 89).

These must suffice as foretastes of the "spoils" to be gathered in the vigilant reading of this Worthy.

I do not deem it expedient similarly to record in this Introduction my margin-markings in the other "Meditations and Disquisitions." Sooth to say, they are more "Meditations" than "Disquisitions," while it is in his excursive and discursive "Disquisitions" that he most of all excels. In his "Meditations" he is rather apt to say things than have things to say. Still, even in the most personal "Meditations" and self-application of the Psalmist's confessions and penitences, aspirations and humiliations, there gleam out fine things. Only very rarely does the reader need to query, yet now and then he will ; *e.g.*, "if he [the believer] ever be in darkness, he shall ever be in darkness" (p. 29) : and "though a wicked man will be counterfeiting to be godly, yet it was never known that a godly man would counterfeit to be wicked" (p. 67). Further : "It may perhaps be true of the angels, in whose mouths we know of nothing there is continually, but Holy, holy, holy Lord God of Sabaoth" (p. 360). The first is out and out false. Many a true child of God knows the terrors and the sorrows of walking in darkness with "no light," and yet emerges from that darkness. Even our Divine Redeemer knew it when He cried, "My God, my God, why hast Thou forsaken me?" The second is mournfully inaccurate. St. Peter was a "godly man," and yet when he went in and "sat among *them*"— the enemies of Christ—and by "oaths and curses" denied Him, how did he "counterfeit to be wicked"? And alas,

alas, so superficial is our transformation, and so common our conformation to the world, that too many "counterfeit to be wicked," and are recreant to their profession. The third (along with the like popular idea of the occupation of the redeemed in heaven) has done more perhaps to *monotonize* conceptions of the state of glory than almost anything else. Plainly it was only the occupation of the heavenly hosts—angelical and human—at the particular time of St. John's vision. Had he returned half an hour after, doubtless he had seen them differently engaged; and so throughout. One ought to lose no opportunity of correcting such nonsense.

"The "Meditations and Disquisitions" on the Lord's Prayer had the following letter prefixed to it :—

"To my loving and learned friend and sometime com-pupil at "Oxford, Sr. Richard Baker, Knight.

"Sir,

"I conceive that you have been pleased, out of our ancient friendship (which was first and is ever best elemented in an Academy), and not out of any valuation of my poore judgment, to communicate unto me your Divine Meditations upon the Lord's Prayer in some several sheetes, which have given me true taste of the whole; wherein I must needs shewe and much admire the very Charity of your Stile, which seemeth unto me to have not a little of the African idea of St. Augustine's age; full of sweet Raptures and of researching conceipts; nothing borrowed, nothing vulgar. and yet all flowing from you (I know not how) with a certaine equall facility. So as I see your worldly troubles have been but Pressing-yrons to your heavenly cogitations. Good sir, let not any modesty of your nature, let not any obscurity of your fortune, smother such an excellent employment of your erudition and zeale: for it as a work of light. and not of darkness. And thus wishing you long health, that can use it so well, I remain,

"Your pious friend, to love and serve you,
"HENRY WOTTON."

THOMAS FULLER says of it (in his "Worthies"), "He wrote an Exposition on the Lord's Prayer, which is coieval with the best comments which professed divines have written on that subject."

His "Meditations and Motives for Prayer upon the Seaven days of the Week" is thinner in its thinking, but is interpenetrated with emotion and devotion. The appended

c

"Disquisition" on Lucifer is disappointing. The Epistle-dedicatory is characteristic, and worthy of preservation here:—

"To my much honoured the virtuous Lady Baker, wife of Sir John Baker, of Sissingherst, in Kent, Bart.
"Madam,
"There are many causes that move me to present this Treatise to your Ladiship. You are the wife of that noble gentleman who is the ornament of our Family. You are the daughter of that worthy Knight to whom, while he lived, I was exceeding beholding; but more than both these, you are a Lady of so great Devotion that the world takes notice of it in a high degree; a rare thing in Ladies of this age, who are commonly noted for no defect more than for excesse of vanitie. This especially makes mee conceive that a treatise of this nature will not bee unpleasing to you: for though you have many godly bookes for the exercise of your pious meditations; yet of this argument perhaps not any; or if you have, yet vanitie oftentimes makes a greater appetite and change of labours is a kinde of refreshing. The booke came once abroad into the world before, but was then so little that it was not fit to goe to some. It is now growne so great that it is able to doe a good daye's worke, or rather if your Ladiship please to entertaine it, will do you service every day of the weeke; and will helpe to set you forward in His service who is the Ancient of Dayes; and will at last turne all dayes into one daye that never shall have night. And seeing it is the employing of the short dayes here, that must make the long day happie it is no lesse wisdome than vertue in your Ladiship that you so piously employ them to that end, and it will be no small service in him. that shall adde but the least graine of furtherance to your doing it. Whatsoever it is, I entreat your Ladiship to account it as coming from him who is no lesse in true affection than in profession

"Your humble Servant,
"RICHARD BAKER."

Surely it is a touching picture that is called up to us in this "decayed" Knight of "gentle blood," and nurture and culture, as a prisoner of nearly ten years in "Fleet Street," occupying himself with such hallowed "Meditations and Disquisitions," with not slightest word of murmuring or fretfulness or blame of ill-willers. It is so far a relief to know that such a man as SIR HENRY WOTTON held true to him; better still, that Dr. THOMAS FULLER sought him out, as we learn by these golden words in his "Worthies' (*s.n.*): "His youth he spent in learning, the benefit whereof he reaped in his old age, when his estate through suretyship (*as I have heard him complain*) was very much impaired. But God may smile on them on whom the world doth frown; whereof his pious old age was a memorable instance, when the storm on his estate forced him to fly for shelter to his studies and devotions."

To me the very mistakes in Bible names and references that the Editor of this collection has had to correct are tremulous with pathos, witnessing as they do to "memory" weakened under his white hairs. The use of the Vulgate—which he very often translates from and builds on—I cannot explain. One thing is clear, he was at no loss for books. Bishop Hacket tells that Archbishop Williams bought his library for £500—equivalent to £2,500 to-day.

Anthony-a-Wood is as nearly sympathetic as his nature would allow, on the close of all: "At length, after he had undergone many cares and troubles in this world, he departed this mortal life in the prison called Fleet, in London, on the 18th day of Feb, 1644, and on the day following was buried about the middle of the south isle joyning to S. Bridget's, commonly called S. Bride's Church, near Fleet Street in London." He left a widow and all his sons and daughters, as herein enumerated, behind him. The widow, it is believed, re-married. It needeth not that I dwell on either her or the children.

And now with relation to this reprint of these old books or selected Psalms of David—I wish it to be understood (because of an inadvertent note at page 303, where I am called Editor) that I am in no way whatever responsible for the editing and reproduction, as I have no claim to any honour that may be won by such. I have read every word from beginning to end. I could not find the time to collate with the original texts; but it seems to me an honest piece of literary work. Personally, I might not have translated some of the Latin quotations and words as the Editor has done, nor given some of his explanations in the notes; but looking at the work broadly, I think the Publisher must be pronounced fortunate in his Editor.

I place below certain words that have been overlooked; and seeing that a large number of others are noted and explained, I venture to hope these will not be thought superfluous.* I also add to these a very few errata that have caught my eye.†

May these fine old books enter on a new lease of useful-

- Page 7, line 26, "*meet with rubs*" = obstacles. So page 128, line 27; page 311, line 10 from bottom.
- ,, 16, line 17, "*shouldered*" = shoved with the shoulder—a favourite word with Bp. Hall and John Marston.
- ,, 19, line 6, "*snake*" = our "sneak."
- ,, 27, line 6, "*leasings*" = falsehoods.
- ,, 34, line 20, "*punctual*" = exact, exacting; line 35, "*scandal*" = stumbling-stone, or baseless objection.
- ,, 38, line 12, "*artificial*" = skilled.
- ,, 44, line 2, "*counters*" = money or coin, in contempt.
- ,, 51, line 27, "*his coming from hell*" = unseen world. To all desirous to master the literature of the question involved, may be recommended Huidekoper's "Belief of the First Three Centuries concerning Christ's Mission to the Underworld." N. York.
- ,, 53, line 32, "*carnally*" = bodily, actually, as distinguished from prior expectation.
- ,, 56, line 20, "*insult*" = triumph, boast. So page 237, line 8; page 299, line 13; page 316, line 3 from bottom.
- ,, 70, line 28, "*entity*" = being, existence.
- ,, 72, line 9, "*strappado*" and relative note. Rather = whip or lash, as in Braithwaite's Strappado for the Devil. See context, "*whirleth* it on high, and then lets it fall," etc.
- ,, 75, line 7, "*abject*" = despicable thing.
- ,, 78, line 10, "*wounds of Abel fall a-bleeding afresh*"—hence the old terrible ordeal of touch, wherein the supposed murderer was brought into the presence of the corpse of the slain and compelled to "touch." If guilty, the wound was supposed to "bleed afresh."
- ,, 80, line 9, "*rout*," = gay mixed ball-like "assembly."
- ,, 84, line 18, "*score*" = debt-book, or markings.
- ,, 100, line 3, "*roundly*" = *ore rotundo*, or with full mark.
- ,, 102, line 20, "*softly*" = soft—common, contemporaneously.
- ,, 103, line 6, "*comfortable*," and related note. Rather = consolatory.
- ,, 127, line 1, "*cried*" = proclaimed.
- ,, 154, line 21, "*chine*" = back, i.e. over-burdened, "heavy-laden."
- ,, 155, line 25, "*long*," line 26, "*long*" = became.
- ,, 162, line 9, "*censure*" = judge. So page 260, line 4 from bottom; and page 274, line 26.
- ,, 187, line 6 from bottom, "*husbands*" = husbandmen.
- ,, 190, line 4 from bottom, "*scammony*" = strong purgative herb.
- ,, 237, line 9, "*apology*" = defence, vindication.
- ,, 260, line 16, the "not" filled in is not required—a common contemporary construction.
- ,, 265, line 6, "*intentive*" = eager, stretching out. So page 273, line 10; page 334, line 1; page 348, line 18.
- ,, 277, last line, "*clawing*" = flattery. See Nares's Glossary, s.v., for a full note.
- ,, 283, line 8, "*mizzling*" = our drizzling.
- ,, 288, line 29, "*affected*" = affectioned. So page 290, lines 3, 11.
- ,, 307, line 6, "*handsomely*" = good favour, or look good.
- ,, 328, line 10, "*tincture*," and related note. Rather an alchemical term = touch.
- ,, 343, line 14, "*prevented*" = anticipated. So page 346, line 24.
- ,, 350, line 8, "*insolent*." Cf. note on p. 56, line 20, etc.
- ,, 355, line 26, "*kindly*," and related note. Rather = congruous or of kin. So page 404, line 1. Cf. Shakespeare, "more than kin and less than kind" (Hamlet 1. ii.)
- ,, 396, line 12, "*retaliation*" = return or recompense.

† Page 17, line 3 from bottom, read "but" for "nut'; page 19, line 18, delete "us": page 30, line 27, read "and by which we shall be judged'; page 37, line

ness! May the memory of good Sir Richard Baker abide green! The facsimile portrait of him showing prison-wornness, from the 1653 "Chronicle," is certainly truthful. ANTHONY-A-WOOD gives this summary description of him: "*He was a person tall and comely*, of a good disposition and admirable discourse, religious and well read in various faculties, especially in divinity and history."

ALEXANDER B. GROSART.

ST. GEORGE'S VESTRY, BLACKBURN,
30*th September*, 1881.

APPENDIX.

SEEING that certain genealogical-biographical data on the Bakers, direct and collateral, have been put at my disposal by Mr. Tarbutt (as before), and somewhat added to by my own researches, I shall preserve them here by way of appendix to this Memorial-Introduction.

The reader will join on the following to the biographical details given in the outset. Sir Richard Baker, second son of Sir John Baker, died 27th May, 1594. He married (1) Catharine, daughter and heiress of John Tyrell, of Heron, co. Essex, son of Sir Thomas Tyrell, and by her mother heiress of the Marquis of Exeter; (2) Mary, daughter of John Gifford (or Gyeforde, or Giffard), of Tiehall, co. Hants. This second wife on his death married (1) Richard Fletcher, Bp. of London, father of Dr. Giles Fletcher, and grandfather of Giles and Phineas Fletcher, the Poets; (2) Sir Stephen Thorne (or Thornie), according to Harleian MS. 840, f. 42 *b*. Sir Richard left issue—a son John is mentioned in the will of his grandfather 1558, buried at Cranbrook, 1574; Thomas, second son, knighted at the Charterhouse 1603 : married in 1592 to Constantia, daughter

---

19, the f in "of" has got turned: page 61, line 17, "is" is misprinted "i?": page 146, line 25, read "heart" not "hear": page 163, foot-note line 3, read "nurse" for "uurse": page 214, line 3, read "may be said to be": page 221, line 26, spell "sacrifices": page 335, line 21, read "If thou . . ." page 338, line 19, spell "fainted": page 340, line 5 from bottom "B" in "But" dropped out: page 355, line 6 from bottom, read "look" for "took": page 432, line 1, the "h" of "then" dropped out.

of Sir William Kingsmill, of Lemm, near Ipswich, and had issue four sons and two daughters. By his second wife, he had two daughters, (1) Cresagon, married to Sir Henry Lennard (or Leonard), afterwards Lord Dacre; (2) ——, married to Richard Blount, son and heir of Sir Thomas Blount.

JOHN, eldest son and heir of Sir Richard Baker (*ut supra*), married Mary, daughter of Sir Thomas Guildfoul, of Hempsted Bondenden, and had issue, two sons and two daughters, viz., Henry, Edward, Joessa (or Jocosa), and Catharine. Edward—of whom nothing more is known—was born in 1597; Joessa (or Jocosa) was married to Sir John Jewill, and Catharine to Edward Yates.

HENRY, eldest son of John Baker, Esq., was knighted before the year 1609; created a baronet in 1611; was next heir to Lord Mountjoy; died in Lime Street, London, and was buried at Cranbrook 1623. He had married Catharine, eldest daughter of Sir John Smith, of Belshanger, and had issue three sons and one daughter, viz., John, Thomas, Henry, and Elizabeth. Henry was posthumous; Thomas died in 1619, aged three years; Elizabeth—unknown.

Sir John Baker—eldest son of Sir Henry, 2nd baronet—to whose Lady our Worthy dedicated his "Motives for Prayer," died in 1653, aged 45; buried at Cranbrook. He married Mary, daughter of a "knight," gratefully recalled by Sir Richard in the epistle-dedicatory of his "Meditations and Motives." She was buried at Cranbrook in 1669. Their issue was two sons and four daughters, viz., John, Robert, Sarah, Catharine, Mary, and Elizabeth;—nearly all died young.

Sir John Baker—eldest son of Sir John, 3rd baronet—was buried at Cranbrook in 1661; had married an Elizabeth (unknown), and left issue four daughters, viz., Sarah, Ann, Mary, and Elizabeth. Sarah died young in 1669; Ann married Edward Beagham, Esq., and died in 1685; Mary married John Dowell, Esq., of Over, in Gloucestershire; Elizabeth married Mr. Robert Spencer. These last three heiresses sold each their share in the Sissinghurst estates to Sir Horace Mann, of Linton, in the co. of Kent; and so ended the direct line.

Returning now to James Baker, brother of *the* historical

Sir John Baker, Chancellor of the Exchequer, etc., etc., these authentic details bring the descent down to our own day, and to—among others—SIR SAMUEL WHITE BAKER, the distinguished Traveller and Author.

1. JAMES BAKER, mentioned in the will of his grandfather, 1493, and of his father in 1504; to whom married not stated; had issue one son, named Walter.
2. WALTER BAKER, of Sherborne, in Dorset, gentleman: his will is dated 19th of April, the 26th year of Queen Elizabeth; proved 28th of May, 1854; married Catherine ——, widow; she was left executrix to her husband's will, and had issue one son.
3. WALTER BAKER, married at Poole, co. Dorset, 22nd January, 1592, to Rebecca, daughter of John Andrew; baptized at Poole 15th July, 1573; had issue eight sons and two daughters. The date of baptism, with their names, as follows: William, 1593; Walter, 1595; John, 1598; Robert, 1601; Andrew, 1604; James, 1605; Nicholas, 1607; Joseph, 1610; Judith, 1596; and Rebecca, 1612. William, the eldest, married Elizabeth Gosselin, of Poole, 1619. No record that any other son or daughter was married except Andrew, the fifth son, and he inherited his father's estate.
4. ANDREW BAKER died at Poole 1662; married Sussanah ——; she died 1665: had issue two sons and two daughters. Of the two daughters, no record beyond name and when baptized, viz., Joane, 1627, and Sussanah, 1630; and the only record of one son, viz., John: his baptism in 1631, and his marriage to Catharine —— in 1660.
5. WALTER BAKER, the other son, inherited his father Andrew's estate: was born 1638; married Magdaline, daughter of Francis Wild. She was baptized at Poole, 1638; had issue three sons and six daughters. The only record in the pedigree of these nine children is as follows: Andrew, baptized at Poole 1660; Joane, bap. at Poole 1663; married in 1698 to James Seager; Elizabeth, bap. at Poole 1665, died 1668; Sussanah, bap. at Poole 1668; married, 1698, to Samuel Russell; John, bap. at Poole 1674; Elizabeth, bap. at Poole 1671; married, 1705, to John Thomson; Magdaline, bap. at Poole 1677; Sarah, bap. at Poole 1680, died 1684; and Joseph, bap. at Poole 1679.
6. JOSEPH BAKER, the youngest son, inherited his father's estate; born in 1679; married 21st of January, 1705; buried 30th of January, 1722. His will is dated 1718: proved at Standford that his children were all under age in 1722: married Mary, daughter of Francis Wild. She was bap. at Poole 1684, and though left executrix to her husband's will, she died the same year, and so did not prove his will. She left issue one son and two daughters, viz., Sussanah, bap. at Poole 1706, mentioned in her father's will 1718; Mary married Capt. Francis Wallis, R.N.; John succeeded to his father's estate.

7. JOHN BAKER, born 1712, mentioned in his father's will 1718; married at Poole, 29th of January, 1732; an officer in the R.N., commanded the letter of marque, *Blood Joke*, 10 guns, afterwards Harbour-master of Bristol; died 1781; married Rhoda Valentine Nicholson, of Poole; born 1709; died in 1800, aged 91 years. [Her father married, in 1699, Dorothy Carter]; she had issue five sons and four daughters, as follows: Mary, born 1733; Joseph, 1735; Valentine, 1737; John, 1739; Francis, 1742; Joseph, 1743; Ruth, ——; Sarah, 1748; Elizabeth, ——. Mary married Capt. Moore, and died 1776; Joseph died young; Valentine succeeded to the estate, and died in 1790; John married Ann ——, Master of his Majesty's ship *Deal Castle*; died without issue; his will proved in 1782; Francis Wallis married a daughter of — Martin, Esq., an officer in the R.N. [He had a son, a commander of an East Indiaman, and died without issue.] Joseph died without issue. Ruth married John Bernard, Esq., of Cork; Sarah ——; Elizabeth married George Oakeley.

8. VALENTINE BAKER, born 1737, Commander letter of marque *Cæsar*, 18 guns; married Eleanor, daughter of Samuel Mattick, and had issue seven sons and four daughters, viz., Eleanor Ruth, born 1776, died same year; James Lockyer, born 1779; Sarah Ellen, married Wildman Goodwin, Esq., Judge of India Civil Service; Eleanor, born 1781, married twice, and died in 1868; Sophia, married John Bernard, Esq., of Cork; George Oakely, born 1782, died 1796; Valentine, born 1784, died 1790; John Samuel, Commander of an East Indiaman, died without issue; William Mattick, born 1791, died 1805; Samuel, who succeeded to the family estate, born 1793, died 1862; Francis, born 1795, died 1832.

9. SAMUEL BAKER, Esq., Lypiat Park, co. Gloucester, and of Thorngrove, Worcester, married Mary Ann, daughter of Thomas Dodson, Esq., as his first wife, and Eliza Maria, relict of Shelton, as second wife, and had issue, five sons and three daughters, viz.,

1. THOMAS, died young.
2. Sir SAMUEL WHITE, born 1821, the African traveller. Sir Samuel has been twice married, and has four daughters by his first wife.
3. JOHN GARLAND, born 1822, married 1863; has issue two sons and two daughters.
4. ELLEN, married Rev. F. Hopkinson, D.D.
5. VALENTINE, born 1827, Col. of the 10th Hussars; married twice, and has issue two daughters. "Silence is golden."
6. JAMES BAKER, born 1830, of the 8th Royal Hussars, Lt.-Col. of the Cambridge University Volunteers; married Sarah Louisa, daughter of Capt. White, and has three sons and one daughter.
7. MARY ANN, married, 1868, Henry Causton.
8. ANN ELIZA, married Capt. Robt. Bourne.

MEDITATIONS
AND
DISQVISITIONS
UPON
The firſt Pſalme of
DAVID.

Bleſſed is the Man.

By *Sir Richard Baker* Knight.

LONDON.
Printed by *Edward Griffin*, for *Francis Eglesfield*
and are to be ſold at the Marigold, in *Pauls*
Church-yard. 1640.

To the
RIGHT HONOURABLE
THOMAS, LORD COVENTRY,*
BARON OF AYLESBOROUGH, AND LORD KEEPER OF THE GREAT SEAL OF ENGLAND.

MY HONOURED LORD,—He may truly be said [to be] a happy man, *Cui omnes bene volunt* [to whom all wish well] : but more truly he, *Cui omnes bene velle debent* [to whom all should wish well]: and in both these rights I may justly pronounce your Lordship happy : yet there is a better title for asserting happiness to you than both these ; that your delight is in the law of the Lord, and in his law [you] will exercise yourself both day and night ;[1] for now it is not the world, it is not I, it is David himself, that pronounceth you happy ; and give me leave, my Lord, to show you the picture of a happy man, drawn here by David ; and let all the world judge if it resemble not you, and that so near, that not any in our age, and I may say nor yet in many ages, hath been more like it. And having showed you this, my part remains only to pray that you may long enjoy this happiness as a fruit of your virtue here, and come at last to be like the tree [2] itself ; which will yield you a fruit of happiness that shall never fade, nor so much as the leaves of it ever wither ; for how should they wither, when *In memoria æterna erit justus*[3] [the righteous shall be in everlasting remembrance] ? Thus he prayeth that is

Your Lordship's humble and devoted servant,

RICHARD BAKER.

[* Son of Thomas Coventry, one of the Justices of Common Pleas ; was born 1578, at Croome d'Abitot, Worcestershire. He became Recorder of the City of London in 1616, then successively Solicitor and Attorney-General, and, under Charles I., Lord Keeper of the Great Seal. He was made a baron of the realm in 1628, under the title of Lord Aylesborough, in Worcestershire. Lord Clarendon says of him, "Though in his own nature he had not only a firm gravity, but a severity, and even some moroseness; yet it was so happily tempered, and his courtesy and affability towards all men so transcendent, and so without affectation, that it marvellously recommended him to men of all degrees ; and he was looked upon as an excellent courtier, without receding from the natural simplicity of his own manners."—Cf. Lord Campbell's " Lord Chancellors," and all the biographical dictionaries, *sub nomine*.

[1] Ps. i. 2.   [2] Ps. i. 3.   [3] Ps. cxii. 6.]

[Blessed *is* the man that walketh not in the counsel of the ungodly, nor standeth in the way of sinners, nor sitteth in the seat of the scornful. 2. But his delight *is* in the law of the Lord; and in his law doth he meditate day and night. 3. And he shall be like a tree planted by the rivers of water, that bringeth forth his fruit in his season; his leaf also shall not wither; and whatsoever he doeth shall prosper. 4. The ungodly *are* not so: but *are* like the chaff which the wind driveth away. 5. Therefore the ungodly shall not stand in the judgment, nor sinners in the congregation of the righteous. 6. For the Lord knoweth the way of the righteous: but the way of the ungodly shall perish.—PSALM i.]

MEDITATIONS AND DISQUISITIONS

UPON THE

FIRST PSALM OF DAVID.

IT may be thought but an idle speculation to observe that the first word of this Psalm, in the Hebrew, begins with *Aleph*, the first letter of the alphabet; and the last word of it begins with *Tau*, the last letter of the alphabet, as though this Psalm should contain whatsoever may be expressed by all the letters of the alphabet. And it may be little better to observe that this first Psalm hath a kind of correspondence to our first parents: for the first word of it is *blessed*, and the last word is *perishing;* and such was their condition; they began in blessedness, but they ended in perishing: they began in blessedness, being placed in Paradise, where they had the Tree of Life; but they ended in perishing, being cast out of Paradise, where they died the death. But although the Prophet perhaps had none of these conceits, yet he had great reason for so placing his words; for *blessedness* is the mark we all aim at; if that be once named, there needs no other rhetoric to make us attentive; most properly therefore it is placed the first word, seeing the first words are the proper place to persuade attention. And as fitly is *perishing* placed the last word; that if the hope of blessedness cannot allure us to godliness, yet the fear of perishing may keep us from wickedness; seeing nothing so much deters from evil doing as the fear of evil suffering; and the word is justly placed the last, that it may last the longer in our memories, seeing the last words ever are best remembered.

But to leave these general aims, and to come to particulars and certainties, we may perceive that this whole Psalm offers itself to be drawn into these two opposite propositions: a godly man is blessed, a wicked man is miserable; which seem to stand as two challenges made by the Prophet: one, that he will maintain a godly man, against all comers, to be the only Jason,[1] for winning the golden fleece of blessedness; the other, that he will make it good upon the heads of all the wicked; that howsoever they make a show in the world of being happy, yet they of all men are most miserable. But lest there should grow litigiousness about the words, he will have it agreed upon—first, what a godly man is; and what it is must qualify this happy Jason. It seems the Prophet had heard of an old description of a godly man: *Declina a malo et fac bonum*—Eschew evil, and do good;[2] but finding this too general, and too much folded up, he thinks it necessary to open the first part of it into two or three negative marks,[3] and the last part of it into two affirmatives. But are not these strange marks to begin withal? as though he could know a godly man by negatives, or that godliness consisted in negation?—as if virtue were only *vitium fugere* [the avoiding vice]? Indeed, the first godliness that ever was—that is, the first commandment of God—was delivered to our first parents in a negative: "Of the tree of good and evil, ye shall not eat;"[4] and if they had well observed this negative, they should never have sinned in any affirmative. As long as it could be said of Adam, "There goes a man that never eat of the forbidden tree," so long it might as well be said of him, "There goes a perfect, righteous man." And even the first written Law of Commandments was delivered likewise, in a manner, all in negatives: "Thou shalt not kill; Thou shalt not steal," and the rest, in which so much godliness is contained as might have brought us all to heaven; as Christ

---

[1] Leader of the Argonauts in the Greek heroic age, type of spiritual heroism, and its quest of goodness. [2] 1 Peter iii. 11. [3] Distinguishing qualities or attributes.
[4] "Of the tree of the knowledge of good and evil, ye shall not eat of it."—Gen. ii. 17.

told the young man, *Si vis ad vitam ingredi, serva mandata* ["If thou wilt enter into life, keep the commandments"].[1] Justly, therefore, the Prophet begins his godliness here with negatives, seeing negatives at first began all godliness.

But as the evil spirit in the Gospel answered the Jewish conjurers, who in their adjuration used the names of Jesus and Paul: "Jesus I know, and Paul I know; but who are ye?"[2] so here, perhaps, some curious spirits may object, and say, "The negative commandments of the first table I know; and the negatives of the second table I know; but what are these?" They are not, indeed, the very mark we aim at, but they are the means that guide us to the mark; and, if by observing those we arrive at the haven, by observing these we avoid the rocks that hinder us from the haven.

But why would the Prophet use any negatives at all, and not rather rely wholly upon affirmatives? as to say, "That hath walked in the counsel of the godly; that hath stood in the way of the righteous; that hath sat in the chair of the humble"? and thus he might have made his argument in Barbara;[3] and never needed to have troubled negatives at all? But negatives in this case could not be denied; for if he had left out negatives, he had left out a great part of the worth and praise of godliness—for a godly man cannot always run in smooth ground—he shall sometimes meet with rubs; he cannot always breathe in sweet airs—he shall sometimes meet with ill savours; he cannot always sail in safe seas—he shall sometimes meet with rocks; and then it is his praise that he can pass over those rubs, can pass through those savours, can pass by those rocks, and yet keep himself upright and untainted, and untouched of them all. Besides, negative precepts are in some cases more absolute and peremptory than affirmatives: for to say, "That hath walked in the counsel of the godly," might not be sufficient; for he might walk in the counsel of the godly, and yet walk in the counsel of the ungodly too; not both

---

[1] Matt. xix. 17.   [2] Acts xix. 15.   [3] A term of logic which signifies that *mode* or form of the syllogism in which from two universal affirmative premisses, a universal affirmative conclusion is reached.

indeed at once, but both at several times; where now this negative clears him at all times. And may it not also be a cause of using negatives, because it seems an easier way of showing what a thing is, by showing what it is not, than by using only affirmative marks; especially where a perfect induction[1] may be made; and herein David not unfitly may be thought to reflect upon himself, and the case [to be] not unlike to Samuel's seeking to find out a king amongst the sons of Jesse?[2] For when Eliab was brought forth, Samuel verily thought that he had been the man; and afterwards, Abinadab, that it had been he; and then that Shammai,[3] without all doubt was he; for these were all goodly personages, likely men in show,[4] to make kings of. But when God refused these, and all the rest, and that there was none left but only David, then was Samuel forced at last to fall upon him. So in our case here, the world is verily persuaded that the likeliest men to be blessed are those that walk in the counsel of the ungodly, or those that stand in the way of sinners, or such as sit in the chair of scorners; for these are all great gallants, and make a goodly show in the world; but when the Prophet hath rejected all these, and none is left but the godly man, then we are forced of necessity at last to fall upon him; and as David was the unlikeliest of all his brothers to be a king, yet he was the man, so a godly man seems the unlikeliest of all others to be blessed, yet he is the man. "In the world ye shall have trouble,"[5] saith Christ; this makes him unlikely; but "be of good cheer, I have overcome the world;" this makes him the man. And thus, as God directed Samuel to elect by rejecting, so David directs us here to choose by refusing; and this is a cause, also, that makes negatives, in many cases, so much in request.

But though some negatives, in some cases, may be fitly used, yet it follows not that these in this; and therefore it will be fit to examine these negatives, and to see what they

---

[1] One "in which there is a complete enumeration of all the individuals, respecting which we assert collectively what we had before asserted separately."—*Whately.*
[2] 2 Sam. xvi. 6—13.   [3] Shammah.   [4] In appearance.   [5] John xvi. 33: "In the world ye shall have tribulation: but be of good cheer, I have overcome the world."

are: that "hath not walked in the counsel of the ungodly; that hath not stood in the way of sinners; that hath not sat in the chair of scorners;"[1] and are not these, in this case, strange marks? As though we should know a godly man by the postures of his body; or as if a godly man should neither walk, nor stand, nor sit. And what remains, then, but that he should do nothing else but lie? and yet this he must not do neither; for lying is the posture of a wicked man, as it is said, He lieth in wait to do mischief.[2] Indeed, walking hath been often branded with notes of miscarrying: Dinah went a-walking in the flowery fields,[3] and returned home deflowered; Cain went a-walking with Abel into the field a brother, and returned home a murderer;[4] and it seems to have been an old exercise of the Devil himself, who answered God, that he came from "walking and compassingt he earth;"[5] and Christ warned his apostles not to walk into the way of the Gentiles,[6] which seems not much different from this caveat [warning][7] here.

But though walking may be a hindrance to godliness, yet standing, perhaps, may be a furtherance; for Christ saith, "when ye stand praying,"[8] and so it is the posture of piety; and it is said of Moses that he stood in the gap,[9] and so it was the posture of charity; and the angels are said to stand before God,[10] and so it is the posture of reverence; and yet, for all this, if standing be not joined with understanding, as if we stand where we should kneel, as when David saith, Let us fall down and kneel before the Lord our Maker;[11] or if we stand in places where we should not, as is the way of sinners; or if we stand amongst persons that we ought not, as in sinners' way;—in all such cases standing may be as great a hindrance to godliness as ever walking was.

Yet, surely, sitting is an innocent posture: sitting never

---

[1] Ps. i. 1: "That walketh not in the counsel of the ungodly, nor standeth in the way of sinners, nor sitteth in the seat of the scornful." [2] Ps. x. 9: "He lieth in wait to catch the poor." [3] Gen. xxxiv. 1, 2. [4] Gen. iv. 8. [5] Job i. 7: "From going to and fro in the earth, and from walking up and down in it." [6] Matt. x. 5: "Go not into the way of the Gentiles." [7] Warning. [8] Mark xi. 25. [9] Num. xvi. 48: "He stood between the dead and the living." Compare Ezek. xxii. 30: "I sought for a man that should . . . stand in the gap." [10] 1 Kings xxii. 19: "I saw the LORD sitting on his throne, and all the host of heaven standing by him," etc. [11] Ps. xcv. 6: "Let us worship and bow down; let us kneel before the LORD our Maker."

committed adultery, never stole, never did any murder; and not only an innocent, but a reverent posture: it is the posture of a judge, as it is said, Ye shall sit and judge the twelve tribes of Israel;[1] it is the posture of a king, as it is said, To the king that sitteth upon his throne;[2] it is the posture of angels, as of the four-and-twenty elders in the Revelation;[3] and yet, as innocent and reverent as it is, it may be abused, for if we sit in the way of lasciviousness, as Thamar did;[4] or if we sit in the chair of injustice, as Pilate did;[5] or if we sit in the seat of pestilence, as it is said here, sitting may prove as great a bane to godliness as either standing or walking was.

But they are not the postures that are here blamed, but the impostures; that we be not drawn abroad a-walking, as to take the fresh air, and then be poisoned with infectious savours; that we be not kept standing in a pleasant way, and then the enemy who lieth in wait continually come suddenly and surprise us; that we sit not idly and take our ease, and in the meantime the bridegroom pass by, and we be shut out of doors. For if there be nothing else in it but walking, a godly man may walk as much as he will, seeing there is not only a godly walking as it is said of Noah, that he "walked with God,"[6] which was a walking in godliness; but there is a blessed walking, as it is said of Enoch, that he "walked with God,"[7] that is, God took him from walking in this vale of misery, to walk with him eternally in Paradise.

The mark therefore to know a godly man consists not in the not walking; but we must walk further to find it; and the next word we come to is *counsel*, and the negative cannot consist in this word neither, for counsel is one of the most excellent gifts that is given to man;—that it is even one of the names of God himself to be called Counsellor,[8] the negative therefore not found here neither. We must yet go further, and the next word we come to is ungodly, and now certainly we shall have a full negative, for ungodliness is the

---

[1] Matt. xix. 28: "Ye also shall sit upon twelve thrones, judging the twelve tribes of Israel." [2] Prov. xx. 8: "A king that sitteth in the throne." [3] Rev. iv. 4. [4] Gen. xxxviii. 14. [5] Matt. xxvii. 19. [6] Gen. vi. 9. [7] Gen. v. 24. [8] Is. ix. 6.

herb that marreth all the *broth*,[1] it poisons all the company that it comes in,—not only walking, a thing in itself indifferent, but even counsel, a thing in its own nature most sovereign: they are both marred by this one ingredient of ungodliness. The like may be said of the other two that follow, for neither standing, nor standing in the way, doth any hurt till we come at sinners; neither sitting, nor sitting in a chair, does any hurt till we come at scorners; all the hurt, like the sting in the tail of a serpent,[2] comes in the last. Walking in counsel had been a safe proceeding, if the ungodly had not given it; standing in the way had been a lawful calling, if sinners had not made it; sitting in a chair had been an easy posture, if scorners had not framed it; but if the ungodly, or sinners, or scorners have any hand at all in our actions, have anything to do in our doings, both safety, and lawfulness, and ease, and all are utterly overthrown.

Or, may we not take a way which crosseth the great highway of the world, and conceive it thus: to walk in the counsel of the ungodly is a pleasant walk, and if pleasure would make us blessed, were likely to do it; to stand in the way of sinners is a profitable way, and if profit will make us blessed, were the way to do it; to sit in the chair of scorners is an honourable seat, and if honour would make us blessed, would serve to do it; but all these courses the Prophet rejecteth: they are so far from making us blessed, that he gives us warning of them as the only impediments that hinder us from blessedness. And, therefore, the voluptuous man is deceived in placing blessedness in pleasures, for howsoever he fare deliciously every day in this life, yet he may hear of a terrible after-reckoning brought in by St. John, How much thou receivest in pleasures here, so much shall be added to thy torments hereafter.[3] The covetous man is deceived in placing blessedness in riches, for howsoever they make him welcome in all companies where he comes in this world, yet he may hear of a grievous repulse to be given him by Abraham: Son, thou hast received thy

---

[1] Cf. 2 Kings iv. 39, 40. [2] Rev. x. 9: "They had tails like unto scorpions, and there were stings in their tails." [3] Luke xvi. 19: The man "fared sumptuously every day." Cf. Rev. xviii. 7. "How much she hath glorified herself, and lived deliciously, so much torment and sorrow give her."

portion in this life, and therefore hast no right of ever coming into my bosom.[1] The ambitious man is deceived in placing blessedness in honour, for howsoever he sit aloft in his chair, and play *rex* [the king] here, yet he may hear of a cruel downfall foretold him by Isaiah, Thou hast said in thy heart, I will climb up above the clouds, and will be equal to the Highest; but thou shalt be cast down to the pit of hell, and to the nethermost lake.[2]

But have then ungodly men counsel? One would think it were want of counsel that makes them ungodly, for who would be ungodly if he had counsel to direct him? Certainly, counsel they have, and wise counsel too; that is, wise in the eye of the world, and wise for the works of the world; but wise in the sight of God, and wise for the works of godliness, they have not; and in that kind of wisdom ungodly men are your greatest counsellors—greatest in the ability of counsel, and greatest in the busying themselves with counselling. For their wisdom in counsel we have a precedent in Achitophel, who was in his time a most wicked man, and yet for counsel was the oracle[3] of his time. And, for their forwardness in counselling, it is a quality they have, as it were *ex traduce* [by ingrafting], from their father the devil, who, no sooner creatures were made that were capable of counsel, but he fell a-counselling; and such, indeed, are all the ungodly, as it is in the Psalm,[4] The poison of asps is under their lips. It serves not their turn to do wickedly in their own persons, but they must be drawing others into wickedness by poisoning and infecting them with wicked counsel. So, then, the not walking in the counsel of the ungodly, is not to hearken to the hissing of the serpent, nor to make wicked men our counsellors, nor in the course and actions of our life to be directed by them.

But, if this be all, what great matter is it? or what needed

---

[1] Luke xvi. 25 : "Son, remember that thou in thy lifetime receivedst thy good things, and likewise Lazarus evil things; but now he is comforted, and thou art tormented." [2] Isa. xiv. 13—15 : "Thou hast said in thine heart, I will ascend into heaven, I will exalt my throne above the stars of God : I will sit also upon the mount of the congregation, in the sides of the north : I will ascend above the heights of the clouds ; I will be like the most High. Yet thou shalt be brought down to hell, to the sides of the pit." [3] 2 Sam. xvi. 23. [4] Rom. iii. 13. Cf. Ps. cxl. 3 : "Adders' poison is under their lips."

so great a caveat to be given of it? Certainly both the danger and the difficulty deserve a principal[1] caveat; and in the caveat itself we may see them both; for there are but three words in it, and every word is as a cord to draw us into sin. If pleasure will entice us, here is walking to do it; if reasons will persuade us, here is counsel to do it; if number will overrule us, here is the plural against the singular to do it: that the air is not more pestilent to be taken in than hard to be kept out; the rock is not more dangerous to be run upon than difficult to be avoided.

We would now proceed to the second mark, but that we know not how to set our feet; for we begin to see, or seem to see, a gradation before us, and, as I may say, a pair of stairs; but whether we go up or down the stairs in this gradation is made a question. But is it not strange [that] we should not know the ground we go upon—whether it rise or fall, whether it be ascending or descending? Yet such is the Prophet's contrivance here, that doctors doubt it, and are divided. Many grave authors there are on both sides, many great reasons on both sides, to maintain their opinions. They which think it an ascent, conceive it thus, that he which walketh in the counsel of the ungodly is yet but wavering, as misled by opinion, and makes but an error; he that stands in the way of sinners, stands out with obstinacy, and makes a heresy; but he that sits in the chair of scorners, is at defiance with God, and makes an apostacy. They who think it a descent, do thus conceive it: he which walks in the counsel of the ungodly, delights and takes a pleasure in his sin; he which stands in the way of sinners, stands in doubt, and is unresolved in his sin; but he who sits in the seat of the scornful, sits down and sins but for his ease, as being unable to suffer persecution. They who think it an ascent, conceive that the ungodly are but beginners in ill; that sinners are proficients in ill; but the scorners are graduates and doctors of the chair[2] in ill. They who think it a descent, conceive that the ungodly are opposite to the godly, and offend generally; that sinners offend, though actually, yet but in particulars; that scorners

---

[1] Emphatic.   [2] College Professors.

might be found at heart, if they did not set themselves to sale, and sin for promotion. The ascent may be briefly thus: that walking expresseth less resolution than standing, and standing than sitting; but in sin, the more resolute, the more dissolute: therefore sitting is the worst. The descent thus: that walking expresseth more strength than standing, and standing than sitting; for a child can sit when he cannot stand, and stand when he cannot walk; but the stronger in sin, the worse; therefore walking is the worst. Many such ways there are of conceiving diversity, either in ascending or descending; but it needs be no question which is the worse, because, without question, they are all stark nought: they are three rocks, whereof the least is enough to make a shipwreck; they are three pestilential airs, whereof the best is enough to poison the heart. This only may be observed, that howsoever the case alter with walkers and sitters, yet standers in the way of sinners keep their standing still; and whichsoever is first or last, yet they are sure to be the second.

But is it not that we mistake the Prophet, and make his words a gradation, when, perhaps, he meant them for level ground? And for such, indeed, we may take them, and do as well, and then there will not be either ascent or descent in the sins themselves, but only a diversity in their causes; as that the first is a sin caused by ill counsel; the second, a sin caused by ill example; the third, a sin caused by the innate corruption of our own hearts. And so we shall have the three principal heads or springs from which all sins do flow, and may probably be exemplified by the three first persons that were in the world: the first, committed by Eve, in following the counsel of that ungodly one, the serpent; the second, committed by Adam, in following the example of the sinful Eve; the third, committed by Cain, who sinned not either by any ill counsel or by any ill example, but only by the inbred corruption of his own heart. And in this we may observe the wonderful proneness of our nature to sin, seeing the three first persons in the world had every one of them a several spring-head of sin of their own opening; as if they thought there were no honour but in being the first founder of sin. And if there had been in nature a fourth spring-head of sin to be found, the fourth man, most likely, would have found it out; but these it seems were all. And so the fourth man, Abel, in his turn, found out a spring-head of another making—the true fountain of life; but the other spring-heads have ever since been so frequented, that Abel's fountain hath been wholly almost neglected, that the Prophet had great reason to give us caveats for drinking at those poisoned springs, and to have recourse to the true fountain of life, which is the law of God.

Or is it that the Prophet alludes here to the three principal ages of our life, which have every one of them their proper vices, as it were, retainers to them?—and therefore the vices of youth, which is the vigour of life, and delights most in motion and society, he expresseth by walking in the counsel of the ungodly; the vices of the middle age, which is *stata ætas* [the steadfast age], he expresseth by standing in the way of sinners; the vices of old age, which, being weak and feeble, is scarce able to go, he expresseth by sitting in the chair of scorners, and it is as if he had said, "Blessed is the man that hath passed through all the ages of his life, and hath kept himself untainted of the vices that are incident unto them; that hath passed the days of his youth as it were the morning of his life, and is not tainted with the stirring vices of voluptuousness and prodigality; that hath passed his middle age as it were the noon of his life, and is not tainted with the more elevated vices of ambition and vain-glory; that hath passed his old age as it were the evening of his life, and is not tainted with the sluggish vices of covetousness and avarice."

Or is it, there being five degrees of sin—concupiscence, consent, act, custom, and pride in sinning; the two first, as incident oftentimes to the godliest men, he forbears to speak of, and intimates only the three last; for to walk in the counsel of the ungodly, what is it but the act of sin? and to stand in the way of sinners, what is it but the custom of sin? and to sit in the chair of scorners, what is it but to take a pride in sin?

Or is it, finally, that by this distinction of postures the Prophet intends an absolute restraint from all manner of conversation with the wicked; so absolute that it may be said, in a proverbial manner, we neither walk, nor stand, nor sit amongst them; for if but the least liberty be taken in conversing with them, it may well be said, the passing of a camel through a needle's eye;[1] exceeding hard, if not altogether impossible, to escape untainted.

We may now consider the second mark, as it is in itself, without gradation; and is not this also a strange mark of a godly man, that he should not dare to stand in the way of sinners? For what hurt can he take by standing in their way? Is it not a broad and a large way,[2] that sinners may go by, and no hurt to him at all? But a godly man is wiser than so; though he know that the way is large and broad, yet he knows also that the press is great;[3] a man cannot stand here, but he shall be shouldered and thrust forward in spite of his teeth. It is not here as in the way of the righteous, where a man may stand long enough before he shall meet with company to thrust him forward; but here is crowding and thronging, that we can neither go here, nor do here, as we would, but must of necessity go as the crowd drives us, must perforce do as the company will have us; that he may justly be counted a happy man that can avoid this rock, which hath been the cause of more shipwrecks than either Scylla or Charybdis.

If the way of sinners were a blind, obscure way, or a man were blind and could not see his way, there might be ways of excuse for standing in it; but seeing all men's eyes are open to this way, and this way lies open to all men's eyes, to stand in it now, is not to stand in the way of sinners, but to sin in the way of understanding; and such sin shall be punished with many stripes.[4]

A man may be in the way of sinners, and be excused; but to stand in the way is unexcusable; for his being there may be by accident, but his standing there must needs be volun-

---

[1] Matt. xix. 24.   [2] Matt. vii. 13: "Broad is the way that leadeth to destruction, and many there be which go in thereat."   [3] *Ibid.*   [4] Luke xii. 47: "That servant, which knew his lord's will . . . shall be beaten with many stripes."

tary; and seeing nearness to a place, and continuance in a place, are great engrossers of the qualities of a place, how fully must he needs engross the way of sinners to himself that stands in it, which contains them both? For whilst nearness works by addition, and continuance by multiplication, the standing in the way of sinners, as gathering heat by both, must needs break forth at last into violent flames of sinning.

It is, therefore, no doubt, a good mark of a godly man that he will not stand in the way of sinners; but why should he not sit in the chair of scorners? for he may sit there and take his ease, and neither do hurt to others nor take hurt himself. He will do both; he will take hurt by brazening his own face, and he will do hurt by poisoning others' hearts. For when a man comes once to sit in the chair of scorners, it hardens him in his sin, it makes him to make a profession of it; he grows to take it in scorn that any man should be wickeder than himself; he sits, as it were, a-brooding of sin; what at first he was ashamed of, that now he glories in; and what before he was glad to do standing, he is confident now to do sitting in his chair. And as he takes this hurt himself, so doth he yet more hurt to others. For when a man in authority gives ill examples, it spreads far and prevails much; it is a pestilent thing to be wicked, *ex cathedra* [in the seat of power]: their chair stands high, and is seen and heard of many. One Pharisee may do more hurt than a hundred Sadducees; and where the poison of ungodly counsel, and the poison of sinful company, reacheth but to men near hand, the poison of this cathedral[1] wickedness reacheth far and near, that he may justly be accounted a happy man that can avoid this rock, which hath been the immediate ruin of many, and the cause of ruin to many more.

There are divers sorts of chairs, and all worth the sitting in, but only this of scorners. There is a chair of majesty; and this is made by God himself,[2] and makes them all as gods[3] that sit in it; for to this chair there is a blessing

---

[1] Enthroned. [2] Ps. lxxxix. 4: I will "build up thy throne to all generations."
[3] Ps. lxxxii. 6: "I have said, Ye *are* gods."

annexed, which makes it sacred: "Touch not mine anointed."[1] There is a chair of doctrine, and this was first set up by Moses, and makes them all reverend that sit in it, for it hath a privilege belonging to it: "Do my prophets no harm."[1] Only this chair of scorners hath none that will avow the making it; it seems to have been broken with the fall of Lucifer,[2] and ever since hath been dangerous to sit in; yet it stands in opposition with both the others, for it scorns to obey the chair of majesty, and makes a mock of hearkening to the chair of doctrine; and therefore this chair is so far from having any blessing belonging to it, that all the curses of Mount Ebal[3] are too little for it.

And as there are divers sorts of chairs, so there are divers of scorners: some scorn their inferiors, and forget that in scorning them they reproach their Maker; some scorn their betters, and seem scholars of the Pharisee, to think none so good as themselves, though none so bad; some scorn to be reproved, as being wise in their own conceit, of whom saith Solomon, "There is less hope than of a fool."[4] Some scorn to hear it said the world shall ever have end; and are herein themselves a sign that it is drawing to an end, seeing such mockers (saith St. Peter) "shall come in the last days."[5] Some scorn the ministers of God's word; and if at any time they hear them, it is but as the Athenians would hear Paul, to hear what this babbler would say.[6] Some scorn God himself, and are ready to answer as Pharaoh answered Moses, "What is God?" and "Who is the Lord that I should obey his voice?"[7] Yet all these scorners have their chair to sit in, set indeed on high, but set in slippery places, and giving them falls as certain as dangerous, or rather most certain, and yet more dangerous, [so] that he may justly be counted a happy man that can avoid this chair, which gives a worse fall than Eli's chair did, in which he fell down backward and brake his neck.[8]

But why should the Prophet speak so scornfully of scorners,

---

[1] Ps. cv. 15. [2] Isa. xiv. 12. [3] Deut. xi. 29. [4] Prov. xxvi. 12: "Sees thou a man wise in his own conceit? *there is* more hope of a fool than of him.' [5] 2 Pet. iii. 3, 4: "There shall come in the last days scoffers ... saying, Where is the promise of his coming?" [6] Acts xvii. 18: "Some said, What will this babbler say?" [7] Ex. v. 2. [8] 1 Sam. iv. 18.

and give them so base a place amongst sinners, seeing not only godly men, but (if with reverence we may say it) even God himself seems to stand in the number of being scorners? For was not Mordecai, the good Jew, a scorner?[1] who scorned so much as to make a leg,[2] or so much as to put off his hat to Haman,—himself a poor snake[3] Jew, to Haman, a prince, and prime favourite of great King Ahasuerus? May not God himself be said a scorner, of whom it is said that he laughs the wicked to scorn, and hath them in derision?[4] And how, then, can scorning be so great a sin, being found in him in whom is nothing but transcendent goodness? Or how, at least, may we distinguish the vicious scorning from that which is the virtue? Is it not that we may distinguish them by their chair? For wicked scorners are set aloft in their chair; they think they cannot be noble unless they be proud; but the good scorners sit not in a chair when they scorn; they keep state indeed, but it is with humility. God may be said to scorn, as he is said to be angry; but as he bids us us to "be angry, and sin not,"[5] so he is angry, but sins not, because his anger is never but for sin; he scorns, but sins not, because he scorns none but sinners; and as such anger, so such scorn, may possibly be and is—is and lawfully may be—in godly men, and to speak ἀνθρωποπαθῶς [after the manner of men], in God himself.

But why would the Prophet say, "Blessed is the man," as though blessedness were entailed to heirs male, or as though the law of God were like the law Salic of France, excluding women from the kingdom of heaven? for else he should rather have said, "Blessed is every man or woman," and not say only, "Blessed is the man." But is it not that David knew better the extent of his words than to be so superfluous; for ever since the time of which Moses saith, God made man; male and female created he them,[6] women have had as good right to the word as men, though it pass in their name; and if we say *more* right, we shall say perhaps but right; for how else could Christ be called the Son of man,

---

[1] Esther iii. 2.   [2] To bow, *flectere genua*, to bend the knees (Vulg.)   [3] Contemptible.
[4] Ps. ii. 4: "He that sitteth in the heavens shall laugh: the Lord shall have them in derision."   [5] Eph. iv. 26.   [6] Gen. i. 27: "So God created man in his *own* image; in the image of God created he him; male and female created he them."

who we all know was the Son of but only woman? And if we look upon examples of blessedness, we shall find as well women as men recorded for blessed; and if any advantage be, it seems rather on the woman's side, seeing we find one woman to have attained a greater degree of blessedness than ever any man did, except only her only Son, "the man Christ Jesus."[1]

If a man have not walked in the counsel of the ungodly, it may probably be thought he hath gone the fairer way; and then he hath a title to blessedness by this rule, "Blessed are they that walk" in the law of the Lord. If he have not stood in the way of sinners, it may charitably be thought he is sorry that ever he came there; and then he may lay claim to blessedness by this rule, "Blessed *are* they that mourn,"[2] and are penitent for their sins. And if he have not sat in the chair of scorners, it may with good reason be thought he hath done it in humility; and then he hath a right to blessedness by this rule, "Blessed *are* the poor in spirit,"[3] for "God resisteth the proud, but giveth grace to the humble."[4] But for all this, and nevertheless, it may be said that these are yet but negative marks, and can make at most but a godliness by negation, which can no more properly be said a godliness than *indolentia* [absence of pain] may be said to be *voluptas* [pleasure]. The true godliness is a positive thing, and cannot be affirmed out of negatives; it is a habit, and cannot be concluded from privations. The Prophet therefore stays not here, but proceeds, and hastens to the affirmative marks; for they, indeed, are the proper characters of a godly man; they are never found but in him, and in him they are ever found. And of these there is but a pair, as they came into Noah's ark, and yet enough to make a breed —enough to bring godliness to its full propagation. And he seems to frame his process in this manner: a man is known what he is by his delight; for such as a man's delight is, such a man himself is;[5] and therefore a godly man delights not to walk in the counsel of the ungodly, nor to stand in the way of sinners, nor to sit in the chair of

---

[1] 1 Tim. ii. 5.   [2] Matt. v. 4.   [3] Matt. v. 3.   [4] Jas. iv. 6.   [5] Prov. xxiii. 7.

scorners, for these are all lawless delights—at least, delights of that law of which St. Paul saith, "I find another law in my members:"[1] they agree not with a godly man's nature, and though a delight there must be, there is not living without it; yet a godly man will rather want it, than take it up in such commodities. *But his delight is in the law of the Lord;* [**ver. 2**] and now the Prophet begins to enter upon his affirmative marks, and the godly man begins to appear in his likeness; for this delighting in the law of God is so essential to godliness, that it even constitutes a godly man, and gives him his being. For what is godliness but the love of God? and what is love without delight? that we may see what a sovereign thing godliness is, which not only brings us to delight when we come to blessedness, but brings us to blessedness by a way of delighting. For the Prophet requires not a godliness that bars us of delight; he requires only a godliness that rectifies our delight; for as the wrong placing our delight is the cause of all our miseries, so the right placing it is the cause of all our happiness; and what righter placing it than to place it in the right? and what is the right but only the law?

But is there delight, then, in the law of God? Is it not a thing rather that will make us melancholy? and doth it not mortify in us the life of all joy? It mortifies indeed the life of carnal delights, but it quickens in us another delight, as much better than those as heaven is above the earth. For there is no true delight which delights not as much to be remembered as to be felt; which pleaseth not as well the memory as the sense; and takes not as much joy to think of it being done as when it was a-doing. For is it not a miserable delight when it may be threatened with this: *Olim hæc meminisse pigebit?* You will one day remember this [with pain]. Is it not a doleful delight, when *extrema gaudii luctus occupat* [grief besets the borders of gladness], —when sorrow follows it at the heels? Is it not a fearful delight when, like a magician's rod, it is instantly turned into a serpent? And such are all worldly delights, either

---

[1] Rom. vii. 23: "I see another law in my members, warring against the law of my mind."

like that of Amnon in loving Tamar—first enjoyed, and presently loathed;[1] or like that of Cain in killing Abel:[2] mad to do it, and then stark mad for having done it; or like that of Esau in eating Jacob's pottage—give at first a blessing for it, and afterwards give it a thousand curses;[3] or like that of Gehazi, in taking gifts of Naaman—leap for joy till we come to Elisha, and loathsome lepers all our lives after.[4] This delight, which the Prophet here speaks of, is the only delight that neither blushes nor looks pale; the only delight that gives a repast without an after-reckoning; the only delight that stands in construction with all tenses;[5] and (like Æneas, Anchises) carries his parents upon his back. And why should not even worldly men be sensible of this delight? They delight in gold and silver, and behold, the law is more precious than gold; yea, than much fine gold.[6] They delight in beauty; and behold, how amiable the tabernacles of the Lord are.[7] They delight in light; and behold, the law is a lanthorn to our feet, and a light to our paths.[8] They delight in knowledge; and behold, through the law we have more understanding than our teachers.[9] They delight in joy; and behold, the law is right, and rejoiceth the heart.[10] They delight in long life; and behold, the law of the Lord increaseth the length of days, and the years of life![11] And where are they now that are afraid of melancholy in the midst of such delights? Certainly if there be, as physicians affirm, a hellebore or a senna to purge away the melancholy and sad humours of the body, this study in the law of God is the true hellebore and senna of the soul; or rather it is the juice of the grape which David in another place speaks of, that exhilarates and "maketh glad the heart of man."[12]

And as in this study of the law of God there is no fear

---

[1] 2 Sam. xiii. 15. [2] Gen. iv. 8 *seqq*. [3] Gen. xxv. 33; xxvii. 34. [4] 2 Kings v. 23—27. [5] Or is suitable to all times. [6] Ps. xix. 9, 10: "The judgments of the LORD . . . more to be desired *are they* than gold, yea, than much fine gold." [7] Ps. cxix. 105: "Thy word *is* a lamp unto my feet, and a light unto my path." [8] Ps. lxxxiv. 1: "How amiable *are* thy tabernacles, O LORD of hosts!" [9] Ps. cxix. 99: "I have more understanding than all my teachers; for thy testimonies *are* my meditation." [10] Ps. xix. 8: "The statutes of the LORD *are* right, rejoicing the heart." [11] Prov. iii. 2: "Length of days, and long life, and peace, shall they add to thee." [12] Ps. civ. 15.

of melancholy, so in the delight that is taken in it there is
no fear of satiety; all other delights must have change, or
else they cloy us; must have cessation, or else they tire us;
must have moderation, or else they waste us: this only
delight is that of which we can never take enough—we can
never be so full, but we shall leave with an appetite, or
rather never leave, because ever in an appetite. It is but
one, yet is still fresh; it is always enjoyed, yet always
desired; or, rather, the more it is enjoyed, the more it is
desired. All other delights may be barred from us, may be
hindered to us; this only delight is free in prison, is at ease
in torments, is alive in death; and indeed there is no
delight that keeps us company in our death-beds, but only
this All other delights are then ashamed of us, and we of
them; this only sits by us in all extremities, and gives us a
cordial when physic and friends forsake us.

The Prophet hath taught us marks how to know a godly
man; but he hath not taught us how to know these marks;
and this is a special matter, for we may as well mistake the
marks as mistake the man; and therefore, though we let
pass the negative marks, and leave them to be taken at all
adventure, yet this affirmative mark, of delighting in the
law of God, would by any means be better marked. For
this is an essential mark, and this mistaken might mar all,
and lead us, perhaps, to Cain instead of Abel. For many
delight in the law, because they which preach the gospel
should live by the gospel.[1] But these are covetous men,
and delight not in the law, but in profit. Many delight in
the law because they desire to sit in Moses' chair; but these
are ambitious men, and delight not in the law, but in
honour. Many delight in the law, because it teacheth
many hidden and secret mysteries; but these are vain men,
and delight not in the law, but in superfluous knowledge.
Many delight in the law, but only to pass away the
time, as thinking it better *otiosum esse, quàm nihil agere*
[to enjoy leisure than to do nothing]; but these are scanda-
lous men, and delight not in the law, but in idle fancies.

---

[1] 1 Cor. ix. 14: "They which preach the gospel should live of the gospel."

Many delight in the law as Neoptolemus in philosophy—*philosophandum sed paucis* [discourse philosophically, but not to many]; a little serves their turn, and if the other sorts were all of them defective in substance, this sort surely is defective in quantity: those had not the right stuff, this hath not the just measure; and so we are little the nearer yet for finding out any marks of true delighting in the law of God. And how, then, shall we come to know the delighting which is true and perfect from that which is counterfeit and defective? Shall we say, it must be a delighting only, or but only chiefly?[1] Not only, for so we should delight in nothing else; and who doubts but there are many other delights which both Nature requires, and God himself allows? therefore, not only, but chiefly; yet so chiefly as in a manner only; for chiefly is properly where there may be comparison; but this is so chiefly as admits of no comparison. In presence of this, all other delights do lose their light; in balance with this, all other delights are found to be light. And this is even intimated in the word itself used by the Prophet here, which is [חֵפֶץ, *hêphets*], and signifies a delight that takes up the whole will, and leaves no *plus ultra* [further (longing)] in our desires; which, as it only is and only can be, so it only must and only ought to be true, of our delighting in the law of God. Other delights may have their fits, but no *hêphets*, but only this.[2] We may take delight in a care of our estates, which is a provident and therefore a commendable delight; for he that provides not for his family is worse than an infidel;[3] yet it must not be our *hêphets*, for *corpus aggravat animam multa cogitantem* [the body burdens the much-meditating mind]; much caring for the world makes the soul heavy, and presseth it down from ascending toward heaven. We may take delight in wife and children, which is a natural and therefore a commendable delight; for no man ever hated his own flesh;[4] yet it must not be our *hêphets*, for he that loves father or mother, wife or children, better than Christ, is not

---

[1] *i.e.*, chiefly, if not only.   [2] None have an engrossing delight, save this only.
[3] 1 Tim. v. 8.   [4] Eph. v. 29.

worthy of Christ.[1] We may take delight in bodily exercises, which is a healthful and therefore a commendable delight, for he that neglects the care of his health is within compass of being *felo de se*, a murderer of himself; yet it must not be our *ḥêphets;* for *nimia cura corporis est incuria animi*, too much care taken of the body, shows there is but little care taken of the mind. But why stand we angling for marks of true delighting in the law of God, when the Prophet himself gives us a mark here that may be *instar omnium* [as good as all other], a mark that never fails—that he who delights in the law of God will be *exercising himself in it day and night;* for it seems to be here, as between faith and works, that as St. James saith, Show me thy faith by thy works,[2] so we may say, Show me thy delighting by thy exercising. For as it is but a dead faith that brings not forth the fruit of good works,[3] so it is but a feigned delight that brings not forth the work of exercising; and as it is but an unsound faith that works but intermittingly and by fits, so it is but an aguish delighting that hath its heat but at turns and seasons; but where we see a constancy of good works, as we may be bold to say there is a lively and sound faith, so where we see a continual exercising, we may be confident to say there is a true delighting. The working shows a life of faith; the constancy of working, a true temper of that life. The exercising shows a delighting; the continuance of exercising, a sincerity of that delighting.

But will not this continual exercising in the law of God get men the name of common barrators,[4] and make them accounted troublesome fellows amongst their neighbours, as of whom it may be said they are never well but when they are going to law? Indeed, the law of man where *summum jus* is *summa injuria* [extreme law is extreme wrong], and where might oftentimes overcomes right, may be subject perhaps

---

[1] Matt. x. 37: "He that loveth father or mother more than me is not worthy of me; and he that loveth son or daughter more than me is not worthy of me."
[2] James ii. 18: "Yea, a man may say, Thou hast faith, and I have works: show me thy faith without thy works, and I will show thee my faith by my works."
[3] James ii. 17: "Even so faith, if it hath not works, is dead, being alone." Also ver. 20: "Faith without works is dead." [4] Stirrers up or setters forward and maintainers of law-suits and quarrels. (Bailey's Eng. Dict.)

to such obloquy, but not the law of God; for this is not a law where the weakest goes to the wall, but this law is a wall to the weakest; the delighting in this law is not a going to law, but a law to our going, as it is said, Thy law is a light to our feet,[1] a light not only to our eyes, to make us see the right way, but to our feet also, to make us walk the right way; and it is so far from making us to become enemies to our neighbours, that it makes us to become neighbours to our enemies; for of this law it is said, it suffers all things, it endureth all things, it seeketh not her own,[2] but if any man will take our coat from us it makes us contented to let him have our cloak also.[3]

The delighting in the law of God is that divine contemplation by which we see God as in a glass,[4] and is the only true way to our only true felicity, though there be men that think they can tell of better contemplations and better ways to happiness than David seems to know, or will at least acknowledge; for if they should but name the contemplation, which is *contemplari nummos in arca* [contemplating money in a chest], or the meditation which is *meditari inania* [meditating vain things],[5] or the pleasure of which is said, *trahit sua quemque voluptas* [every one is led by his own delight], the worst of these would be a better delight and a better way of happiness than this of David's. But these men's blindness must not lead us into the ditch;[6] for these delights they speak of are the very blocks that lie in our way and hinder us from happiness; they are the very weights that hang heavy upon the soul, and keep it from rising to the true height of divine contemplation; and if a man whose mind were once raised up to this height should afterward descend and take a view of the world, he would even be astonished to see men that pretend to reason, and would be thought wise, be so simple as to take delight in their weights, and to take a pleasure in their clogs, and so sillily to leave the delight of heavenly meditation to follow these vain and foolish things which the world admires.

---

[1] Ps. cxix. 105: "Thy word *is* a lamp unto my feet."   [2] 1 Cor. xiii. 4, 5, 7.
[3] Matt. v. 40.   [4] 1 Cor. xiii. 12: "For now we see through a glass darkly."
[5] Ps. ii. 1.   [6] Matt. xv. 14: "And if the blind lead the blind, both shall fall into the ditch."

And, indeed, what but this made our Prophet here, in another place, break out into his passionate exclamation, "O ye sons of men, *how long* will ye love vanity, *and* seek after leasing?"[1] For look into the world, and to all things that are in the world, and see if there be anything in it (as to the purpose of making us happy) but only lies and leasings. Pleasure bears thee in hand, it can make thee happy; but it lies; for do not all pleasures hasten to their end, and that end either in sorrow or satiety? Honour vaunts it can make thee happy; but it lies; for hath honour any being but in others not being, where it is part of our happiness that others be happy? Riches make thee believe they can make thee happy; but they lie; for they cannot so much as ease the least pain of thy body, or the least anguish of thy mind. Learning persuades thee it can make thee happy; but it lies; for "in much wisdom *is* much grief; and he that increaseth knowledge increaseth sorrow."[2] The flesh tells thee it can make thee happy; but it lies; for the worms stand waiting continually for it, and are sure erelong to have it to eat. O that men would consider this, and not put the Prophet to his exclamation, "O ye sons of men, how long will ye be in love with vanity, and seek after leasings?" For this indeed would be a good preparative, and but a preparative, to divine contemplation; it might serve to strew branches in the way, but not to cry Hosanna;[3] for to raise the soul up to this height of contemplation, it is not enough to put off these weights that draw it down, but there must be a pulley also to draw it up, as Christ saith, No man can come unto me, except the Father draw him;[4] and therefore many heathen philosophers could cast off these clogs, could put off these weights; for they despised riches, they scorned honours, they hated pleasures, they contemned the world, and yet for all this they could never but flutter a little in the low region of the air; they could never rise up to the firmament of contemplation; and all because they wanted this pulley, which they that delight in the law of God shall never want. For *Honorantes me honorabo*, saith God; They which

---

[1] Ps. iv. 2.   [2] Eccl. 1. 18.   [3] Matt. xxi. 8, 9.   [4] John vi. 44: "No man can come to me, except the Father which hath sent me draw him."

honour me, I will honour them;[1] and if they delight in my law, I will delight in their study. And then, if by delighting in the law of God, we can bring God to delight in us, oh, what joy, what excessive joy, what happiness, what transcendent happiness, will this be unto us!

But why would the Prophet speak of delighting in the law of God, and not speak rather of delighting in God himself? for this, no doubt, is a better delight, and this delight would be a greater blessedness. Is not the answer to this question made by Christ [John] himself? If you love not your brother whom you see, how can you love God whom you do not see?[2] If we delight not in the law of God which we know, how can we delight in God whom we do not know?—not know, but as the law teacheth him unto us and showeth him unto us. This life is but the means to a better life, and the chief delight of this life is but to delight in the means to a better life. We see God now but as in a glass,[3] and though there be many glasses to see God, yet the brightest of these glasses is the law, and how then can we delight in the seeing of God if we delight not in the glass in which we may best see him? To see him as he is,[4] and in himself, is reserved till we shall have better eyes: these eyes we have are carnal and corruptible, and cannot see God till they have put on incorruption;[5] but when those eyes come, and that we shall see God face to face,[6] then the means will give place to the substance, and then the delighting in the law of God will be turned into the delighting in God himself. Till then the Prophet, though with his Prophet's eyes he might see more himself, yet could not inform us to make us see more; but he hath truly told us the height of our delight in this life, if the delight of our life be in the law of God.

But let the delight be what it will, it is but only contemplation, and contemplation sets but only the eyes a-work; it leaves all the rest of the body idle. But godliness is an exercise for the whole man, both body and soul; and there-

---

[1] 1 Sam. ii. 30: "Them that honour me I will honour."   [2] 1 John iv. 20: "He that loveth not his brother whom he hath seen, how can he love God whom he hath not seen?"   [3] 1 Cor. xiii. 12.   [4] 1 John iii. 2.   [5] 1 Cor. xv. 53.   [6] 1 Cor. xiii. 12.

fore, not only David saith, My soul, praise thou the Lord,[1] but St. Paul saith, Make your bodies a living sacrifice;[2] for our godliness must be perfect, that our blessedness may be perfect; and even in heaven (if they could be separated) we should not be blessed in beholding the blessed face of God, if we did not as well glorify him in beholding him as behold his glory. Contemplation brings us but to *video meliora proboque* [I see and approve the better]; and if *deteriora sequor* [I pursue the worse] do follow, then godliness is stopped in her race at the very goal: the building is left unperfect when it is come to the roof. We cannot make a demonstration of true godliness out of all the premises, unless that be added which follows, "And in his law he will exercise himself day and night;" but if this be added, then the roof of the house is set on, and then the goal of godliness is won. And though it may seem a wearisome thing, summer and winter, day and night, all a man's life long, to do nothing else but always one thing, yet this is the godly man's task; he must do so, or he cannot be the man we take him for. For to be godly but sometimes, is to be ungodly always; and no man is so wicked but he may sometimes have good thoughts, and do good works. But this serves not our godly man's turn; his sun must never set,[3] for if he ever be in darkness, he shall ever be in darkness; at least, he shall find it more work to kindle his fire anew than to have kept it still burning. For if a man should water his bed with tears all night,[4] and go next day to the house of laughter,[5] that man's godliness would be but as the morning dew—rise to a cloud, and so vanish.[6] Or if he should bestow the whole day in the exercise of godliness, and yet at night return to his vomit,[7] that man would be but as a half-moon—bright on one side, and horrid blackness on the other. For godliness is a thing entire; it cannot be had in pieces. We must have it together, or not at all; and by this a godly man is made *totus teres atque rotundus* [com-

---

[1] Ps. ciii. 1, 22: civ. 1, 35: "Bless the LORD, O my soul." [2] Rom. xii. 1: "I beseech you therefore, brethren, by the mercies of God, that ye present your bodies a living sacrifice, holy, acceptable unto God." [3] Isa. lx. 20. [4] Ps. vi. 6. [5] Eccl. vii. 2: "The house of feasting." [6] Hos. vi. 4. [7] Prov. xxvi. 11.

pletely smooth and round]. All the former make but lines; this only consummates godliness, and brings it to a circle.

It seems here as if the Prophet went about to make men think that the readiest way to be a happy man were to be a lawyer, if we may call him a lawyer that studieth and practiseth the law; for after his negative marks of a godly man, he comes next to this, that "his delight is in the law of the Lord," which is his studying of the law; and because a student in the law can make no benefit by it till he come to be a practiser, he therefore, by these next words, "And in his law he will exercise himself," seems to call him to the bar, and enables him to practise, that having learned the law himself, he may now teach it to others, or at leastwise practise it towards others. But is not this a paradox in David, seeing it is against our own experience? for we have known many that by the law have grown rich; many that by the law have gotten honour; many that by the law have grown famous; but we never yet knew any that by the law grew happy; for, notwithstanding their honour, their riches, their fame, yet they ever had something whereof to complain. We must therefore remember what law this is. It is not our common law, nor our canon law; it is not the civil law, nor the law of the twelve tables; it is not the law of the Medes and Persians,[1] nor the law of nations. It is the law of the Lord; a law pure and undefiled; a law that was given by angels, in the hand of a Mediator;[2] a law by which we shall judge,[3] and by we shall be judged.[4] It is *imperatoria lex;* not the emperor's law, but an imperial law —*lex architectonice,* a law that gives rules to all other, and is itself ruled by none. And here now there opens itself, as it were, a *novus orbis* [a new world], for if we should enter into the main to speak of laws, we should never make an end; our best is, therefore, to keep close to David, and to go no further than he goes, and yet so we shall have law enough to make us happy. Only we may consider what these exercises are in which this godly lawyer is so diligent all day, and so vigilant all night, to exercise himself; and as

---

[1] Dan. vi. 8.   [2] Gal. iii. 19: "*It was* ordained by angels in the hands of a mediator."   [3] 1 Cor. vi. 2, 3.   [4] Rom. ii. 12.

the marks before, so the exercises here, may be distinguished into negatives and affirmatives; but, seeing the godly man mingles them together in his course, we may as well mingle them together in our discourse. A godly lawyer will not boast himself to know that of which he is ignorant, nor feign himself to be ignorant of that he knows. He will not discourage a man in a good cause, nor encourage him in a bad. He will not overreach a man that is shorter than himself, nor undermine a man that is shallower than himself, nor supplant a man weaker than himself. He will not rise by other men's falls, nor make a gain of other men's losses. He will give counsel to a poor man without a fee, as reckoning a poor man's cause his own, and a good conscience the best fee. If he have taken any other fee, he hath mortgaged his time, and will not sell it again till he have first redeemed it. He gives fees himself to get him clients, and grows richer by giving than others do by taking. He is ready to end suits, but not to begin them; and he had rather want work than make it. He is glad when he can use the law, but would be more glad there were no use of it. It is a booty to him when he can find opportunity to do a good deed. If there want counsel to set forward a good cause, he gives it; if pains or care, he takes it. He keeps his terms duly, as preserving the Sabbath day before all other days; and yet as his piety makes every day to him a Sabbath, so his practice makes it term to him all the year long. He turns over books and searcheth records, not so much to look out dead precedents as to find out the reasons that gave life to the precedents; for he makes it not a reason of his action that others have done so, but he makes it his actions, if he find there was reason, for the doing so. He inquires and hearkens out the poor, and relieves them; the naked, and clothes them; captives, and redeems them; men oppressed, and succours them; men that mourn, and comforts them; men a-dying, and revives them. The law is both his study and his recreation, and one cannot tell whether it be more his work or more his pastime; for, as the Prophet saith here, it is his exercise, so he said before, it is his delight. And it is well it is so, for without this delight it were impossible he should ever go through with such incessant labours as are imposed upon him, or, rather, he imposeth upon himself, day and night. But delight makes burdens light, makes labours easy; which, perhaps, made Christ say that his burden was light, and his yoke easy.[1] And in this manner, indeed, if a man be a student and a practiser in the law, it will be no paradox to say, it will be no violence to the text to make David say, that the best and readiest way to be a happy man is to be a lawyer.

When it is said, "His delight is in the law of the Lord, and in his law he will exercise himself day and night," is it not a kind of solecism[2] to double the word law, without any lawful occasion? It may, perhaps, be a solecism in grammar, but it is none in affection; for, therefore, he doubles the word (the law) to express the wonderful delight he takes in the law; and this is more fully expressed in Psalm cxix., where he seems so fond of the word, and so loath to leave it, that he cannot endure it should be out of his mouth, and therefore at every third or fourth word is up with it again. Or is it that he therefore doubles the word (the law), because, indeed, there is a double law, which though as a man he could not see, yet as a prophet he might foresee; and the words day and night are here joined to the later law, because although there were in the old law a *juge sacrificium* [continual sacrifice] in representation; yet there never was any *juge sacrificium* in reality and execution, but only in this later law; therefore where David speaks it as a great matter to pray his seven times a day,[3] we in this law are put to our *semper orate* [pray always],[4] and *sine intermissione orate* [pray without ceasing];[5] continual prayer is expected from us, day and night.

But why should the Prophet require day and night to be spent in the doing of God's law? seeing, for the day, God himself allows us six days to do our own work; and for the night, there is no *opus tenebrarum*, no fit work to be done in darkness? Yet a godly man will do as the Prophet requires

---

[1] Matt. xi. 30. [2] An error in speech. [3] Ps. cxix. 164: "Seven times a day do I praise thee." [4] Eph. vi. 18: "Praying always with all prayer." [5] 1 Thess. v. 17.

him; he will do it in the day, that men, seeing his good works, may glorify his Father which is in heaven;[1] and he will do it in the night, that he may not be seen of men,[2] and that his left hand may not know what his right hand doeth.[3] He will do it in the day to show he is none of those *qui fugiunt lucem* [who shun the light]; and he will do it in the night to show he is one of those *qui cum in tenebris mices*[4] [who, when in darkness, shine]. He will do it in the daytime, because the day is the time of doing, as St. Peter [the Lord] saith, "Work whilst it is day;"[5] and he will do it in the night lest his master should come as a thief in the night[6] and find him idle. Indeed, this day and night of David's amounts but to St. Paul's continually, Watch continually, Pray continually,[7] for though the sun in the firmament set, and make it night to our eyes, yet the Sun of Righteousness must never set, to make it night in our hearts; but it must be here as it was in the beginning, the evening and the morning must make but one day.[8]

The Prophet hath used much circumstance to tell us of the man that should be blessed; and when he hath said all he can, it is all but a godly man; and why could he not do this at first, and have saved himself and us a labour? We cannot, perhaps, tell for what reason the Prophet did it, but we may easily tell for what reason he might do it, for many reasons may be given of it. If he had only said, A godly man is blessed, it would have made but a new business, for we should presently have asked him, And what is a godly man? and then he must have come to this which he delivers now; so the Prophet went the nearest way, though we may think he went about. And if he had said, A godly man is blessed, and had not told what a godly man is, it would have bred a world of controversy, for then every man would have come and put in his claim to blessedness, under pretence of godliness, and there would never have been quiet. Cain[9] would have come and pretended devotion for making oblations and offering sacrifices to God; Korah

---

[1] Matt. v. 16.   [2] Matt. vi. 1.   [3] Matt. vi. 3.   [4] So in original edition.
[5] John ix. 4.   [6] 1 Thess. v. 2.   [7] Eph. vi. 18: "Praying always .... and watching thereto with all perseverance."   [8] Gen. i. 5 (Heb. one day).   [9] Gen. iv. 3.

and Dathan[1] would have come, and pretended zeal for opposing governors, as taking too much upon them. The Pharisee[2] would have come, and pretended pureness for only fasting twice a week, and giving tithes of all he possessed. Judas[3] himself would have come, and pretended charity for taking care of the poor, and finding fault with the cost bestowed upon Christ; and there would have been so many pretenders to godliness, and thereupon such snatching and catching at blessedness, that if this had been suffered, both godliness would have been in danger to be adulterated, and blessedness itself to suffer violence. To stop, therefore, the mouths of these pretenders, and utterly to damn all such false claims, the Prophet proclaims here the true title, and sets down, as it were, in *terminis terminantibus* [in definite terms], how the man must be qualified that will lay claim to blessedness, for, if any of the conditions here expressed be wanting, it will be in vain to have a thought of blessedness; for this the Prophet delivers for law, and of this we may be sure there will not be anything abated.

But if the Prophet be so punctual, and require such precise performance of such precise points, he might as well have held his peace and said nothing; for what is this but to build castles in the air, to tell us of a man that should be blessed, when there never was in the world, nor ever shall be, any such man; and so, by the course he takes, blessedness must either fall to the king, by escheat,[4] for want of a right heir, or at least *cedere primo occupanti* [pass to the first taker], for want of a lawful claimer. But the Prophet had more knowledge than these men are aware of; he had read the chronicles, and found there many such men upon record, —Abel, Enoch, Noah, Abraham, Samuel; many others. And since his time we ourselves find many recorded for such men,—Hezekiah and Josiah, kings of Judah; Zacharias and Elizabeth of later time. It is, therefore, but a mere scandal; blessedness can never want an heir, for in all ages past there have been such men, and, by God's grace, are

---

[1] Numb. xvi. 1—3.   [2] Luke xviii. 12.   [3] John xii. 4, 5.   [4] A writ for the recovery of any land or profits that fall to a lord within his manor, either by forfeiture or the death of a tenant without heirs. (Bailey, Eng. Dict.)

many such at this day, and shall be many such in the ages to come, as long as the world shall last, for the devil must not have all; God will have his congregation; and that must consist of such as are here described, a "congregation of the righteous."[1]

And now we may say, the Prophet hath, as it were, his prize; he hath set a spell[2] to all posterity for a perfect description; for though some may think that Xenophon, in his Instruction of Cyrus, and Cicero, in his description of an orator, have become his equals, yet let the matter be examined fairly, and we shall find that the Prophet here, in a few plain words, hath made a perfecter godly man than either Xenophon a prince, or Cicero an orator, with all their long elaborate discourses.

The Prophet set "blessed" as it were a sign at the entrance of his Psalm; and where blessed is hung out for a sign, we might be sure to find a godly man within; and so he hath well quitted himself of the first part of his proposition in showing us what a godly man is; and now, if he can quit himself as well of the second part, in showing us that he is blessed, we shall then say he hath truly played his prize indeed, and worthily deserves to be called the godly man's champion; for in so doing he shall set a more glorious crown upon a godly man's head than that which Samuel set upon his. He is blessed; *and he shall be like a tree.* [**ver. 3.**]

But here, by the way, we may observe a grammatical difference which the Prophet intimates between blessedness and godliness; for to blessedness he assigns but only two tenses or times; a present tense, He is blessed; and a future, He shall be like a tree. Preterperfect tense, he assigns none; for indeed, *fuisse felicem miserrimum est* [to *have been* happy is most unhappy]; and to say *fuimus Troes* [we *were* Trojans], is as much as to say, We are not so now. That which is past is dead in time; and in the body of true happiness there must be, there can be, no dead flesh. But to godliness he assigns three tenses or times:[3] a preterperfect tense, That hath [not] walked in the counsel of the ungodly; a present tense, His delight is in the law of the

---
[1] Ps. i. 5.   [2] Challenge.   [3] In the Vulgate.

Lord; and a future, In his law he will exercise himself; for godliness is a habit, and cannot be had but by often repetition and reiteration of actions; that if the time past do not prompt and give example to the present, and the present to the future, we may have flashes of godliness, but a true habit of godliness we can never have.

And here now the Prophet begins to show himself a prophet, and to speak like a prophet: all he had said before, he might have spoken as a doctor of the law, for they were but caveats and informations to godliness. This he speaks now, he could not speak but as a prophet, for he comes to speak of things to come, and what shall become of the godly, and of the wicked, in the times hereafter; and this, neither doctor of law, nor yet astrologer, nor any human artist could do, but only a prophet of God. And we may not the less believe him because he speaks of future things, which to man's understanding are always uncertain; seeing he speaks it not as of himself, or as having learned it of men; but he speaks it as taught by God, with whom all future things are present, all things to come as come already. For these prophets of God had, as I may say, perspective glasses, given them by God, in which they could see things afar off, and far off both in place and time; and we may be allowed to call them glasses, seeing themselves were called *videntes*, seers, as seeing the things they were to speak; and then prophets, foretellers, as communicating that to others which in their glasses they saw themselves. And as themselves were called *videntes*, seers, so their work or faculty was called *visio*, or seeing; and yet in this there was distinction, for not every prediction of a Prophet was called *visio*, a vision, but such only as came with joyful tidings; for when they came with heavy news, it was not properly called *visio*, a vision, but *onus*, a burden; and our Prophet here sings both tunes,—he hath *visionem*, a vision, for the godly; and *onus*, a burden, presently after, for the wicked; but he tells his vision, his good news, first; and this it is—A godly man shall be like a tree.

But is this such good news for a godly man? must this be the height of a godly man's expectation, to be like a tree?

Will the Prophet serve us thus,—make us take such pains for godliness, and bear us all this while in hand, that by being godly we shall be happy, and now bring us to no better a happiness than to be like a tree? If he would needs use a similitude, could he by his glass make no better choice, or is a godly man's happiness no better worth than to liken him to a tree?—a tree, which grows out of the earth, and creeps into the earth?—a tree, that is exposed to wind and weather?—a tree, that is subject to worms and cankers?—a tree, that for all its being planted by the water, is sure at last to come to the fire? But we must not, with our ignorance, lay aspersion upon the Prophet's knowledge, (for it is not the worthiness of the subject, in a similitude, that dignifies the thing that is compared to it; for what honour was it to Nebuchadnezzar that he was likened to Lucifer,[1] the morning star? or what more did Christ express of the kingdom of heaven by comparing it to a pearl, than by comparing it to a grain of mustard seed?)[2] but it is the good qualities in which they sympathise; and of such good qualities we shall find so many in a tree, that happiness may think itself happy to be compared to it; for was it not a tree that bore the fruit of life in the Garden of Eden?[3]—was it not a tree that bore the Lord of life,[4] in the field of Golgotha? O happy tree! well worthy to be made the similitude of our happiness, which was the instrument to procure our happiness. But we need not to go so far to show the worth of the comparison; there are circumstances enough in a tree itself that may sufficiently justify the Prophet's choice, for though a tree be but dust in substance, and have the lower part fixed in the earth, yet it riseth above the earth, and hath boughs and branches aspiring towards heaven, transformed into a substance as though they were no earth, expressing plainly the condition of the godly, who though they be of earthy mould, and dwell in houses of clay, yet their aspiring is to heaven, and their con-

---

[1] Isa. xiv. 12: "How art thou fallen from heaven, O Lucifer, son of the morning!"
[2] Matt. xiii. 31, 45: "The kingdom of heaven is like unto a grain of mustard seed," etc. . . . "like unto a merchant man, seeking goodly pearls," etc. [3] Gen. ii. 9; iii. 22. [4] Acts v. 30.

fidence is to be transformed into the image of Christ, and to have their bodies made like to his glorious body.[1]

But this is a common resemblance that may be found in every tree; the Prophet here sets his similitude closer upon a godly man than that *ex quovis ligno fiat Mercurius* [a god may be made out of any log]; every tree will not serve to do it; but as before he delivered certain characters to know what a godly man is, so here he delivers certain marks to know what kind of tree it is that must make his similitude; for it is not a tree that grows up wildly of itself, as having no other education but nature, but it is *planted* by an artificial hand, and as it were civilized by transplanting; and it is not planted amongst rocky cliffs where it may be choked with drought, and where it must eat stones, or else be starved, but it is planted *by the waters'* side, where it hath drink to its meat, and where the soil is made supple, to give the root readily both passage and nourishment. And it is not a barren, vain-glorious tree, that makes only a show, and is nothing but words, as bearing nothing but leaves;[2] but it is a just-performing tree, that follows his leaves with fruit, as a just man's deeds do follow his words. Neither is it an unseasonable tree, that brings forth abortive fruits, and sets our teeth on edge with sourness; but it goes the full time out, and nourisheth the fruit up till it hath gotten sweetness by maturity, and tastes most pleasantly. And that we may know it to be no ordinary tree, the very leaves continue still, and do not wither.

But what matter is it, when the fruit is gathered, whether the leaves continue still or no? For the work the leaves come about, is but to defend the buds, and to keep the young fruits from the violence of the sun and wind; and when they have seen them brought up and come to a ripe age, that they can shift for themselves, the leaves then may take their leave, as we see them fall away by one and one, as taking notice that their work is done. There are, perhaps, some barren trees that bear no fruit, and these sometimes have leaves continuing still, and hanging on, both

---

[1] Phil. iii. 21: "Who shall change our vile body, that it may be fashioned like unto his glorious body."   [2] Matt. xxi. 19: "Nothing thereon, but leaves only."

summer and winter, as if they stayed waiting for employment, and looking still when fruits would bud forth, but with as idle an expectation as the Jews stand waiting for the coming of their Messiah. But this is not the case of our leaves here, which therefore continue still, because they are still in office; for our tree bears fruit continually, and therefore hath need of leaves continually: when one fruit is ripe and gone, another is green and coming on; and therefore the leaves, which are necessary attendants upon the fruits as long as there are young fruits that need attendants, cannot be discharged, and therefore do not wither. And yet, perhaps, the Prophet had a further reason why he would give the leaf a place in the similitude of a godly man's happiness, seeing a leaf was the first angel of liberty to the prisoners in the ark;[1] their daybreak of comfort came from the light of a leaf; and if it had not been for a leaf, the tyrannizing waters would have more kept their minds in the dark than their bodies in the ark, and have drowned them with despair, when they could not with their waves; and when the waters overcame all other creatures, both men and beasts, yet the leaf continued constant to the tree, and overcame the waters; and as it perished not in the inundation of the world, no more shall it wither in the conflagration of the world.

But what happiness can a godly man expect from this similitude of a tree? for he can have no more than the similitude will afford. He can look for no more than the tree hath itself; and where hath the tree any resemblance of happiness in anything that is here expressed? It hath none in being planted by the water's side; for happiness is *summum bonum* [the chief good], and this at most but *inferius bonum* [an inferior good]; therefore only good because it serves to do the tree good; it hath none in bringing forth fruit, for happiness is *bonum proprium* [one's own good], and this but *bonum alienum* [the good of another]; for what good is it to the tree to bring forth fruit for others to gather? for so the tree shall be no happier than a bee,

---

[1] Gen. viii. 11.

that makes honey indeed, but for others to eat; a godly man shall be no happier than a sheep, that bears wool indeed, but for others to shear; and for anything appears yet, a godly man, by this similitude, is like to lose his happiness. But the Prophet cannot be so much mistaken; the similitude, therefore, would be better looked into: for there is *felicitas medii* and *felicitas finis* [a happiness of the means and of the end]; there is *felicitas viæ* and *felicitas patriæ* [a happiness of the journey and of the home-land]; and this tree, indeed, enjoys them all. It hath in this life *felicitatem medii* and *felicitatem viæ*, in being planted by the water side, for this moistens, cools, cleanses, and gives an easy and a happy passage to the journey's end. It shall have in the life hereafter *felicitatem finis* and *felicitatem patriæ*, in bringing forth fruit; for this shall not be as the bee makes honey for others to eat, nor as the sheep bears wool for others to shear; but this fruit shall be for its own use only, and only for itself to gather; for this fruit is that of which Christ saith, Your joy shall be full, and none shall be able to take it from you.[1] Your joy shall be full; there is *plena felicitas* [a complete bliss]; and none shall be able to take it from you; there is *secura felicitas* [a secure bliss]. And now the Prophet need not be ashamed of choosing his similitude; the godly man need not be afraid of losing his happiness.

But is it not strange to see how contrary the Prophet proceeds here, to our expecting? for when he propounded his similitude of a tree, we looked he should have begun at the top boughs, which are the highest parts, and commonly bear the ripest fruits; and he begins clean contrary, at the lowest part, at the very root; for, indeed, although the root be not seen of men, and have no outward glory, yet it is the root that gives the praise to the tree; it is the root the tree may thank for all he is worth; for though the branches bring the fruits, yet they are but messengers; it is the root that sends them; and indeed if there be not a root of humility, and that root planted by grace, the aspiring

---

[1] John xvi. 22: "Your heart shall rejoice, and your joy no man taketh from you." er. 24: "Ask, and ye shall receive, that your joy may be full."

boughs are but sprigs of pride, and will never bring forth the fruit of glory.

We looked he should have set our tree, if not in *torrida zona*, in the very fire, yet at least in some sunny place, as it were by the fire's side; and he sets it, clean contrary, by the water's side; for, indeed, a tree fears nothing so much as want of moisture: it can ill spare the radiancy of the sun, but it can worse spare the moistening of the water, for death hath a spite at nothing so much in anything as at the *humidum radicale*, the natural moisture. He kills more with the drought of too little moisture, than with the drought of too much heat or cold; for this is a dart which death hath from nature; all his other darts are from violence; and though the water be external to the tree, yet when it enters and moistens the root it becomes radical.[1] And it may not be the least reason why the Prophet sets the tree, which is our symbol of eternal life, by the water's side, seeing the water seems the most productive element of life, as that which produced the first living creatures[2] that were in the world; although we may raise our thoughts yet higher, and remember there are waters as well above the firmament as under the earth;[3] and there indeed must the tree be planted that shall bring forth the fruit of our expected happiness.

We looked he should have set our tree, like the trees of Eden, with present fruits hanging upon them; and he talks of tarrying the time till the tree bring them forth; for indeed our Eden is past. There was at first no time there, and therefore the fruits there were not children of time, but as soon born as their parent the tree. But we are in a world of time; our tree will bear no fruit but by the help of time; and no help of time neither, till the fulness of time come; and that is only in him who came in the fulness of time.[4] For Christ is our time, and our fulness of time will be when we shall meet Christ full in the air, and be taken with him into the new Eden, where time shall be no more, and where our tree shall bring forth fruit in the present tense, which shall never fade into preterperfect tense.

---

[1] Essential.   [2] Gen. i. 20.   [3] Gen. i. 7.   [4] Gal. iv. 4.

But seeing the Prophet meant afterwards to make chaff a similitude of the wicked, why would he take a tree for his similitude of the godly, and not rather take wheat, as in a plainer opposition; and as Christ, it seems upon better advice, did take it afterwards?[1] Christ indeed took wheat for a similitude of the godly, but to another purpose. The purpose of the Prophet here is to show the great distance that shall be of glory between the godly and the wicked; and in the points of glory we shall find the wheat to come far short and to be far inferior to a tree; for the wheat, though it rise flourishing up, yet it riseth out of the ground but the same it was cast into the ground; but the tree, of a little, small seed, riseth up to a substance that one could never have expected such an issue for such a parent. The wheat, though it rise flourishing up, yet it riseth but to a small height, as loth to leave the earth too much, and afraid to go too far from the root; but the tree riseth up to an eminent height, as scarce acknowledging the root from which it springs, and far surmounts all growing things upon the earth. The wheat, though it rise flourishing up, yet it riseth but to a slender small stalk, that quakes and trembles at the voice of the wind; but the tree riseth up to a vast and firm body, that scorns the threatenings of the wind, and is not once moved for all the wind can do. The wheat, though it rise flourishing up, it is quickly down again: if it be not reaped in summer, it dies in winter; but the tree is a laster for many ages, and of all things that grow out of the earth comes nearest to everlastingness.

And now, if we cannot choose but think it a blessed thing to be such a tree, we cannot, as little, choose but think it a blessed thing to be a godly man; for whatsoever is seen or said of this tree, is true, and more true, of a godly man. He is more fixed and immovable than this tree, for where this tree is rooted but in the earth, a godly man is founded upon a rock.[2] He is planted by a better gardener than this tree, for where this tree is planted but by Adam, a natural

---

[1] Matt. iii. 12: "He will throughly purge his floor, and gather his wheat into the garner; but he will burn up the chaff with unquenchable fire." (Cf. Luke iii. 17.)
[2] Ps. xxvii. 5.

man, a godly man is planted by Paul,[1] or rather, as Christ saith, by God himself.[2] He is moistened with better waters than this tree, for where this tree is watered but by springs from the earth, a godly man is watered with the dew of heaven. He riseth to a greater height than this tree, for where this tree is stinted in its rising, and stays in the air, a godly man riseth up, and never stays till he come at heaven. He bears more fruit than this tree, for where this tree hath many leaves besides fruits, the very leaves of a godly man are themselves fruits. He is longer in season than this tree; for where this tree is in season but some part of the year, godliness is in season all the year long. This tree is in season but for a time, but godliness is in season to all eternity.

The similitude of a tree is sufficiently justified, but why would the Prophet express happiness by any similitude at all, and not deliver it rather in the very substance? Why would he not rather tell us what it is, than what it is like? May we not be bold to say, because it was more than he could do? for seeing the happiness of a godly man is such as neither eye hath seen nor ear heard,[3] certainly we may conclude it is such also as neither words can express nor tongue utter. And if we should heap up words upon words, laying Pelion upon Ossa,[4] and making mountains of volumes, yet we should never be able to express the happiness ordained by God for godly men. If the happiness consisted of finite parts, and were a stinted thing, either in number, or magnitude, or continuance, we might by the help of arithmetic and geometry express it, perhaps, in some proportion; but seeing it consists of parts, in number innumerable, in magnitude infinite, in continuance eternal, what man of art, what art of man, can now come near it? Or if the happiness were to continue but so many thousand years as there be sands in the sea, though this were a vast incomprehensible extension of time, yet it were but a continuance that would not continue; there would one day be an end. But seeing it shall be for ever, everlasting, eternal—*in æternum et ultra*

---

[1] 1 Cor. iii. 6.   [2] Matt. xv. 13.   [3] 1 Cor. ii. 9.   [4] Mountains in Greece.

[for ever and evermore]—what stars of heaven, what sands of the sea, can now be counters enough to sum it? And now tell me if the Prophet were not well advised to make use of a similitude; but tell me, rather, if godly men be not well advised to make use of godliness; tell me, if wicked men be not ill advised to make account of vanities; oh, tell me, if the serpent be not a devil, the flesh a traitor, the world an impostor, that, for pleasures of sin, not worth the speaking of, would make us to forfeit this unspeakable happiness.

But now to consider it in allegory, what may we think is meant by this tree? Is it not the tree figured by the tree of life in the garden of Eden?[1] And what by this planting?—our ingrafting into Christ.[2] And what by this water's side?—the water that was shed out of Christ's side.[3] And what by this fruit?—our everlasting happiness. And what by these leaves?—the leaf of a good conscience, and the leaf of a good fame; for a good conscience never withers, but accompanies a godly man to another world; and a good fame never withers, but *in memoria æterna erit justus* [the righteous shall be in everlasting remembrance].[4] And what by the time? when time is no more; for time is but the measure of motion and mutation, but happiness hath nothing to do with these, and therefore nothing to do with time; her time is eternity.

And indeed is it not strange that men who have outlived yesterday should think there can be happiness where there is time? For let the day past be spent in all the pleasures of the world, yet what is yesterday to us to-day? and what will to-day be to us to-morrow? and so the days of happiness should come at last to be all lost, and be no more to us than if they never had been ours; wherein in true happiness, to-day is to us as it was yesterday, and to-morrow will be as it is to-day, and what we are now we shall be for ever. Time and happiness are things incompatible; for happiness is permanent, time always in mutation; for what is time but a very changeling, or, rather, makes very change-

---

[1] Gen. ii. 9.   [2] Rom. xi. 17—24.   [3] John xix. 34.   [4] Ps. cxii. 6.

lings of us? It is long[1] of time that we continue not long in one state; it is always bringing some new thing, but ever carries away more of the old; it runs over all things, but never tarries with any; we cannot see it till it be gone out of sight; and by this only we find it hath been here, because we find not that here which hath been. The happiness of this life is like Joseph's coat, parti-coloured,[2] to express variableness, a mixture of weal and woe, but turns at last all to a stain; and such happiness wicked men may have. The true happiness is in a long white robe;[3] long for durableness, and white for joyfulness; and this keeps the colour still, and is only to be had in heaven;[4] for there this changeling, time, shall not be suffered to come, to set diversity of colours upon our robe of happiness.

And now, if any man ask for happiness, here it is; it grows upon the tree of godliness; but though it have its beginning, and as it were its blooming, in this life, yet it comes not to its growth till another life. This present world is too cold a climate to bring it to ripeness; it must have the sun to shine more directly upon it. We have here *spem rei* [the hope of its substance], but shall not have *rem spei* [the substance of our hope], till we come to see[5] the blessed face of God; for this indeed is the true sun that only can bring the fruit of this tree to its full maturity.

But is not this hard dealing in the Prophet, to make us promise of a present possession of blessedness, and now turn us off with little more than a bare reversion? Will he be so a prophet as that he will be no more than a prophet,—tell us only of things to come, and not keep his word in things present? It was his saying, at the very first, that a godly man is blessed; and seeing he thought good to say it then, we look he should make it good and show it now; for as yet there appears but little to make it appear that the godly are in this life any more blessed than the wicked; and if any advantage be, it seems to most men to be of the

---

[1] Because. [2] Gen. xxxvii. 3. [3] Cf. Dan. vii. 9: "The Ancient of days did sit, whose garment *was* white as snow," etc., with Rev. i. 13: "Clothed with a garment down to the foot." [4] Rev. iii. 5: "The same shall be clothed in white raiment." [5] 1 John iii. 2: "We shall see him as he is."

wicked's side. But is not this rather to deal hardly with the Prophet, to put him to his proofs for every word he speaks, as though the word of a prophet were not of itself an authority sufficient to command our assent? But since we are so hard of belief, at least, *propter duritiem cordis* [because of the hardness of our hearts], let it be considered that there is great difference between having of blessings and being blessed. A wicked man may have many, perhaps very many, blessings, and yet it shall never be truly said of him that he is blessed; for who doubts but that strength and beauty, riches and honours, are blessings and the good gifts of God? And all these, and many more than these, a man may have, and yet walk in the counsel of the ungodly, and stand in the way of sinners, and sit in the chair of scorners; and he that doth such things, the Prophet would have us know, though he be as strong as Samson, though as beautiful as Absalom, though as rich as Solomon, though as full of blessings as the world can make him, yet he cannot be blessed. Such things may entitle men, *benedicti* [endowed with blessings], perhaps, but not *beati* [blessed]; or, if *beati*, it is but *falso clamore* [in lying words]. The true blessedness is nowhere found growing, nor can anywhere be made to grow, but only upon this tree of godliness; and therefore you shall never hear any such word to come from David, as to say, Blessed are the rich, or Blessed are the honourable and great men of the world; but all his blessedness is ever with some relation or other unto godliness. Blessed are they whose sins are forgiven.[1] Here godliness is made legitimate.[2] Blessed is he whom the Lord chasteneth.[3] Here godliness is set to school. Blessed are they who walk in the law of the Lord.[4] Here godliness is at its exercise. Blessed is the man that considereth the poor.[5] Here godliness is making a purchase. Blessed is he that putteth his trust in the Lord.[6] Here

---

[1] Ps. xxxii. 1: "Blessed *is he whose* transgression *is* forgiven, *whose* sin *is* covered." [2] Dependent on the law. [3] Ps. xciv. 12: "Blessed *is* the man whom thou chastenest, O Lord." [4] Ps. cxix. 1: "Blessed *are* the undefiled in the way, who walk in the law of the Lord." [5] Ps. xli. 1: "Blessed *is* he that considereth the poor." [6] Ps. lxxxiv. 12: "O Lord of hosts, blessed *is* the man that trusteth in thee."

godliness is taken sanctuary; and so godliness ever, in one kind or other, or blessedness never, in any kind whatsoever. Not all the smiths of Egypt, not all the temporal blessings of the world, will serve the turn; godliness must turn the key, or the door of blessedness, the gate for the King of glory to enter,[1] will never be opened.

And as a man may have many blessings, and yet not be blessed, so he may want many blessings, and nevertheless be perfectly blessed. He may want the riches of worldly pomp, and yet be blessed; for "Blessed are the poor in spirit;"[2] and this was David's case with Michal.[3] He may want a quiet life, and yet be blessed; for "Blessed are they that are persecuted for righteousness' sake;"[4] and this was David's case with Saul. He may want good report, and yet be blessed; for Blessed are ye when men rail upon you and revile you;[5] and this was David's case with Shimei.[6] But is not this strange, that a man should want, and yet be perfect? should want blessings, and yet be perfectly blessed? Indeed, no more strange than that Adam should lose one of his ribs,[7] and yet continue a perfect body still; for these temporal blessings are to a godly man as the rib was to Adam of which Eve was made, not superfluous to him when he had it, nor making him defective when he wanted it; and so are all temporal blessings, not superfluous to a godly man to have them, because he can make good use of having them; nor making him defective to want them because he can make good use of wanting them. And this, perhaps, might make St. Paul to say, I can want, and I can abound;[8] as much as to say, I can have a rib more or a rib less, and yet in both estates continue perfect still.

But is it not, then, that we are all this while mistaken in blessedness, and that David hath set a gloss upon it, to make us esteem more highly of it than there is cause? seeing

---

[1] Ps. xxiv. 7, 9. [2] Matt. v. 3. [3] 1 Sam. xviii. 23: "Seemeth it to you a light *thing* to be a king's son-in-law, seeing that I *am* a poor man, and lightly esteemed?" [4] Matt. v. 10. [5] Matt. v. 11: "Blessed are ye, when *men* shall revile you, and persecute *you*, and shall say all manner of evil against you falsely, for my sake." [6] 2 Sam. xvi. 5—8. [7] Gen. ii. 21. [8] Phil. iv. 12: "I am instructed both to be full and to be hungry, both to abound and to suffer need."

Christ, who knew blessedness better than David, proclaims it openly that they are blessed that mourn;[1] and surely mourning can make but an untoward blessedness; for what is mourning but a deploring of misery? That to say, They are blessed that mourn, is all one as to say, They are blessed that are miserable; and so, blessedness no such goodly thing as David goes about to make us think it. But it is not that we mistake blessedness; the mistaking is in mistaking Christ's speaking of blessedness; for Christ saith not, They are blessed that mourn, because they mourn, but because they shall be comforted. The blessedness consists in the comforting, not in the mourning; and not all neither that mourn shall be comforted, for then the damned in hell, and even the devil himself, than whom there is not a greater mourner, should come at last (as some have erred to think) to have their shares in comfort. But their mourning is in despair and upon wrong causes. They only shall be comforted that mourn upon just cause, and that in hope; and such are only the saints on earth who mourn for the Bridegroom's departing from them,[2] and cry with St. Paul, I desire to be dissolved, and to be with Christ.[3] Indeed, comforting is to mourning a plain relative,[4] and cannot be without it, for where no mourning is, there can be no comforting; for what is comforting but a wiping away of tears from the eyes, and how can tears be wiped away if there be no tears to wipe away? And seeing the Holy Ghost (the author of all blessedness) is the Comforter,[5] and no comforting where no mourning, it follows that where no mourning, no Holy Ghost, and where no Holy Ghost, no blessedness. Therefore, Blessed are they that mourn, for they shall be comforted. And so, between Christ and David there will be found but this difference, that David seems to consider godliness as a jubilee, and therefore expresseth it by delighting in the law of God, and exercising in it; but Christ seems to consider it as a funeral,

---

[1] Matt. v. 4.   [2] Matt. ix. 15: "Can the children of the bridechamber mourn, as long as the bridegroom is with them? but the days will come, when the bridegroom shall be taken from them, and then shall they fast."   [3] Phil. i. 23: "Having a desire to depart, and to be with Christ."   [4] Correlative.   [5] John xiv. 26: "The Comforter, *which is* the Holy Ghost."

and therefore expresses it by mourning, as by which a godly man is crucified to the world, and the world to him.[1] And, indeed, this jubilee, and this funeral, must both meet in a godly man, or there will not be a godliness that can produce a blessedness; but where these two meet and kiss each other,[2] there the delighting in the law of God will cause a mourning for our sins, and the mourning for our sins will cause a joy in the Holy Ghost,[3] that we may be confident to say we have a comfortable blessedness, seeing we have the blessing of the Holy Ghost the Comforter. And now, if any man slight this joy as not deserving the name of blessedness, is it not because he feels it not in himself? for without being felt, it is not possible to be understood; but he that feels it and understands it will find this joy to be that jewel which the wise merchant sold all that he had to buy;[4] for what avails it a man to enjoy the whole world,[5] and to want this joy? for this joy is not an influence from the stars, which yet can do great wonders for breeding joy in the world, but it is an influence from that spirit which moved upon the waters,[6] before the stars were made, and is only able still to move upon the waters, and to remove the waters of a weeping soul. It is a joy begotten in our hearts by motion of the Holy Ghost, which, moving upon the waters of a true repentance, works in us the joy of this assurance, that we have an Advocate and Intercessor for us with God the Father;[7] which joy was thought so great, when time was, that no messenger was thought fit to bring the news of it but an angel from heaven: Behold, I bring you tidings of great joy;[8] and great indeed it must needs be which an angel calls great, that scarcely would call the whole earth great; and seeing St. Paul exhorts us to rejoice evermore,[9] we may know the joy to be exceeding great that can make us able to hold out rejoicing so long together, in

---

[1] Gal. vi. 14: "By whom the world is crucified unto me, and I unto the world." [2] Ps. lxxxv. 10: "Righteousness and peace have kissed *each other*." [3] Rom. xiv. 17. [4] Matt. xiii. 45, 46: "The kingdom of heaven is like unto a merchant man, seeking goodly pearls," etc. [5] Matt. xvi. 26: "What is a man profited, if he shall gain the whole world, and lose his own soul?" [6] Gen. i. 2. [7] 1 John ii. 1: "We have an advocate with the Father, Jesus Christ the righteous." Rom. viii. 26: "The Spirit itself maketh intercession for us." [8] Luke ii. 10: "And the angel said unto them, Fear not: for, behold I bring you good tidings of great joy." [9] 1 Thess. v. 16.

all tempests and calms, in all actions and passions; joy enough to maintain a feast of rejoicing all our life long. And then, if this joy can make a blessedness (as certainly a greater cannot be had on earth), and none partakers of it but the godly, we must needs confess the Prophet had great reason to make it his challenge, and that in the present tense : A godly man is blessed.

And will not this blessedness appear yet plainer if we consider the divers sorts of blessedness? for there is a blessedness of the law, and this was delivered by Moses, who, delivering the law but *in litera* [in the letter], delivers a blessedness but *in cortice* [in the bark] : Blessed shalt thou be in the field, and blessed in the city, blessed shall be the fruit of thy body, and the fruit of thy cattle,[1] etc. There is a blessedness of grace, and this was delivered by Aaron, who being the minister of our atonement with God delivers a blessedness in this atonement :[2] The Lord bless thee, and keep thee ; the Lord make his face to shine upon thee, and be merciful unto thee ; the Lord lift his countenance upon thee, and give thee peace.[3] And there is a blessedness of glory, and this was delivered by Christ, who being himself the perfection of blessedness, delivers a blessedness in perfection : Come, ye blessed of my Father, inherit a kingdom prepared for you.[4] And now that we have these divers sorts of blessedness laid out before us, which of them, may we think, was thought upon by David in saying, Blessed is the man ? Not Moses' blessedness, for that is too imperfect; nor yet Christ's blessedness, for that is too consummate. Moses' blessedness is imperfect; for gold (one of the best of his blessings) hath commonly proved but *aurum Tolosanum*,[5] ominous to the owners, and apt to bring them to utter ruin ; at most, to blessedness it hath never been but neutral, only as a cipher in arithmetic, no

---

[1] Deut. xxviii. 3, *seqq*.   [2] Reconciliation.   [3] Numb. vi. 24—26: "The LORD bless thee, and keep thee : the LORD make his face shine upon thee, and be gracious unto thee : the LORD lift up his countenance upon thee, and give thee peace."
[4] Matt. xxv. 34.   [5] The gold of Toulouse or *Tolosa:* the temples of this city had immense treasures of both gold and silver. Q. Servilius Caepio seized the enormous booty, and owing, as was thought, to the anger of the gods, was in the following year defeated and taken by the Cimbri. His goods were sold, and he himself died in prison.

value but from the placing it; for if it be placed in a godly hand, it serves *in subsidium virtutis* [as a succour to virtue], and may prove a means for augmentation of blessedness; but if it fall to be the lot of the wicked, it is but *incentivum vitiorum* [an origin of faults], and serves but *in majorem damnationem,* for an augmentation of misery. And as Moses' blessedness is too imperfect, so Christ's blessedness is too consummate; for the blessed face of God (in which that blessedness chiefly consists) is no fit object for corruptible eyes. God must make himself *capabilis* [receptible], which now he is not, and us *capaces* [receptive], which now we are not, before we can arrive at the haven of that blessedness. And so, Moses' blessedness being suspended, and Christ's blessedness not yet to be expected, what remains but that we lay hold on Aaron's blessedness? and this, indeed, we shall find to sympathise and suit well with this of David; for Aaron's blessedness is a confidence in God's mercy for remission of sins, and a peace of conscience in being at peace with God in Christ. And it is no wrong to Aaron's peace to add "in Christ," for though Aaron express it not, as speaking it, but in figure, yet we may well think he understands it, as meaning it in substance, seeing no peace without Christ is safe unto us. All peace without him is but dangerous security; for *Christus est pax nostra,* he only is our peace,[1] and this peace he hath ever used as his proper good. It was the present he brought the apostles at his coming from hell: "Peace be unto you;"[2] and it was the legacy he left the apostles at his going to heaven: My peace I leave with you.[3] This peace made Job upon the dunghill blessed, and the want of this peace made Saul upon his throne miserable; this peace the world cannot give, and the wicked cannot have; for there is no peace to the wicked, saith the Lord.[4] And now, if any man slight this peace, as not thinking it to deserve the title of blessedness, is it not because he hath no feeling of it in himself? for, not being felt, it can never

---

[1] Eph. ii. 14.   [2] Luke xxiv. 36.   [3] John xiv. 27: "Peace I leave with you, my peace I give unto you."   [4] Isa. xlviii. 22: "*There is* no peace, saith the LORD, unto the wicked." Cf. Isa. lvii. 21.

be understood; but he that feels and understands it will find this peace to be that purchase which Christ so dearly bought for us with his precious blood, and is that in substance which Aaron's peace was but in figure, for to this peace it is not enough to have a *nil conscire sibi*, a clear conscience in us, seeing St. Paul knew nothing by himself, yet was not thereby justified;[1] but we are justified by faith in Christ, and thus justified we have peace with God,[2] and being at peace with God we have peace of conscience within ourselves. And then, if this peace can make a blessedness (as certainly a greater cannot be in earthly tabernacles), and none partakers of it but the godly, we may speak it as well from Paul as from David or Aaron; and so priest and prophet, apostle and all, agree in this, A godly man is blessed.

And if we take another way to go, will it not come to all one journey's end? only, as having now taken the Prophet's words in this manner, A godly man is blessed, and he shall be like a tree, there have appeared two distinct blessednesses, one present and another future; so if we take the words in this manner (as some will have it), A godly man is blessed, for he shall be like a tree, there will then appear but one main blessedness, the present being only a hope of the future; and yet thus it shall still be justly said, A godly man is blessed; for this hope is not wavering that may make ashamed,[3] seeing it hath faith to guard it, and patience to wait upon it, but it is the anchor of the soul[4] that keeps it upright in all tempests of temptations. And if we pass from the hope itself to that which is hoped for, oh, then, how transcendent a blessedness will be found in hope! for is it not an armour of steel against all blows of fortune and wracks of time, that I have hope continually to stand prompting me with this: *Durate et vosmet rebus servate secundis* [endure and keep yourselves for better days]; Be constant to the end, and be assured it will not be long ere thou shalt reign with Christ? Is it not a shield of brass against all the terrors of death and hell, that through hope I

---

[1] 1 Cor. iv. 4.   [2] Rom. v. 1.   [3] Rom. v. 5.   [4] Heb. vi. 19.

can say with Job, I know that my Redeemer liveth, and though that worms destroy this body, yet I shall one day see God in my flesh?[1] but most of all, is it not a rock of defence against all afflictions in body or goods, against all disgraces in fame or fortunes, that with St. Paul I can say in hope, There is a crown of righteousness laid up for me, which the just Judge will give me at the last day?[2] And now, if any man slight this hope, as thinking it not worthy the name of a blessedness, is it not because he hath no feeling of it in himself? for not being felt, it cannot be understood; but he that feels and understands it shall find that this hope is the true cordial of a fainting soul; as David saith, I had fainted if I had not hoped to see the goodness of the Lord in the land of the living.[3] And then, if such a cordial it be, as such a cordial most certainly it is, and none partakers of it but the godly, we may justly conclude the Prophet had just cause to make it his conclusion, A godly man is blessed.

And yet more expressly to show the dignity of a godly man's blessedness, we may observe that as, *ratione personarum* [with respect to persons], God is said to be the God of Abraham, the God of Isaac, and the God of Jacob,[4] so, *ratione rerum* [with respect to things], he is said by St. Paul to be the God of joy, the God of peace,[5] the God of hope,[6] that we cannot think much to have a blessedness made us up of those things, of which St. Paul thinks not much, to make up God himself a title.

The joy which Abraham took when his sacrificed son, Isaac,[7] was restored to him alive, was no doubt a wonderful joy, yet but a type of ours, that Christ, the true Isaac, is restored to us alive by his rising again. The peace of mind[8] which Simeon felt when he bare the babe Jesus carnally in his arms was, no doubt, a blessed peace, yet but an inchoation of ours,[9] who bear the man Christ Jesus (our full

---

[1] Job xix. 25, 26: "For I know *that* my redeemer liveth, and *that* he shall stand at the latter *day* upon the earth: and *though* after my skin *worms* destroy this *body*, yet in my flesh shall I see God."   [2] 2 Tim. iv. 8: "Henceforth there is laid up for me a crown of righteousness, which the Lord, the righteous judge, shall give me at that day."   [3] Ps. xxvii. 13: "*I had fainted*, unless I had believed to see the goodness of the LORD in the land of the living."   [4] Exod. iii. 6.   [5] Phil. iv. 9.   [6] Rom. xv. 13.   [7] Gen. xxii. 12, 13.   [8] Luke ii. 29.   [9] Beginning.

reconcilement) spiritually in our hearts. The hope which Jacob had,[1] to enjoy the beautiful Rachel, was a comfortable hope, yet but a shadow of ours, who hope to enjoy the transcendent beauty of the blessed face of God in the kingdom of heaven. And shall not the truth of joy make us more blessed than the type made Abraham? Shall not the consummation of peace make us more blessed than the inchoation made Simeon? Shall not the substance hoped for [2] make us more blessed than the shadow made Jacob? Oh, then, the happiness of a godly man, in whom these blessings are all united, which, singly enjoyed, made such mirrors of blessedness,—a joy in the Holy Ghost [3] which no temptation of Satan can dismay, a peace of conscience which no worldly tumult can disturb, a hope of heaven which no delay of expectation can discourage! And now let Solomon tell us if this be not a wreath of three that far exceeds his threefold cord,[4] and can never be broken. And if, again, to this wreath of three we add a fourth (as the Prophet is going about to do), the blessedness of prosperity, will it not then be a blessedness with admiration, and a wreath of four that we can never say, *O terque, quaterque, beatus*, [O thrice, yea four times blessed!] so justly of anything under heaven as of a godly man, that not only we may proclaim it in Gath, and publish it in Askelon,[5] A godly man is blessed, but with the asseveration of Isaac, in blessing Jacob, even to Esau's face, redouble it in the ears of all the wicked: A godly man is blessed; "yea, and he shall be blessed." [6]

And now that we have found out a godly man *in hypothesi* [in definition], where may we look to find him out *in thesi* [in realized fact]? Not amongst the heathen philosophers, for their peace of conscience was only *nil conscire sibi* [being conscious of no guilt]; they knew nothing of any reconcilement with God in Christ. Not amongst the Turkish Mussulmans, for they believe no Holy Ghost, and therefore can have no joy in the Holy Ghost.[7] Not amongst the Jewish Sadducees, for they deny the resurrection,[8] and

---

[1] Gen. xxix. 18.   [2] Heb. xi. 1.   [3] Rom. xiv. 17.   [4] Ecc. iv. 12.   [5] 2 Sam. i. 20.   [6] Gen. xxvii. 33.   [7] Rom. xiv. 17.   [8] Matt. xxii. 23.

therefore can have no hope of heaven. And where then? Only amongst the Christian believers, for in them only is found this wreath of four, which though singly perhaps they may, yet joined together they can never be broken: that if a philosopher thought it cause enough to cry out in exultation, εὑρηκα [I have found it], for finding out the quadrature of a circle in geometry,[1] we much more justly may think it cause enough, in exultation, to cry out εὑρηκα for finding out this quadrature of blessedness in Christianity.

The Prophet might well rest now in his similitude as containing sufficiently a godly man's happiness; but he seems to be afraid it is not capacious enough, and therefore pieceth it out with a blessedness of another making: *And whatsoever he doeth, it shall prosper,*—a blessedness much like the manna [2] in the wilderness, that fits the relish of all tastes; for who but will easily admit prosperity indeed to be a blessedness? and he seems to have provided it specially for the meaner capacities, such as are not well able to apprehend the former, as being too spiritual. But this is a blessedness so visible to be seen, so palpable to be felt, that even the veriest worldling that is cannot choose but acknowledge it; yet we may perceive the Prophet brings it in but as a fag-end of blessedness, as choosing rather to add a coarse piece than that it should be said he had made it too little.

But doth not the Prophet's adding of this piece make the Prophet himself defective? Doth he not, by showing the blessedness to be the more, show his own judgment to be the less? For if this were true, there should not be a godly man to be found in the whole world; for are not all men generally subject to crosses,—some in body, some in goods, some by enemies, some by friends, some in all, but all in some? All this is true; and yet the Prophet nevertheless saith true, for crosses are our sufferings, not our doings. The adversity of a godly man in that he suffers, is no contradiction of prosperity in that he doth; and yet even crosses and sufferings and all, as St. Paul saith, shall be

---

[1] A problem which involves the (impossible) discovery of a precise numerical ratio between the lengths of the diameter and circumference of the circle.   [2] Exod. xvi.

made useful and prosperous to the godly;[1] for though martyrs cannot well be said to prosper in their suffering because it is grievous, yet they are truly said to prosper by their suffering because it is glorious; though Lazarus did not prosper in his suffering because it brought him but to Dives' gate, yet he truly prospered by his suffering because it brought him into Abraham's bosom.[2]

But may not the Prophet preach this doctrine long enough before he meet with an auditory that will believe him? Godliness to be a means of prospering?—a stranger paradox was never held. It is a greater miracle for men to draw prospering out of godliness than for Moses[3] to draw water out of rocks. *Probitas laudatur et alget* [goodness is praised, but suffers cold]; godliness may have the world's good word, but he that useth it shall die a beggar. Thus the wicked, through the Prophet's sides, stand goring and galling the goodness of God; and never remember, or never regard, the saying of St. Peter [Paul], that godliness hath the promise both of this life and of the life to come.[4] But most of all they insult upon the Prophet, as thinking they can take him tripping in his words, and can prove him manifestly in two tales; for that which he saith here of the godly, he affirmeth the very same, in another place, of the wicked: Their ways always prosper;[5] they are not in trouble like other men;[6] they have more than their hearts can wish.[7] And is it possible the Prophet should ever be able to answer this? Can these words of his be ever possibly reconciled? Indeed, with a word, for it is but mistaking a word (taking the present tense for the future) that makes all this difference,—it is but breaking time that makes this discord. Keep time with the Prophet, and all will go well; for he saith not of a godly man, All his ways do prosper, but they shall prosper. He meddles not with the present tense, nor with the prosperity of the present tense; he leaves that for the wicked to make merry

---

[1] 2 Cor. iv. 17. [2] Luke xvi. 20, 22. [3] Numb. xx. 10. [4] 1 Tim. iv. 8: "Godliness is profitable unto all things, having promise of the life that now is, and of that which is to come." [5] Ps. xxxvii. 7: "Fret not thyself because of him who prospereth in his way." [6] Ps. lxxiii. 5: "They *are* not in trouble *as other* men." [7] Ps. lxxiii. 7.

with, for it is a prosperity not worth the envying; for who would envy Jonah his gourd, that is gone in a night?[1] The present tense of this life cannot make a prosperity that is worth the having: it is the future tense must do it, for this is the lasting tense; and though it show not all his wares at first, as the present tense doth, you cannot see yet what it will prove; yet give it time, let things come to a ripeness, and you shall find it true in the end, that whatsoever a godly man doeth it shall prosper. And in this tense and in this sense it is that the Prophet speaks of the prosperity of the godly; but if he come to speak of the wicked in this tense, he then alters his key, he speaks in another tune: Thou shalt look after his place, and it shall not be found.[2]

Or may we not, perhaps, reconcile the Prophet's words as well, if we only say that in speaking of the prosperity of the wicked, *loquitur ut vulgus* [he speaks popularly], and as it is in appearance, because in the eye of the world it seems to be so; but when he speaks of the prosperity of the godly, *loquitur ut veritas* [he speaks as truth itself], because it is in truth and really so. The Prophet, we may perceive, makes this account, that nothing can be truly said to prosper which hath not a prosperous ending; but if it have a prosperous end, it may truly then be said to prosper. And it is a very just account, for else we might say that a cup of cold water prospers in a fever because it cools and easeth for the present, though it infinitely increase the burning afterward. And we could not say that a sovereign medicine prospers in a sore because it aches and pains us for a while, though afterward it work a perfect cure. And now bring the wicked and the godly to the trial of this account, and you shall find it true that the wicked never prosper, and that the godly prosper always. Did Ahab prosper in seeking Naboth's vineyard? He got, indeed, the vineyard, but the dogs licked up his blood.[3] Did Judas prosper in betraying his Master? He got, indeed, the thirty pieces of silver, but his bowels would not tarry in his belly after he had done it.[4]

---

[1] Jonah iv. 6, 7. [2] Ps. xxxvii. 10: "Thou shalt diligently consider his place, and it *shall* not *be*." Also ver. 36: "I sought him, but he could not be found."
[3] 1 Kings xxi. 16, 19; xxii. 38. [4] Matt. xxvi. 15; Acts i. 18.

And so the most that can be said of the prosperity of the wicked is but this, that they have a prosperity indeed, but it is a tragical one; begins in jollity, and hath some mirth for a while, but ends at last in blood and death. And such, it seems, the Prophet means is the prosperity of the wicked, if he mean not, rather, that a prosperity it seems, but is not; for the wicked may have children, like olive branches, round about their table,[1] and in this may seem to prosper, but yet they do not; and Job tells why: For their children are to the sword, and shall be buried in death.[2] They may heap up treasure and flow in wealth, and in this may seem to prosper, but yet they do not; and Solomon [David] gives the reason: For they know not who shall gather it.[3] Themselves, they are sure, shall carry away nothing. They may rise in honours and be set aloft, and in this may seem to prosper; but yet they do not, and David shows the cause: For they are set in slippery places,[4] and their ending commonly falls out in falling. And this is not only to be observed in single persons, but even in whole families. A generation or two may flourish, and hold their heads high, and in this may seem to prosper, but yet they do not; for of this is grown a proverb: *Non gaudet tertius hæres.* The third generation pays for all. So it is true here which Abner said to Joab, There is bitterness in the end.[5] But with the godly is clean otherwise: For many are the afflictions of the righteous, but the Lord delivers them out of all.[6] So here is prosperity in the ending yet: They may sow in tears, but they shall reap in joy.[7] Prosperity in the end still: They may go forth weeping, and carrying precious seed with them, but they shall return rejoicing, and bring their sheaves with them.[8] Still prosperity in the end: Daniel may be cast

---

[1] Ps. cxxviii. 3: "Thy children like olive-plants round about thy table" (spoken of him "that feareth the LORD"). [2] Job xxvii. 14, 15: "If his children be multiplied, *it is* for the sword.... Those that remain of him shall be buried in death." [3] Ps. xxxix. 6: "He heapeth up *riches*, and knoweth not who shall gather them." [4] Ps. lxxiii. 18: "Surely thou didst set them in slippery places." [5] 2 Sam. ii. 26: "Shall the sword devour for ever? knowest thou not that it will be bitterness in the latter end?" [6] Ps. xxxiv. 19: "Many *are* the afflictions of the righteous; but the LORD delivereth him out of them all." [7] Ps. cxxvi. 5: "They that sow in tears, shall reap in joy." [8] Ps. cxxvii. 7: "He that goeth forth and weepeth, bearing precious seed, shall doubtless come again with rejoicing, bringing his sheaves *with him*."

into the lion's den, but he shall come forth untouched; his danger shall be his glory.[1] Jonah may be swallowed up of a whale, but he shall be cast up safe on shore; his destruction shall be his safety.[2] Job may have his children slain,[3] his goods taken from him,[3] and his body afflicted,[4] but his children shall be restored,[5] his goods doubled,[6] and his life trebled.[7] And, to make short, the Prophet in another place makes it a rule of infallibility: Mark the upright man, and behold the perfect man, for the end of that man is peace.[8] And so it is verified here which is said by the Prophet: Sorrow may be overnight, but joy cometh in the morning.[9] And this, again, is another advantage of the prosperity of the godly, that their sorrow comes but overnight, when they may sleep it out and pass it over; but their joy cometh in the morning, when they come fresh unto it, and have the whole day before them to enjoy it.

And now, if we ask the Prophet what reason he can give of this prospering of the godly, do not his words themselves answer for him, and carry in them the very reason of it? For in saying, Whatsoever he doeth, he seems to intend a godly man's service; and in saying, Shall prosper, he seems to intimate God's wages; and if this be so, then is the prospering as sure as check;[10] for as God is a Lord that looks his servants should do their work, so he is a Master that never fails to pay his servants their wages. And then, if blessedness be God's wages, and godliness the man's service, what is this but ὅπερ ἔδει δεῖξαι [what he has to show], the very thing the Prophet takes upon him to demonstrate—A godly man is blessed?

And here now we may stand and admire the great bounty of God, and consider how good a service it is to serve him, and what great wages he gives his servants; for the meanest of them all may reckon upon this, that all he doeth shall prosper. The wages are not stinted by the Master,

---

[1] Dan. vi. 10—28. [2] Jonah i. 15, 17. [3] Job i. 13—19. [4] Job ii. 7. [5] Job xlii. 13. [6] Job i. 3; cf. xlii. 12. [7] Job xlii. 16: "After this lived Job an hundred and forty years, and saw his sons, and his sons' sons, *even* four generations." [8] Ps. xxxvii. 37: "Mark the perfect *man*, and behold the upright, for the end of that man *is* peace." [9] Ps. xxx. 5: "Weeping may endure for a night, but joy *cometh* in the morning." [10] As an audited or checked account.

but by the servant : that if he have not prosperity enough, he may thank himself that would be idle, and do no more ; for all he doeth shall prosper, but nothing but what he doeth ; the Prophet promiseth no further ; for if he do nothing, he must look for no prospering. But what, have good thoughts, then, and good words, no promise of prospering? If they [be] followed by doing, then are they *præviæ actiones* [pioneer deeds], and as part of the doing shall have their reward ; otherwise they are but abortives, and come not to life to give them capacity, for the life of words and thoughts is actuated by the acting. And yet, even thus, the service is so small, the wages so great, that if it were told us by any but by a prophet, or told us of any but of God, we might justly doubt it ; but hearing it from such a reporter, and of such a Master, if we should doubt it now, it might justly be said unto us, What doubt ye of, O ye of little faith?[1] Yet it must be observed here, though we call it wages, that yet it is not so much earned as given, being more of favour than of merit ; and cannot be exacted, though it may be expected ; for though the wages of sin be death,[2] yet we cannot properly say the wages of godliness is life. The antithesis hath not place, because our godliness hath not weight ; but eternal life is the gift of God, through Jesus Christ our Lord.

And now, if we should ask the world what it says to all this,—whether it think not these blessings to be far more worth than all their gilded vanities,—what do we think would the world answer to such a question? We may be sure the world would answer thus : It likes the blessings well, and thinks them all good ; but one circumstance in them it doth not like, that they are all in the future, none in the present ; all birds in the bush, none in the hand ; never a bird in the hand amongst them all. " Blessed are they that mourn, for they (are not, but) shall be comforted."[3] The tree is planted by the waterside, but bears no fruit yet ; but will do. A godly man's actions (do not prosper, but they) shall prosper. This delay the world doth not like ; it cannot

---

[1] Matt. xiv. 31.   [2] Rom. vi. 23 : " For the wages of sin *is* death ; but the gift of God *is* eternal life through Jesus Christ our Lord."   [3] Matt. v. 4.

away with these future tenses—so much talking of what shall be, and nothing of what is; and therefore they have a question to ask too, the same which the disciples asked Christ: "But when shall these things be?"[1] for if the blessedness be long a-coming, it can then come but to this, that it may be said, A godly man shall be blessed, but is miserable; and miserable, too, for God knows how long. Therefore, give us the present, say they, and (as Christ also seems to teach us[2]) let hereafter shift for itself. This, indeed, is the hinge the world still turns upon; and it is a hard matter to take it off. But may we not answer these men, as Christ answered his disciples, *Non est vestrum, nôsse tempora*, It is not for you to know the times and seasons, which God hath kept in his own hand?[3] It may suffice you to know that these things shall be; when they shall be, is more than the portion of your knowledge comes to. It is indeed an earthly question, and moved only by such, of whom it is said, Earth thou art, and to earth thou shalt return;[4] for when we move such questions, we return to earth; for if we stayed with God, we should know that, as the darkness and the light is all alike to him,[5] so to him the future and the present is all one; that we may marvel what St. Peter meant to say, A thousand years with God are as a day,[6] as though there were a proportion between eternity and time; when Isaiah speaks it out plainly, All nations are to God as nothing,[7] and put in the balance are less than nothing; and we may say as well, All time is to him as nothing, and put in the balance with eternity is less than nothing. And therefore, when we meet with these words (will be, and shall be) in relation to God, we may take them rather as words of order than of time, as in order of nature the tree must first be planted before it can bring forth fruit; a deed must be done before it can be rewarded. And yet even this order also is in God's disposing, either to divert it, or wholly to

---

[1] Luke xxi. 7. [2] Matt. vi. 25, 31, 34. [3] Acts i. 7: "It is not for you to know the times or the seasons, which the Father hath put in his own power." [4] Gen iii. 19: "Dust thou *art*, and unto dust shalt thou return." [5] Ps. cxxxix. 12. [6] 2 Peter iii. 8: "One day *is* with the Lord as a thousand years, and a thousand years as one day." [7] Isa. xl. 17: "All nations before him *are* as nothing; and they are counted to him less than nothing and vanity."

reverse it, at his own pleasure. As in the garden of Eden, there was bearing of fruit as soon as planting of trees, this was a diverting of order; but when God said, Esau have I hated, and loved Jacob,[1] before they had done either good or evil, here was a prospering before a doing, and we may say a bearing of fruit before a planting the tree; and this was an absolute reversing of order. The world therefore must take notice, that Will be, with God, is as much as with men, It is; and when he saith, It shall be, it is as good as if it were already. We all know there is to be *dies retributionis*, a day of account; and this day to be, God knows how soon—sooner, perhaps, than the world thinks, but certainly sooner than the world would have it; and we are sure that this Will be, and Shall be, shall not exceed that day; but how much it shall be sooner (as oftentimes much sooner, and always to the godly, in whose spirits there is an influence of the future in the present, by the presence of that spirit with whom the future is present,) we must leave to God, in whose only hand it is, to dispose of all things, both for time and order.

But lest the godly should be slighted, as men only of expectation, and wholly excluded from any part of blessedness in present, let it be remembered what God's promise to the godly is, "I will never leave thee, nor forsake thee;"[2] and if never leave us, then always with us; and so indeed doth Christ expound it: And lo, I am with you always to the end of the world.[3] And lest his presence should be thought to serve for directing only, and not as well for comforting, hear him in this also: And I will send you another Comforter;[4] but Christ could not send another comforter, if he were not himself a Comforter first. And may it not then be truly said of the godly, *nullum numen abest* [no divinity is absent]; there is not a person in the whole Deity but is present with them? And can blessedness be absent where the whole Deity is present? And yet more mediately to show God's care over them, he gives his angels charge over them, to keep them in all their ways,[5]

---

[1] Rom. ix. 13: "Jacob have I loved, but Esau have I hated." Cf. Mal. i. 2, 3.
[2] Heb. xiii. 5. [3] Matt. xxviii. 20: "Lo, I am with you alway, *even* unto the end of the world." [4] John xiv. 16: "He shall give you another Comforter." [5] Ps. xci. 11.

where the wicked in the meantime, as things forlorn, have neither part nor portion in any of these promises. It was not to the wicked that God said, I will never leave thee nor forsake thee; it was not to the wicked that Christ said, And lo, I am with you always to the world's end; it was not to the wicked that Christ promised to send another Comforter; it was not to the wicked that God promised a guard of angels; and may it not then be truly said of the wicked, *nullum numen adest* [no divinity is present]; there is not a person in the whole Deity, there is not an angel in the whole choir of heaven, that is present with them? And what is then the present possession they so much stand upon, and so much boast of? Alas, poor wretches! what is it but as a dream; as Isaiah saith, They dream they are full, and when they awake, behold, their soul is empty.[1] What is it but as a mist upon their souls that makes them, as St. John speaks, to think they are rich, and fair, and strong,[2] when yet they are poor, and naked, and miserable? For what is their present possession but possession of the present? and what is the present but a transient thing, a thing next to nothing; no sooner begun but ended; that before you can say it is, it is not—the future hath taken its place, and put it from being? And say we allow them to take the whole extent of their present life for the latitude of their present possession, yet what is all this latitude but a breadth made up of narrow minutes, which, being impossible they should be all one like to another, makes it impossible they should make a blessedness that can be certain? Where the blessedness of the godly is more certain than all the assurances of the world can make it. For what are the greatest assurances of all worldly things? Do we not count ourselves sure if we have a good man's word? and here we have the word of God—so sure a word, that heaven and earth shall fail, but his word shall never fail.[3] And if his word will not be taken, have we not then

---

[1] Isa. xxix. 8: "It shall even be as when an hungry *man* dreameth, and, behold, he eateth; but he awaketh, and his soul is empty."   [2] Rev. iii. 17: "Thou sayest, I am rich, and increased with goods, and have need of nothing; and knowest not that thou art wretched, and miserable, and poor, and blind, and naked."   [3] Matt. xxiv. 35: "Heaven and earth shall pass away, but my words shall not pass away."

a sufficient man's bond, the bond of the man Jesus Christ, and that in the highest kind of obligation, bound body for body? And if bond be thought too little, have we not then a good pawn besides, *arrham Spiritus Sancti*, a pawn and pledge of the Holy Spirit.[1] And lest there should be defect for want of witnesses, have we not a whole army of martyrs, and confessors innumerable?[2] that, unless the apostles and martyrs should all prove false witnesses, unless the pawn of the Spirit should prove a counterfeit, unless the obligee,[3] Christ Jesus, should prove *non solvent* [insolvent], unless God himself should prove no man of his word (all which are far greater impossibilities than that the sky should fall), it is impossible that the hope of the godly should be frustrate, or that these blessings should not be accomplished to them in the fullest measure. And now let the world itself judge if the Prophet had not all the reason of the world to make it his challenge against the world that a godly man is blessed.

But now that the world may seem to be satisfied for the security, now comes in the flesh with her objection: These blessings indeed are sensible to the soul, but insensible to the body; and seeing a man is a compound thing, consisting of a body and a soul, how can these blessings, which reach but only to the soul, make more to be said than this, A godly man is blessed in soul, but is miserable in body; and why, then, should the Prophet shuffle them together, and, as if the body were nobody, say, Blessed is the man? But is it not that, *animus cujusque is est quisque* [the mind of a person is the person himself]? and when the progeny of Jacob went down into Egypt, is it not said that so many souls went down,[4] without making reckoning of their bodies? and did not Christ say to the thief on the cross, This day thou shalt be with me in paradise,[5] which yet was meant but only of his soul? And why then should not the Prophet, though but in respect of these blessings, say, Blessed is the man? The body indeed in this life is subject to corruption; and as long as it is so, it is not in itself, nor can be of itself,

---

[1] 2 Cor. v. 5: "Who hath also given us the earnest of the Spirit." [2] Heb. xii. 1: "So great a cloud of witnesses." [3] Person bound. [4] Exod. i. 5. [5] Luke xxiii. 43: "To-day shalt thou be with me in paradise."

capable of blessedness; all the blessedness it hath, or can have, it must have from the participation it hath with the soul, and from the influence it receiveth from the soul, which influence is so strong, which participation so powerful, that it even confounds the distinction of body and soul, and makes them considered but as one entire thing, that even heathen capacities could apprehend how, the body being *in equuleo*, upon the rack, might yet by the strength of this participation be made able to say, *Quàm suave est hoc!* [How delightful is this!] and therefore the Prophet can never be justly blamed for saying (as in this and many other respects he may and must say), A godly man is blessed.

Though this Psalm be most properly understood of a godly man, yet there are some will needs have it primarily to be meant of the man Christ Jesus; and there may be reasons found to make probable their opinion; for it is most true indeed of Christ that he prospered in all he did. He prospered in his mother's womb, for at the salutation of the Virgin Mary the babe sprang in the womb of Elizabeth;[1] he prospered at his birth, for he was presently adored of the wise men of the East;[2] he prospered in his infancy, for he grew in favour with God and men;[3] he prospered in his baptism, for there came a voice from heaven, This is my well-beloved Son, in whom I am well pleased.[4] He prospered in his temptations in the wilderness, for he triumphed over Satan, and the angels ministered unto him;[5] he prospered in his death, for he was manifested by miracles to be the Son of God;[6] he prospered in the grave, for God suffered not his holy one to see corruption;[7] he prospered in his rising, for he ascended into heaven;[8] he prospered in ascending, for he sitteth at the right hand of God, in the glory of his Father.[9] And thus also shall a godly man, as ingrafted into Christ, be carried with him through the like passages: he shall prosper in temptations,

---

[1] Luke i. 41. [2] Matt. ii. 11. [3] Luke ii. 52. [4] Matt. iii. 17: "This is my beloved Son, in whom I am well pleased." [5] Matt. iv. 11. [6] Matt. xxvii. 50—54. Cf. Acts ii. 22—24. [7] Acts ii. 31. [8] Acts i. 9—11. [9] Acts vii. 56: "The Son of man standing on the right hand of God." Also Rom. vi. 4: "Christ was raised up rom the dead by the glory of the Father."

for God will give the issue[1] with the temptation; he shall prosper in hunger, for he shall be fed with bread from heaven:[2] he shall prosper in mourning, for he shall receive comfort;[3] he shall prosper in sickness, for God himself will make his bed,[4] and lay him at ease; he shall prosper in death, for he shall rest from his labours, and his works shall follow him;[5] he shall prosper in the grave, for he shall sleep in quiet till God awake him, and give him light:[6] he shall prosper in his resurrection, for he shall meet Christ in the air,[7] and be carried with him into his kingdom of glory.

And now it may be time, both for the Prophet and us, to rest awhile, and take breath; for of us it may be said that we have now passed over the Mount Gerizim, and are come to the foot of the Mount Ebal;[8] for we are entering upon his second proposition, which is his *onus*, or burden, for the wicked; and of the Prophet it may be said, that he hath now finished his second prize, and hath put a godly man in quiet possession of his blessedness, and is now entering the lists again, to make good his second challenge—*The wicked are not so* [ver. 4].

Where, first, we may observe that the Prophet observes here a different course in handling of this proposition from that he held in handling the former; for there he only described a godly man, but named him not; here, he only names the wicked, but describes them not; and, indeed, it needed not, for *Rectum est index sui et obliqui* [Justice defines both the just and the unjust]; by telling what a godly man is, he tells, by virtue of the law of contraries, what the wicked are, for if that be affirmed of a wicked man which was denied of a godly, and that denied which was affirmed, the description is made ready to your hand, and you have him deciphered in his fulness. And yet we may take notice of a further reason, for godliness is subject to many falsifications; it may suffer much alloy by mixture

---

[1] 1 Cor. x. 13. [2] Ex. xvi. 4: "I will rain bread from heaven for you."
[3] Matt. v. 4. [4] Ps. xli. 3. [5] Rev. xiv. 13. [6] Eph. v. 14: "Awake thou that sleepest, and arise from the dead, and Christ shall give thee light." [7] 1 Thess. iv. 17. [8] Josh. viii. 33.

of base metals, and then there is need of a touchstone to try whether it be right or no. Many colours may be laid upon wickedness, to make it seem godliness, as Satan can transform himself into an angel of light;[1] and then there is need of marks to know whether it be a good angel, whether it be true godliness or no; but in the case of wickedness, it is not so; there is no need of any such marks, for there cannot a worse vizard be put upon wickedness than its own face, there is no baser metal to be mingled with it; and though a wicked man will be counterfeiting to be godly, yet it was never known that a godly man would counterfeit to be wicked; and therefore the Prophet, who is no waster of words in vain, would not give marks where there needed none, but left wickedness to be known by its own ill face, which is seen plainly enough by the law of contraries.

And now, what means the Prophet by saying, The wicked are not so? Means he not, They are [not] like a tree? and what care the wicked whether they be like a tree or no, as long as they may be like to something else, as well to be liked as a tree? as to be like a flower, or to be like the grass, or like a stone, for they may be so, though they be not so; they may be like these, though they be not like that; and any of these will serve their turn, and please them as well, as to be like a tree. This indeed might be their hope, if the Prophet should stay here; but he quickly takes them off from this hope, for he finds he cannot make use of the law of contraries here as he did before; though the negation of godliness might well enough express the nature of wickedness, yet the negation of blessedness of the godly is no sufficient expressing of the misery of the wicked; but as their misery is a positive thing, so it must have a positive expressing; it is not enough to say, They are not like a tree, but he must tell what they are like; and he cannot say, They are like a flower, for a flower, when time serves, is the prime beauty of the earth, where wickedness is never but deformity. Nor he cannot say, They are like to grass, for the grass is thought a fit similitude as well for the godly as the wicked, as it is

---

[1] 2 Cor. xi. 14.

said, All flesh is grass.[1] Nor he cannot say, They are like a stone, for a stone is serviceable for many excellent uses, and especially for building up, where wickedness can serve for nothing but destroying and pulling down; and to what, then, can he say they are like? To speak it at once (as Joab struck Amasa),[2] and not to speak again, he may justly say, *They are like to chaff*, for chaff as fully expresseth the misery of the wicked, as a tree expressed the blessedness of the godly; for though the likening them to so light a thing as chaff may seem to import but a light misery, yet being well weighed, it will appear that, though he say not in plain terms, A wicked man is miserable; yet by saying he is like to chaff, he intimateth more misery than the word miserable is capable of.

But may we not make a stand here, and question the Prophet about his similitude? for look upon the wicked, do they look like chaff? One would think them rather, in all appearance, to be clean wheat, and the best wheat too, for they only are flourishing—they only carry the price in all markets. But the Prophet speaks not how they look, but what they are; he saith not, They look like chaff, but, They are like chaff; and before he hath done, for all their appearance, he will make it appear they are like chaff, and chaff they are like to have for their similitude. Well, be it so let the Prophet have his will, and let them be like chaff; what hurt take they by this? for doth not the chaff grow up, and is it not brought up with the wheat? and when harvest comes, are they not both reaped together, and both together laid up into the barn? and what more misery in all this to the chaff than to the wheat itself? All this is true; the Prophet sees it well enough, and therefore stays not here neither; he ends not with saying, They are like to chaff, but, They are like to chaff *which the wind scatters*. For this is that which perfects the similitude; and now let any man except against it if he can; for there was a time, indeed, when the chaff was united to the wheat, and made one body with it, and enjoyed then some privileges for the

---

[1] Isa. xl. 6.   [2] 2 Sam. xx. 10.

wheat's sake which were proper to the wheat, and nothing at all belonging to the chaff; and all this while it could not justly be said, The wicked are like to chaff; but when it is divided from the wheat, and is no longer countenanced by it—when it is not borne out by the greatness of the wheat against the power of the wind, but is wholly cast off, and left alone to itself, then it becomes subject to the scattering of the wind, and then, and not till then, is it made fit to be a similitude for the wicked; for then it shows itself what it is—the most contemptible and abject thing, the most unquiet and restless thing, that is in the world; so contemptible and abject, that if it fly in the air all men shut their eyes against it, and if it lie on the ground all men tread their feet upon it; so unquiet and restless, that even Cain, the man that had the first taste of this similitude, makes this complaint upon it: I am now a vagabond in the earth;[1] for what is his being a vagabond but his being like chaff? For who knows not that a vagabond is properly one that roams about from place to place, but is never in his proper place? and how great a misery it is to be *extra locum proprium*, out of the natural place, may appear by the striving and struggling of all natural bodies to attain it; but if any such thing be that hath no *locum proprium*, as it were, no home at all to go to, the unquietness of that thing must needs be infinite, seeing it hath not so much as capacity of quietness; and such a thing is chaff, for the air is not the natural place—it is too heavy for that; nor the earth is not its natural place —it is too light for that; and so, as having no home at all to go to, it must of necessity remain a perpetual vagabond still. And such was the state of Cain; and such is the state of all the wicked, that the Prophet could never have met with such another similitude to express the state of the wicked, as to say, They are like to chaff, which the wind scatters.

But here, by the way, we may let the wicked know they have a thanks to give they little think of; that they may thank the godly for all the good days they live upon the earth, seeing it is for their sakes, and not for their own, that

---

[1] Gen. iv. 14: "I shall be a fugitive and a vagabond in the earth."

they enjoy them. For as the chaff, whilst it is united and keeps close to the wheat, enjoys some privileges for the wheat's sake, and is laid up carefully in the barn, but as soon as it is divided and parted from the wheat it is cast out and scattered by the wind, so the wicked, whilst the godly are in company and live amongst them, partake for their sake of some blessings promised to the godly, but if the godly forsake them, or be taken from them, then either a deluge of water comes suddenly upon them, as it did upon the old world when Noah left it and went into the ark,[1] or a deluge of fire, as it did upon Sodom, when Lot left it and went out of the city.[2] And even one good man is oftentimes enough to moralize the fable of Atlas, and to stay the wrath of heaven from falling down upon the world. For though Abraham in good manners would not press God under the number of ten,[3] yet the angel told Lot plainly he could do nothing against Sodom till he were out of it, and far enough from it.[4]

But though we cannot say that a tree and chaff are such contraries as godliness and wickedness are, where denying the one infers affirming the other, and affirming the one denying the other; yet if they be laid together, and well examined, there will be found so infinite odds between them that they may well pass for contraries, which comes so near to being so. For, take but a leaf, which seems, as it were, but the chaff of a tree—at least, the meanest part of it,—and see how infinitely it exceeds this chaff in anything that is of value, as in entity, in use, in goodness. For everything hath so much entity in it, as it hath influence from the *Primum ens* [First Being], and as it is degrees removed from not being; but such [5] degrees we may conceive, in a leaf, infinite; in chaff or dust, none at all, for it is the very bottom and dregs of all being; and if you would conceive less than dust or chaff, you must conceive just nothing; and in this it resembles sin—at least, comes nearest of anything to resemble it. For sin hath no influence at all from the *Primum ens;* it is no creature of God's making; but when

---

[1] Gen. vii. 11.   [2] Gen. xix. 22.   [3] Gen. xviii. 32.   [4] Gen. xix. 22.   [5] *Pulvis* (Vulg.), dust.

the devil would be counterfeiting God, and take upon him to be a maker, he brought forth sin : other creatures he could make none, and therefore, so much as a man sins, so much he recedes from the *Primum ens;* so much he approacheth to annihilate himself; so much he is made a creature of the devil ; and so much he becomes chaff. In matter of use, the odds between a leaf and chaff is yet more evident ; for a leaf, besides the service it doth the tree, is serviceable also for food, for medicine, for clothing. A leaf was the first clothing of our first parents,[1] and (as much as we scorn it now) it is our finest clothing still ; for what are all our silks but mulberry leaves—at least, by propagation ? whereas of chaff or dust there was never any use made since the world was made, but only that by the curse of God it was ordained to be the devil's food.[2] And in this also it resembles sin ; for ever since God said to man, for his sin, Dust thou art, and to dust thou shalt return,[3] the devil hath taken, as common dust, for his common food, so wicked men, as the finest dust, for his *escæ delicatæ*, his daintiest food, as Isaiah calls them.[4] And this, perhaps, in contracts with witches, makes the devil so eager to be sucking their blood, setting his mark upon them as dainty morsels reserved for his own tooth. Lastly, for goodness, do we not see in the leaf a kind of gratefulness and good-nature, that when it can do the tree no more service by hanging upon it, it then falls off, and lies as near to the root as it can, warming and fattening all the ground about it, as it were, to pay the tree for the juice and nourishment it had received from it ; where the chaff is so ungrateful a thing, and of so vile a nature, that wheresoever it lights it makes the very ground barren that receives it ; even the ground itself that bore it. And in this also it resembles sin, which, though it be hurtful even to strangers, as appears by the deluge, which brought ruin upon all creatures for the only sin of man, yet it is most hurtful to them that commit it, as it were, to its own parents; and this ungratefulness is so general a symptom to all vice, that it seems to have as large a latitude as vice itself : *Nam*

---

[1] Gen. iii. 7.   [2] Gen. iii. 14.   [3] Gen. iii. 19.   [4] Query Jer. li. 34: "He hath swallowed me up like a dragon, he hath filled his belly with my delicates."

cum ingratum dicis ; omnia vitia dicis [In saying "ungrateful," you name all faults].

Thus the wicked have for their similitude the chaff; and the chaff hath for its persecutor the wind ; and as the wind, or air, tyrannizeth over the chaff, so the prince that ruleth in the air [1] tyrannizeth over the wicked. This tyrannical wind hath not power over anything so much as over this chaff, for it tumbles and tosses it from post to pillar ; and we may even say it gives the chaff, as it were, a strappado,[2] for it whirleth it on high, and then lets it fall at leisure to give it the longer pain. It hath no such power over our tree when it comes to a tree ; it doth it more good than hurt, more pleasure than annoyance ; for when the wind blows, we may justly say the trees are then at their exercise ; for having no local motion in themselves, they are agitated and stirred by the wind, which stirs up their vital vigour as exercise stirs up natural heat in the bodies of men. But the wind hath no such meaning towards the chaff ; it comes not to exercise it, but to vex it ; it makes it not a traveller, but a vagabond ; for if it but happen to light anywhere, the least air that moves removes it again : the east wind drives it forward, the west wind turns it backward, the north wind crosseth them both, that the poor chaff hath no standing, but to stand amazed ; it is held up but by contrary motions ; it is of [on] all hands, under the hand of violence ; it hath no natural rest, but as it is natural to it never to rest ; it must be somewhere, yet it can be nowhere ; it hath a place, but no mansion ; a being, but no abiding ; no refreshing but while the wind is weary ; no resting but till the air be up and ready ; that as long as the air is an element, and hath to do in the world, there is no hope for the miserable chaff to be ever at quiet. And such is the condition of the wicked ; a gale of prosperity hoisteth them up, that they neither know themselves, nor where they are ; a blast of adversity blows them down, and makes them tear the heavens with murmuring, and themselves with impatience. No state, no time, no place contents them ; that it may be truly said, There is

---

[1] Eph. ii. 2.   [2] An ancient punishment wherein the victim was drawn to the top of a beam and then let fall, whereby a limb was sometimes dislocated.

no ungodly man that is not a kind of a fool; their being like chaff makes them lightheaded; they are only witty to show they have no wit; only ingenious to do themselves hurt; their brains, that should rest in their heads, are always a-working to find out heads [1] of unrest; adversity doth not please them, because they are in a storm; prosperity doth not please them, because they are becalmed; a mean degree doth not please them, because it leaves them in the dark; honour doth not please them, because it sets them in too much light; labour doth not please them, because it breaks their rest; ease doth not please them, because it gathers rust; life doth not please them, because it is always going away; death doth not please them, because it never suffers them to come again; that let come what will come, the wicked make sure work to be never contented: where the godly are as a cube; toss them and tumble them how ye will, yet they have a bottom still to light upon; and we may truly say, there is no godly man that is not truly wise; their wits are always employed to find out reasons of contentment; poverty pleaseth them, because they have nothing to lose; riches please them, because they have something to give; adversity pleaseth them, because they may show patience; prosperity pleaseth them, because they may show charity; a mean estate pleaseth them, because they may be quiet; honour pleaseth them, because they may be humble; labour pleaseth them, because it is a good exercise; ease pleaseth them, because it is a good recreation; life pleaseth them, because they have something to do; death pleaseth them, because they rest from their labours; that let come what can come, the godly make sure work to be ever contented. Let Fortune appear in what shape she will, yet a godly man is *faber fortunæ suæ* [the maker of his own fortune]; he can work her and frame her to his own liking, that the Prophet may well justify his similitudes: The godly are like a tree, which stands fixed and immovable; the wicked are like to chaff, which is scattered about.

It is a miserable thing to be in slavery, much more to be

---

[1] Occasions or grounds.

in slavery to a tyrant; but to a malicious tyrant, a misery most intolerable. If the Prophet had only said, The wicked are like to chaff which is scattered about, though this had been a slavery, yet there had been hope they might have lighted on a gentle master; but when he saith, They are like the chaff which the wind scatters, this makes them in a desperate case; they are now in slavery to a malicious tyrant, and no possibility of any good for ever. We may observe there are divers kinds of scatterings. It is said of a liberal man that he scatters abroad when he gives to the poor;[1] and it is said of a husbandman that he scatters abroad when he sows his seed;[2] and these are good scatterings, for they are ways to gathering; though they be scatterings for a time, yet they be gatherings in the end, and such scattering is a blessed thing; but the scattering of the chaff by the wind is not a way to gathering: you may as soon gather the wind in your fist, as gather the chaff when the wind hath once scattered it; it is a scattering first and last, and such scattering is a miserable thing. And we may know the condition of the scattering by the conditions of the scatterer; for alms are scattered by a merciful hand, and seed is scattered by a provident hand, but this chaff is scattered by a malicious hand—the hand of Satan, that will never leave scattering them till he have scattered them for his own gathering, which is the final yet the endless scattering. And therefore it seems well observed in Scripture, that when the godly die it is said, They are gathered to their fathers;[3] but when the wicked die, there is no gathering to their fathers spoken of, but their scattering must be understood to be first and last,—a scattering both here and in another world.

And now, if you cannot choose but think it a miserable thing to be this chaff, you can as little choose but think it a miserable thing to be a wicked man; for whatsoever is seen or said of this chaff is true, and more true of a wicked man. The chaff is light, and makes no weight in the balance, but

---

[1] Prov. xi. 24: "There is that scattereth, and yet increaseth." [2] Isa. xxviii. 25: "Doth he not . . . . scatter the Cummin." [3] Jud. ii. 10: "All that generation were gathered to their fathers."

the wicked are lighter than vanity itself;[1] they are not worth putting in the balance. The chaff is not moved but when the wind blows, but the wicked are moved when there is no wind at all; they are afraid where no fear is.[2] The chaff hath the wind without it that disquiets it, but a wicked man hath the wind within him (his own passions) that disquiet him. The chaff is an absolute abject, and can never rise in value; but the wicked are more absolute reprobates, and shall never rise in judgment. The chaff is not suffered in the heap of the wheat, but the [wicked[3]] shall be less suffered *in the congregation of the righteous* [**ver. 5**]. The chaff is persecuted but by the wind of the air, but the wicked are persecuted by the prince that ruleth in the air; the chaff is trodden under foot but by men and beasts, but the wicked shall be trampled upon by the devil and his angels.

If that which is spoken of the godly man may be applied to the man Christ Jesus, then certainly that which is spoken of the ungodly may be applied to the wicked Jews; for no chaff was ever more trodden under foot—no chaff more scattered upon the face of the earth; that it seems verified of them which David speaks in another place: Let them be as chaff, and let the angel of the Lord persecute them.[4]

The Prophet hath now said fully as much as need to be said in proof of his two positions, A godly man is blessed, a wicked man is miserable; and why, then, will he use any more words? Is it, that as a good mathematician, he will not only make a demonstration, but add a corollary?[5] or is it, that considering it is the office of a prophet chiefly to tell of things to come, he insists not upon the present misery of the wicked, but, as more properly belonging to his office, he discovers the misery they shall have hereafter? And, indeed, who but a prophet could have made this discovery? Or is it that the present misery of the wicked, as a thing more obvious and apparent, he leaves to be gathered from the

---

[1] Ps. lxii. 9: "Surely men of low degree *are* vanity, *and* men of high degree *are* a lie: to be laid in the balance, they *are* altogether *lighter* than vanity." [2] Ps. lii. 5: "There were they in great fear, *where* no fear was." [3] The edition of 1640 erroneously reads, "the *wheat* shall be less suffered," etc. [4] Ps. xxxv. 5: "Let them be as chaff before the wind: and let the angel of the Lord chase *them*." [5] A further theorem the proof of which is deduced directly from the demonstration just given.

similitude itself; but their future misery, as a thing less known and more concealed, he will not leave to the venture of others' construction, but for more surety will bring it in himself? And therefore, as the similitude consisted of two parts, They are like to chaff, and to chaff which the wind scatters, so he brings in an inference consisting of two parts, to answer them : They are like to chaff; therefore they shall not rise [1] in the judgment; and to chaff which the wind scatters ; therefore they shall not be of the congregation of the righteous.

But is not this a strange inference,—the ungodly are like unto chaff, therefore they shall not rise in the judgment, for being as chaff, they should rise the rather ; for what is apter to rise than that which is light, and what is lighter than the chaff? And yet the inference [is] not so strange as the consequence dangerous, for if the ungodly shall not rise in the judgment, what shall then become of two articles of our faith, the general resurrection and the general judgment? How will the Prophet avoid the imputation of [being] a Sadducee? How will he hold fellowship with St. Paul, who makes a solemn protestation that he believes the resurrection shall be both of just and unjust? [2] Yet let not this trouble us, for both the inference will be plainly enough justified and the dangerous consequence easily avoided. For take the inference as it is intended—and what can be plainer—the ungodly are like to chaff, therefore they shall not rise in the judgment, for the judgment is as a balance ; but to rise in the judgment is not to rise in the balance, which is a work of lightness, and makes rejected ; but it is a pressing down the balance, which is a rising in value, and makes accepted. And as the inference is thus justified, so the dangerous consequence not only is easily avoided, but the directly contrary consequence necessarily inferred : The ungodly shall not rise in the judgment, therefore there shall be a general resurrection. For the judgment indeed is as a balance to try the weight of things ; but how can the weight of anything

---

[1] Our author adopts the reading of the Vulgate, *Ideo non* RESURGENT *impii in judicio.* [Therefore the wicked shall not rise in the judgment.]   [2] Acts xxiv. 15 : " And have hope toward God . . . . that there shall be a resurrection of the dead, both of the just and unjust."

be tried if it be not put into the balance, and how can it be put into the balance if it come not where the balance is? When, therefore, the Prophet affirmeth that the ungodly shall not rise *in* the judgment, is it not a necessary consequence that they shall rise *to* the judgment? For how can it be tried whether they shall rise in the judgment or no, if they come not to the judgment where they are to be tried? The general resurrection shall be before the judgment, and therefore this rising in judgment is a rising after the resurrection; and so the not rising here no hindrance to the rising there, but rather enforcing that general, that there may be this particular.

But what say we, then, to that saying of Christ, He that believeth not, is judged already?[1] for being judged already, he need not come any more to judgment, seeing none shall be judged for one cause twice. We say this is no consequence neither, for what greater unbelievers than those in the Gospel who cast out devils in Christ's name,[2] yet did not so much as profess Christ's name? And yet even those shall come to judgment, for Christ tells what answer shall be made them when they come there. How, then, is it true that they be judged already? Not by the sentence of the Judge, but by the prejudice of their cause; and this is no hindrance for their coming to judgment. If the Prophet had said, The ungodly shall not rise *to* the judgment, the Sadducees indeed might have taken hold of this, and justly claimed him to be of their side; but when he only saith, They shall not rise *in* the judgment, this is no more than St. Paul would have said himself if he had been in the Prophet's place, for who ever thought the ungodly should rise in the judgment, who are sure to fall in the judgment, seeing their judgment shall be to condemnation, and not to deliverance? To rise *to* the judgment is to be brought to public trial, and this is the general resurrection that we believe; but to rise *in* the judgment is upon trial to come off with credit, and, by the sentence of the Judge, not only to be justified, but advanced. And who ever believed this

---

[1] John iii. 18 : "He that believeth not is condemned already."   [2] Matt. vii. 22.

rising to belong to the wicked? It is, therefore, well observed by one that St. Paul calls the resurrection of the just ἐξανάστασιν,[1] to show that every one who shall have their ἀνάστασιν,[2] to be raised up; but none but the just shall have ἐξανάστασιν, to be raised up and be exalted.

And indeed, in this kind of rising, how can any of the ungodly rise who have so many standing ready to pull them down? Cain cannot rise here, and with him no murderer nor malicious person; for if he but offer to come in place, the wounds of Abel fall a-bleeding afresh, and cry out for vengeance. Saul cannot rise here, and, with him, none that trust in the world and distrust in God; for though the witch of Endor could raise up Samuel to Saul,[3] yet she cannot here raise up Saul to Samuel. Dives cannot rise here, and with him no glutton nor covetous person, for the blisters of Lazarus are rising upon them, and keep them from rising. Simon Magus cannot rise here, and, with him, none guilty of simony or bribery, for Simon Peter hath stopped all their rising with this, Thou and thy money perish together.[4] The like may be said of all other ungodly ones, as many as the chaff can challenge to be like it, that it is no hard matter to prove the Prophet's saying true—it is impossible it should be false—The ungodly shall not rise in the judgment.

But may we not draw the similitude, and will not the similitude draw the wicked into a further degree of not rising in judgment than this now spoken of? For cast both wheat and chaff into the ground, and after a few days you shall see the wheat rise flourishing up, and rise up daily more and more, till it come to a fit ripeness to be brought into the barn; but you shall never see more of the chaff than to lie dead in the place, sweltering and mouldering in its own corruption. And this is even intimated in the similitudes themselves, for in the similitude of the godly the Prophet first expresseth passion, and then action: first the

---

[1] Phil. iii. 11 : "If by any means I might attain unto the resurrection (*exanastasis*) of the dead." In all other passages the word resurrection represents the Greek, *anastasis*, except in Matt. xxvii. 53, where the word *egersis* is used of the Lord's rising.   [2] Acts xxiv. 15.   [3] 1 Sam. xxviii. 12—14.   [4] Acts viii. 20: "Thy money perish with thee."

tree is planted, and then it brings forth fruit; but in the similitude of the wicked he expresseth nothing but passion: They are like to chaff which the wind scatters; and seeing the wicked are like to chaff, in which there is nothing but passiveness, how should they rise in the judgment, which is a work of activeness? But will not this bring us again into a relapse of denying the general resurrection? Not at all; for though the chaff cannot rise by any principle of motion it hath in itself, as the tree doth, yet it may be raised up by the working of the wind; so, though the wicked cannot rise by any seed of life remaining in themselves, as the godly shall, yet they may be raised up by the help of some outward operation. The godly have *semen spiritus* [the seed of the spirit] sown in their hearts by faith; they are members of Christ's body; they have this promise made them by Christ, that he will raise them up at the last day;[1] and therefore their rising shall be a rising to judgment, and a rising in judgment. But the wicked have no such *semen* [seed] in them; they are no partakers of Christ's body; they have no such promise made them by Christ, and therefore their rising shall be to judgment, but not in judgment. Their rising shall be by a violent dragging by some other, it shall not be a voluntary motion of their own; it shall be by infirmity of passiveness, it shall not be by any strength of activeness; it shall be by the power of Christ's resurrection, it shall not be by participation of Christ's ascension. And so the Prophet's denying the rising of the ungodly in judgment is no negation of their rising to judgment, and therefore neither joins hands with the Sadducees nor shakes hands with our belief, nor yet opposeth St. Paul's protestation.

And as there shall be a general judgment, in which the ungodly shall not rise, so, after the judgment, there shall be a particular congregation of the righteous, in which sinners shall not stand. And, indeed, what society can there be between a tree and chaff? or who can think it fit that trees and chaff should be made companions? And as there is no reason that the ungodly, having made others by their

---

[1] John vi. 39.

counsel to fall here, should rise themselves in judgment hereafter, so there is no reason, seeing the righteous could not be suffered to stand here in the way of sinners, that sinners should be suffered to stand hereafter in the congregation of the righteous. And here now a multitude of reasons seem assembled, as it were, to make it good, that sinners neither can nor ought to stand in this assembly. It is a congregation which none can make but the righteous; for sinners are all rebels, and would make it a rout. It is a court where all must be neat and clean; and so are none but the righteous; for sinners are all lepers, and would make it a spital.[1] It is an assembly of such only as are chosen, and come when they are called; and such are only the righteous; for sinners are all intruders, and scorn to come at any one's call. It is a company that makes a communion, and that can none do but saints, for sinners seek every one their own, and are all for themselves. They must be some hands, some feet, some head, yet all members of one body; and so are only the righteous; for sinners are dismembered members; they would be all head, yet cannot all make a body. They must be all God's friends; at least, such as he knows; and such are only the righteous, for sinners are all mere strangers and aliens from God.

Indeed before the judgment, the wheat and the chaff made both but one heap; but after the judgment, the wheat is received into the barn, and the chaff is cast upon the dunghill, and scattered about. Before the judgment, the ungodly and the righteous made both but one assembly; but after the judgment, the righteous make a city by themselves, which is the new Jerusalem, into which no sinners shall be suffered to enter.[2] The righteous shall be taken, with the Bridegroom, into glory; and the ungodly with shame shall be shut out of doors.[3] For the Judge hath a fan in his hand to winnow the chaff from the wheat,[4] and to separate the ungodly from the righteous; and this is his fanning, when to the comfort of all comforts he shall say to the godly, *Venite benedicti patris,* Come, ye blessed of my Father;[5] and to the

---

[1] Hospital. [2] Rev. xxi. 10, 27. [3] Matt. xxv. 10—12. [4] Luke iii. 17. [5] Matt. xxv. 34.

terror of all terrors, shall say to the wicked, *Ite maledicti in ignem æternum*, Go, ye cursed, into everlasting fire.[1] And when Christ the Judge hath once said the word, there can be no tarrying; they shall presently be parted; they must presently part; and so be parted, and so part, as never to stand together, never to come together any more for ever.

But seeing the future misery of the wicked shall consist in two main points—*in pœna damni et pœna sensus*, in pain of loss and pain of sense,—why would the Prophet speak here of only their *pœna damni*, as their not rising in judgment, and their not standing in the congregation of the righteous; but speak nothing at all of their *pœna sensus*, when yet to speak of their pain of sense would make us more sensible of their pain, and more readily assent to the Prophet's assertion that wicked men are miserable? Is it that he would not go further than the line of his similitude would lead him, and he saw that his similitude would not reach to *pœna sensus*? For how can chaff, which is a thing without life or sense, be able to express a misery in which there is life only, that there might be sense; and sense only, that there might be pain? Or is it that indeed it needed not, seeing the pain of loss is misery enough to make a hell of itself, and able to bring upon the wicked as much as Christ affirmed, even weeping, and wailing, and gnashing of teeth?[2] For if ever misery deserved weeping of eyes, if ever loss deserved gnashing of teeth, this is the misery, that they shall not rise in the judgment, by which they shall never come to see the blessed face of God; and this is the loss, that they shall not be of the congregation of the righteous; by which they shall for ever be excluded from all society with saints and angels. Ahasuerus asked Haman what should be done to the man whom the king would honour; and Haman, supposing himself should be the man, made answer, Thus and thus shall be done unto him; but when the king appointed Mordecai to be the man, and himself the man to see it executed,[3] oh, what torment, what anguish and vexation did then surprise the soul of

---

[1] Matt. xxv. 41: "Depart from me, ye cursed, into everlasting fire." [2] Matt. viii. 12; xiii. 42, 50. [3] Esth. vi. 6—10.

Haman; to be himself thus basely employed, and the man he most scorned so highly exalted! Such, and infinitely greater, shall be the torment and anguish of mind to the wicked, when, rising to the judgment, they shall not rise in the judgment; but they which sat before in the chair of scorners, shall now be scorned themselves; and, to disgrace them the more, God himself shall turn scorner; as it is said, God shall laugh them to scorn, and have them in derision.[1]

And now let the great men of the world please themselves, and think it a happiness that they can rise in honours, can rise in riches and estimation in the world; yet, alas! what is all this, if they fail of rising in the judgment to come? Let them please themselves, and think it a happiness that they are honoured in all companies where they come, and have the solace of all the good fellowship the world can afford; yet, alas! what is all this, if they fail to be admitted into the congregation of the righteous?

This rising in judgment is that high glory whereof Christ showed a pattern to St. Peter and John, in his transfiguration;[2] so high, that they were fain to be carried up into a mountain to see it; so glorious, that it put them into ecstasies to behold it, and yet but the lower region of this rising neither; but when St. Paul was taken up into the third heaven,[3] where he might see much more than Peter and John could see upon the mountain, he then saw so much glory as made him afflicted to express it, and could not express it but by afflictions. The afflictions of this life are not worthy of the glory that shall be revealed;"[4] not all the afflictions of the prophets, of whom it is said, They were stoned, they were sawn asunder, were slain with the sword;[5] not all the afflictions of the martyrs (of whom some were broiled upon gridirons, some roasted upon spits, some broken in pieces upon racks and wheels) put all together, and confined upon one man, yet can never make him worthy of the glory that

---

[1] Ps. ii. 4: "He that sitteth in the heavens shall laugh: and the LORD shall have them in derision."   [2] Matt. xvii. 1—6.   [3] 2 Cor. xii. 2--4.   [4] Rom. viii. 18.
[5] Heb. xii. 37: "They were stoned, they were sawn asunder, were tempted, were slain with the sword.

is to come. And how then, O my soul, canst thou avoid the ecstasy of Peter and John, but to think of this? how canst thou give David cause to say, Why art thou cast down, O my soul, and why art thou so disquieted within me?[1] for this rising there will make ample amends for all the fallings that can be here; for though it be a great fall to be laid low in the earth, where the worms shall eat this flesh of thine, yet it will be a greater rising to be raised up into the mount, where thy body shall be made like to Christ's glorious body,[2] and thou mayest say of thyself now, as St. Paul said, O wretch that I am, who shall deliver me from this body of death?[3] yet when the time of this rising comes, it shall be said of thee, even of thee, O my body, as was said of Mordecai, Thus shall be done to the man whom God will honour.[4]

This congregation of the righteous is that new Jerusalem of which it is said, Great and glorious things are spoken of thee, thou city of God.[5] Great and glorious indeed, for if we conceive in our minds the happiness of a city where there are millions of millions of citizens, yet all as loving mutually together as David and Jonathan;[6] where there is holiness immaculate, peace inviolate, joy ineffable, pleasure inexpressible; no time but eternity, no place but immensity, no noise but of music with songs of Hallelujah, no sickness but of love with the spouse in the Canticles,[7] no motions but of mildness where the Lamb is the leader,[8] no words but of wonder where the angels are silent,[9] where God is all in all, and all and every one in God; this congregation is that city; but because no tongue can so well express it as his whose eyes did clearly behold it, hear St. John in his own words: God shall wipe away all tears from all eyes; there shall be no more death, neither sorrow nor crying, neither shall there be any more pain; there shall be no need of the sun nor of the moon, for the glory of God shall

---

[1] Ps. xlii. 11: "Why art thou cast down, O my soul? and why art thou disquieted within me?" [2] Phil. iii. 21. [3] Rom. vii. 24: "O wretched man that I am! who shall deliver me from the body of this death?" [4] Esth. vi. 9. [5] Ps. lxxxvii. 3: "Glorious things are spoken of thee, O city of God." [6] 1 Sam. xviii. 1. [7] Song ii. 5. [8] Rev. vii. 11: "For the Lamb .... shall lead them." [9] Rev. viii. 1: "There was silence in heaven."

lighten it, and the Lamb shall be the light thereof.[1] Now therefore, O my soul, why art thou cast down, and why art thou so disquieted within me?[2] What though thou fly as a bird to the mountains,[3] what though thou dwell awhile in the tents of Mesech,[4] this congregation will make amends for all; not only for John Baptist's desolateness in the wilderness, but even for Job's despisedness on the dung-hill. We may well be contented to serve a prenticeship here, so we may come to be free of this city hereafter: here we sweep kennels, there shall wear crowns; here we are militant, there shall be triumphant; for Christ the crucified is our captain, and God our glory. And now we may see there was no need at all why the Prophet should aggravate the hell of the damned by adding their sense of pain, seeing no bottom of hell can be so deep as this, to be barred for ever from this rising in judgment, and to be excluded for ever from this congregation of the righteous. And so all this goes on upon the score still to make up the full measures of the blessedness of the godly, and of the misery of the wicked, that no art can show principles so irrefragable, positions so infallible, as these of the Prophet, A godly man is blessed, a wicked man is miserable.

But how happens this sudden alteration in the Prophet? He was so reserved at first, and made so dainty but only to name a righteous man, that he would not do it, though it were to bring him to inherit blessedness; and now, on a sudden, he brings them in by troops, a whole congregation of the righteous at once! Is it not that he durst not presume to use the name of righteous till it were first determined of in the judgment, and till they had their station assigned them amongst the saints? not only because it cannot till then be known whether any such title be due or no (for who knew Judas for any other than a holy apostle till Christ discovered him to be a traitor? or who

---

[1] Rev. xxi. 4, 23: "And God shall wipe away all tears from their eyes; and there shall be no more death, neither sorrow, nor crying, neither shall there be any more pain. And the city hath no need of the sun, neither of the moon, to shine in it: for the glory of God did lighten it, and the Lamb *is* the light thereof."   [2] Ps. xlii. 11: "Why art thou cast down, O my soul? and why art thou disquieted within me?"   [3] Ps. xi. 1: "Flee *as* a bird to your mountain."   [4] Ps. cxx. 5: "That I sojourn in Mesech, *that* I dwell in the tents of Kedar."

knew the seven thousand that bowed not their knees to Baal [1]
to be no idolaters, till God, by his own mouth, made them
known to Elijah?), but because, indeed, the name of
righteous can by no right be given to any till they be tried,
and have their approbation in the judgment, to make us
know that righteousness stands not so much in merit as in
acceptance; and though many may be so qualified by
delighting in the law of God as to inherit blessedness, yet
till by the judge they be pronounced righteous, they cannot
rightly claim the title; and therefore David, who is no
herald to decide men's titles, would not use a style that
might not be due, and as little would detract from it, being
once adjudged.

All the Prophet hath hitherto said seems to be but [**ver. 6**]
bare affirmations only, words that we must take upon his word;
but now comes in a word of authority, this rational particle,
"for," or because—a little word, but of great command,
which in all this Psalm hath not been seen till now; and
now that it is come, we cannot well tell why it is come;
we know it brings a reason with it, but cannot easily find
where this reason should lie; for if we take the reason as it
seems to lie, the ungodly shall not rise in the judgment,
because God knoweth the way of the righteous, is it not as
unreasonable a reason as if one should say a malefactor
shall be punished because the judge knoweth another to
be an honest man? And who would ever look for such a
blind reason from a prophet? But is it not that the Prophet
hath a good opinion of our understanding, and therefore
trusts us to supply that which, by the law of contraries, may
plainly, or rather must necessarily, be inferred; for having
said, Therefore the ungodly shall not rise in the judgment,
nor be of the congregation of the righteous, he leaves us
to supply, Therefore the godly shall rise in the judgment,
and make a congregation by themselves; and then the
reason stands ready to tell wherefore: For the LORD knoweth
the way of the righteous.

But if this be a reason to make the godly rise in the

---

[1] 1 Kings xix. 18.

judgment, because God knoweth their way, why is it not, then, as well a reason to make the ungodly to rise in the judgment, seeing we are sure that God knoweth their way as well? And if God's knowing the way of the righteous be a sufficient cause to exclude the wicked, why is not his knowing the way of the wicked as sufficient a cause to exclude the righteous? Here, perhaps, we must be fain to do as astronomers feign to do—make use of certain *phenomena* [appearances]; not that such things be indeed, but that we may conceive them to be, for the better helping of our capacities. As to conceive that there is in God (as to the purpose here) a twofold kind of knowledge, *scientia cognitionis, et scientia dignationis* [a knowledge of perception and a knowledge of approval]; that, common to God with men; this, proper to God alone; that, simple, and without influence or operation; this, operative, and bringing blessings with it. *In scientia cognitionis*, God knows the wicked so well that makes him say, *In scientia dignationis*, he knows them not; but his *scientia dignationis* is as a link that draws with it the whole chain of God's goodness; for whom he knows he regards, whom he regards he preserves, whom he preserves he blesses; and with this kind of knowing God knows none but the righteous, and therefore none but the righteous can have these blessings—to rise in the judgment and to be made a member of the congregation of the righteous. And now the Prophet's reason is found where it lies—the godly shall rise in the judgment, because God knows their way, *In scientia dignationis;* but the ungodly shall not rise in the judgment, nor be of the congregation of the righteous, because, although God knows their way in his *scientia cognitionis*, yet in his *scientia dignationis* he knows it not.

But did not the Prophet give a sufficient reason before why the godly shall rise in the judgment, and make a congation by themselves, when he said, They are like a tree—seeing a tree hath boughs and branches aspiring towards heaven, united in one root, and making one body? But this, perhaps, as being but a reason drawn from the similitude, the Prophet counts but a similitude of a reason, and takes it but upon a liking; the true reason, and which he insists upon, is this, which he allegeth here, For the Lord knoweth the way of the righteous. For this indeed is the true reason of all the blessings that are or ever shall be to the godly; all their praises that went before, their delighting in the law of God, their exercising themselves in it, and whatsoever else. They are good conditions necessarily required in them that must make this congregation; but the true cause and reason of making it is this which the Prophet brings here,—because the Lord knoweth the way of the righteous. For though it were a good likely reason to say, The godly shall rise in the judgment, and make a congregation by themselves, because they are like a tree; yet it may be asked, What makes them like a tree? Godliness indeed procures them to be made like a tree, but what makes them? For that which makes a thing is a superior cause to that which procures it to be made; and this superior cause the Prophet allegeth here, For the Lord knoweth the way of the righteous. And though it were a likely reason to say, The ungodly shall not be of the congregation of the righteous, because they are like to chaff which the wind scatters, yet it may be asked, what makes them like to chaff? Wickedness, indeed, procures them to be made like chaff, but what makes them? Here the Prophet is silent, and says nothing, and by saying nothing seems to acknowledge there is nothing to be said. Wickedness both procures them to be made like chaff, and makes them like chaff; they are both their own ruin and their own ruinousness. God in this kind hath no hand at all in it; it is all their own doing: *Perditio tua ex te, O Israel* [Thy destruction, O Israel, is from thyself].[1]

And may not a reason also be conceived thus, why the ungodly can never come to be of the congregation of the righteous, because the ungodly and the righteous go two contrary ways? The righteous go a way that God knows, and the wicked go a way that God destroys; and, seeing these ways can never meet, how should the men meet that go these ways? And to make sure work that they shall

---

[1] Hos. xiii. 9: "O Israel, thou hast destroyed thyself."

never meet indeed, the Prophet expresseth the way of the righteous by the first link of the chain of God's goodness, which is his knowledge; but expresseth the way of the wicked by the last link of God's justice, which is his destroying. And though God's justice and his mercy do often meet, and are contiguous one to another, yet the first link of his mercy and the last link of his justice can never meet; for it never comes to destroying till God be heard to say, *Nescio vos* [I know you not];[1] and *Nescio vos*, in God, and God's knowledge, can certainly never possibly meet together.

But why doth the Prophet say, The Lord knoweth the way of the righteous; and saith not rather, The Lord knoweth the righteous? why saith he, The way of the ungodly shall perish; and saith not rather, The ungodly shall perish? Is it not that he saith not, The Lord knoweth the righteous, because in another place it is said, There are none such for him to know;[2] but he knoweth the way of the righteous; and what is this way but he which said, *Ego sum via, veritas, et vita*—I am the way, the truth, and the life?[3] And the Prophet might well say that God knoweth this way, seeing Christ saith that none knoweth it but he: None knoweth the Father but the Son, and none knoweth the Son but the Father.[4] But what is this to us? That if we be engrafted into Christ, who is this way, then God, in knowing this way, knows us that are engrafted in this way; and this way indeed must God know us, or not know us at all; for if he know us not in Christ, in ourselves we are sure he can never know us. Or is it that the Prophet saith not, God knoweth the righteous, but the way of the righteous; perhaps lest men, for doing one or two good deeds in all their life, should claim to be righteous, and for such righteousness claim acquaintance with God; and so indeed God might have acquaintance enough, seeing no man is so wicked but he may sometimes have good thoughts, and do good deeds; but this will not serve; it must be a way of righteousness before God will

---

[1] Matt. xxv. 12. [2] Rom. iii. 10. [3] John xiv. 6. [4] Matt. xi. 27: "No man knoweth the Son, but the Father; neither knoweth any man the Father, save the Son."

know it. Abraham had forsaken his country, and sacrificed his only son with his own hands, in obedience to God, before God came to say of him, *Nunc cognivi te;* [1] and therefore it is not a turn or two that will serve the turn; it must be an exercising day and night, a continual walking in the law of God, that must make it a way for God to know. Indeed this way is something of a strange condition; for sometimes much and long walking will not make it a way, and sometimes, again, a turn or two will do it. Sometimes the giving of all a man's goods to the poor will do but poor good,[2] and sometimes the giving but of a small mite will have no small might in it;[3] sometimes the giving one's body to be burnt will have but cold entertainment,[4] and sometimes the giving but a cup of cold water shall be counted a hot service.[5] Saul seems to have walked long in a course of godliness, and yet with all he could do, he could not make it a way for God to know, where the thief on the cross, fetched, as I may say, but a turn about; and he made such a way of righteousness, that Christ presently knew it, and took notice of it. It seems the matter is all, with what feet we walk; for if we walk with the feet of the body only (if there be no other goodness in our good deed but only the outward act of doing it), we may walk long enough before we make it a way of righteousness for God to know; but if we walk with the feet of our hearts (in faith and love), then, perhaps, small walking may sometimes serve; for the heart indeed is a hard treader; it leaves prints behind that will not easily be gotten out; and with these feet of the heart, the good thief walked; or else he could never have made a way of righteousness for Christ to know, upon such a sudden as he did. Howsoever, when it is once made a way, whether with much walking or with little, yet God presently knows it; and knowing it, delights in it; and as in the garden of Eden, will walk in it himself;[6] then indeed it will be a full measure of blessedness, pressing down, and running over;[7]

---

[1] Gen. xxii. 12: "Now I know that thou fearest God." [2] 1 Cor. xiii. 3. [3] Mark xii. 42. [4] 1 Cor. xiii. 3. [5] Matt. x. 42. [6] Gen. iii. 8: "They heard the voice of the LORD God walking in the garden in the cool of the day." [7] Luke vi. 38.

for if in the presence of God there be fulness of joy for evermore,[1] how pressing down, how running over, must that joy be where we enjoy his presence, not only as walking by us, but as walking in us!

And if the Prophet had said the ungodly shall perish, and not the way of the ungodly, it would have made us all afraid; we could hardly have found eight persons to put into Noah's ark; for the best that are, have a spice of ungodliness, enough to taint them with the name of ungodly; but this is the measure of God's mercy, pressing down, and running over, that he will not suffer it to be a way of perishing, unless it be a way of ungodliness first. And here the godly may take this comfort by the way, that it is not their slippings or treading awry, which may be by ignorance, or infirmity, that can make, with God, this shipwreck of perishing; it must be a way of ungodliness, which is not usually made without much walking and exercising, without resolute intentions and endeavours, without set purposes and persistings, that if a man be sure he is free from these, he may then be confident he is safe from perishing. And though this way of the ungodly and the way of the righteous be very unlike, yet they are like in this, that this way also is not made sometimes with much walking; and sometimes, again, it is made with a turn or two; for David walked in adultery and murder a whole year together,[2] and yet it made not a way of perishing, because he had the tears of repentance to wash away the prints of the steps, and charity to cover them. But Judas walked a turn or two, but for anything we know, and it made a way that made away himself,[3] because he neither washed it with repentance, nor covered it with charity. Howsoever the way be made, with much walking or with little, yet if once it come to be a way of ungodliness, there is no way then but perishing; all the world cannot save him; he shall never be forgiven in this world, nor in the world to come.[4] And here again is the measure of God's justice pressing down and running over; 'pressing down,

---

[1] Ps. xvi. 11: "Thou wilt shew me the path of life: in thy presence *is* fulness of joy; at thy right hand *there are* pleasures for evermore." [2] 2 Sam. xii. xiii.
[3] Matt. xxvii. 5. [4] Matt. xii. 31, 32.

because it presseth down to the bottom of the bottomless pit; and running over, because it runs for ever. For then the way of the ungodly is said to perish, when there is no way left to save them from perishing; for such and so desperate is the state of the ungodly, in the state of ungodliness, that no way is left them either for help or hope. For wherein should they hope for help? Compassion will not help them, for the Lord will laugh them to scorn in his high displeasure.[1] Mediation will not help them, for God hath sworn, though Noah, Daniel, and Job should speak for them, yet he will not hear them.[2] Time will not help them, for they shall perish everlastingly.[3] Place will not help them, for they shall fall into a bottomless pit.[4] Death will not help them, for they shall call for death, and it shall flee from them,[5] that they may live to be tormented with the worm that never dies.[6] And here now, for very pity's sake, let me put all poor souls in mind that they be careful to remember that warning of Christ, Agree with thine adversary whilst thou art in the way;[7] for whilst we are in the way, there are ways left to keep us from perishing. There is a way of compassion, for God delights not in the death of a sinner, but that he should turn from his wickedness and live.[8] There is a way of mediation, not of the men Daniel and Job, but of the Mediator between God and man, Christ Jesus.[9] There is a way of repentance, for if a sinner repent him of his sin, God will put away his sin out of his remembrance.[10] But if it once come to this, that the way of the ungodly do perish, alas! then there is nothing left but woe upon woe; no way left for help, no way left of hope, nothing to be talked of, nothing to be thought of, but perishing, not only whilst the world endures, but when the world itself shall perish.

---

[1] Ps. ii. 4, 5: "He that sitteth in the heavens shall laugh: the LORD shall have them in derision. Then shall he speak unto them in his wrath, and vex them in his sore displeasure." [2] Ezek. xiv. 14: "Though these three men, Noah, Daniel, and Job, were in it, they should deliver *but* their own souls by their righteousness, saith the Lord GOD. [3] Athanasian Creed. [4] Ps. cxl.: "Let them be cast into the fire; into deep pits, that they rise not up again." Cf. Rev. ix., xi., xvii., and xx. [5] Job iii. 21: "Which long for death, but it *cometh* not." [6] Is. lxvi. 24; Mark ix. 44, 46, 48. [7] Matt. v. 25: "Agree with thine adversary quickly, whiles thou art in the way with him." [8] Ezek. xxxiii. 11: I have no pleasure in the death of the wicked; but that the wicked turn from his way and live." [9] 1 Tim. ii. 5. [10] Ezek. xviii. 21, 22.

The Prophet gave a good reason before, why there shall be a congregation of the righteous, because God knoweth the way of the righteous; but why would he give no reason here why the way of the ungodly shall perish? For to draw a reason from the law of contraries, as to say, Because God knoweth not the way of the ungodly, will not serve; for God's knowing may well be a strong reason, seeing it is a strong cause—a cause that is operative, and that to many degrees. For whom God knows, he regards; whom he regards, he preserves; whom he preserves, he blesses: but what cause can God's not knowing be? for what operation can be in a negative? Yet so it is: God's not knowing, works by not working; for whom he knows not, he regards not; whom he regards not, he preserves not; and whom he preserves not, they presently fall, and perish of themselves. And the Prophet had great reason to give a reason there, because it was an effect that needed a cause; but he had no reason to give a reason here, because it is an effect without a cause; without a cause efficient, though not deficient; and why then should he give a reason why the ungodly shall perish, seeing, God not knowing them, there can be no reason given why they should not perish?

When it is said, The way of the ungodly shall perish, the wicked take occasion by these words to conceive a hope, as wicked as foolish, that if the way of the ungodly shall perish, then the ungodly shall have no way to stand in; and if they have no place to be in, then they shall be nowhere; and if they be nowhere, then they shall not be at all, which is as much as they desire; for it never troubles them not to be at all, so they may be sure not to be troubled at all. But this is a conceit not only vain but wicked; for by perishing is not meant an utter annihilating and dissolving into nothing; but they are then said to perish when they are forsaken of God and delivered over into the hand of Satan.[1] For when the judgment is once past, and the chaff separated from the wheat, then there shall be a new heaven and a new earth;[2] but the old hell shall continue still, and

---

[1] 1 Tim. i. 20.   [2] Rev. xxi. 1; cf. xx. 14.

there the ungodly and their way shall lie; for in the new earth there shall be no way for either the ungodly to walk in or for sinners to stand in; but all shall be holy ground, and no feet shall walk or stand there but such only as have put off the shoes of corruption, or rather, indeed, as have put on the shoes of incorruption.[1]

The Prophet in the beginning of his Psalm noted in the wicked a triplicity of sinning—walking in the counsel of the ungodly, standing in the way of sinners, and sitting in the chair of scorners; and here in the end of his Psalm he noteth a triplicity of their punishments: they shall not rise in judgment, they shall not stand in the congregation of the righteous, and their way shall perish; and it may be thought, when the scorners heard they should not rise in the judgment, this never troubled them, for they are not for rising; they are well enough as they are; they have a chair to sit in, and they scorn to rise. And when the sinners heard they should not stand in the congregation of the righteous, this did not much move them neither; for they like better to be by themselves, in the way of sinners, than be bound to keep company with such precise fellows; but when the ungodly hear that their way shall perish, and that they shall not have that way to walk in, this strikes them dead; their hearts are clean done; and now would they be begging of Abraham to send Lazarus to their father's house,[2] to warn their friends from following their courses, for fear of their curses.

And may it not now be truly said that the Prophet hath performed both his prizes to the full? for as before he did not leave a godly man till he had brought him to receive his portion in heaven, so now he hath not left a wicked man till he hath brought him to receive his portion in hell. For the wicked have a portion too, though they were better be without it; a miserable portion, to have misery for a portion; yet so the Prophet in another place calls it. This is their portion: fire and brimstone, and a stormy tempest.[3] And now we may indeed say the Prophet hath well ended his task, and

---

[1] 2 Pet. iii. 13. [2] Luke xvi. 27, 28. [3] Ps. xi. 6: "Upon the wicked he shall rain snares, fire, and brimstone, and an horrible tempest: *this shall be* the portion of their cup."

we might say happily, but that he ends it miserably; for he hath delivered his Psalm, as it were, in a tragical form, making it to begin with blessedness and to end with perishing; but yet he hath so framed it that we may easily reduce it, by help of the law of contraries, into a more comical form (if I may so speak), making it to begin with misery and to end with blessedness; and this, perhaps, will be a form more capable of a *plaudite*[1] from our hands, and of an *Io pæan*[2] from our tongues, and may thus be framed: Miserable and wretched are the men that have walked in the counsel of the ungodly, and have stood in the way of sinners, and have sat in the chair of scorners; but have no delight in the law of the Lord, nor in his law will exercise themselves, either day or night; and they shall be like to chaff which the wind scatters. The godly are not so; but they are like a tree planted by the water's side, which will give its fruit in its time; the leaves also shall not wither, and whatsoever they do it shall prosper. Therefore the godly shall rise in the judgment, and (parted from the wicked) shall make a congregation by themselves. For the Lord knoweth not the way of the wicked, and the way of the godly shall be established.

---

[1] A demand for applause.   [2] A shout of triumphant praise.

MEDITATIONS
AND
DISQVISITIONS
UPON
The Seven Pfalmes of DAVID, commonly called the Penitentiall PSALMES.

By Sr. RICHARD BAKER, *Knight.*

LONDON,
Printed by *Iohn Dawſon*, for *Francis Eglesfield*, and are to bee ſold at the Marigold, in *Pauls* Church-yard. 1639.

*Recensui Meditationes has in Septem
  Psalmos Davidis, & Typis
     mandari permitto.*
                              SAMUEL BAKER.

*Ex Ædibus Londinens:
   Iunii* 5, 1638.[1]

---

[1] I have revised these Meditations on Seven Psalms of David, and allow them to be printed.
                              SAMUEL BAKER.
At my house in London, June 5th, 1638.

To the
RIGHT HONOURABLE
MARY, COUNTESS OF DORSET,
THE VIRTUOUS LADY OF THE RIGHT HONOURABLE EDWARD, EARL OF DORSET.

MOST HONOURED LADY,—It is not the least of your virtues, that you are not proud of your virtues; which if it had been in the angels that fell, they had perhaps not fallen. And because you delight so much in humbleness, it makes me bold to present unto you these Psalms of David's humiliation. How happy were I, if I could make a descant,[1] answerable to David's plain-song:[1] but what is wanting in mine, your own meditations will happily supply; which cannot but be excellent, being followed by the practice of so virtuous a life; of which I wish I could as well make a monument to remain to all posterity for their example, as it will certainly remain to your own posterity for their glory. But lest I should add the offence of tediousness to boldness, I humbly crave pardon for having said so much, but more, for having said no more; and make it my aspiring suit to be accounted, as I truly am,

Your Ladyship's devoted servant,
RICHARD BAKER.

---

[1] *Plain-song*, the air; *descant*, the harmonious accompaniment.

O LORD, rebuke me not in thine anger, neither chasten me in thy hot displeasure. 2. Have mercy upon me, O LORD; for I *am* weak: O LORD, heal me; for my bones are vexed. 3. My soul is also sore vexed: but thou, O LORD, how long? 4. Return, O LORD, deliver my soul: oh save me for thy mercies' sake. 5. For in death *there is* no remembrance of thee: in the grave who shall give thee thanks? 6. I am weary with my groaning; all the night make I my bed to swim; I water my couch with my tears. 7. Mine eye is consumed because of grief; it waxeth old because of all mine enemies. 8. Depart from me, all ye workers of iniquity; for the LORD hath heard the voice of my weeping. 9. The LORD hath heard my supplication; the LORD will receive my prayer. 10. Let all mine enemies be ashamed and sore vexed: let them return *and* be ashamed suddenly.—PSALM vi. (Auth. Vers.)

MEDITATIONS AND DISQUISITIONS

UPON

THE SIXTH PSALM.

O MY soul, what is it thou hast done? Hast thou been striving with the angel about the body of Moses? For why else shouldst thou be afraid of the angel's imprecation to Satan, when he strove with him about it, "The Lord rebuke thee"?[1] Certainly either the angel was very mild in his imprecation, or thou art very sharp in thy deprecation. But oh, wretch that I am! if Satan deserved rebuking for striving with an angel, how much more do I deserve it for striving with the Creator[2] of angels, and not about taking away the body of Moses, but about taking away the glory of his holy name? For such and so execrable are my sins, that through them the holiness of God's glorious name is blasphemed among the Gentiles;[3] and have I not just cause, then, to fear that he will, and therefore just cause to pray that he will *not rebuke me in his anger, nor chasten me in his heavy*[4] *displeasure*.

But though rebuking were an imprecation to Satan, yet to me it is not so, seeing I do not more deserve it than I need it. As I deserve it for my sin, so I need it for my amendment, for without rebuking what amending?—what amending, indeed, without thy rebuking? for, alas! the flesh flatters me, the world abuseth me, Satan deludes me; and now, O God, if thou also shouldst hold thy peace,[5] and wink at

---

[1] Jude 9. [2] Isa. xlv. 9. [3] Isa. lii. 5. [4] "Hot" (A.V.) [5] Ps. lxxxiii. 1

my follies, whom should I have—alas! whom could I have—to make me sensible of their foulness? If thou shouldst not tell me, and tell me roundly, I went astray, how should I ever—alas! how could I ever—be brought to return into the right way? To thy rebuking, therefore, I humbly submit myself. I know thou intendest it for my amendment, and not for my confusion; for my conversion, and not for my subversion. It may be bitter in the tasting, but is most comfortable in the working; hard, perhaps, to digest, but most sovereign being digested. Yet I cannot endure thou shouldst rebuke me in anger; I cannot endure it in affection, but I can less endure it in ability. It is grievous to me to think thou art angry, but it is insupportable to me to feel thou art angry. The hand of thine anger is heavy; and though of thyself thou be, as it were, a sweetly breathing air, yet anger makes thee a consuming fire;[1] that if thine anger be kindled, yea, but a little,[2] Blessed are all they that put their trust in thee.

When I consider with myself the many favours—undeserved favours—thou hast vouchsafed unto me, and consider withal how little use, how ill use, I have made of them all, though I know I have justly deserved thy rebuking, yet my hope is still thou wilt add this favour also, not to rebuke me in thine anger. But when I think how unkind a thing thy rebuking is, but how terrible a thing thine anger is; when I think what a pain it is to have thee chasten me, but what a death it is to have thee chasten me in displeasure, then I fall a-trembling in all my joints, and never think I can make haste enough to say, and to say with sighing, O Lord, rebuke me not in thine anger, neither chasten me in thy heavy displeasure.

But why may not God rebuke me, as Eli rebuked his sons? For he rebuked his sons for their sins, and yet no anger appeared in him at all.[3] O my soul, wilt thou make Eli a pattern for God? Because God is a loving Father, wilt thou, therefore, make him, like Eli, too indulgent a

---

[1] Deut. iv. 24. [2] Ps. ii. 12: "Kiss the Son, lest he be angry, and ye perish *from the way*, when his wrath is kindled but a little. Blessed *are* all they that put their trust in him." [3] 1 Sam. ii. 23—25.

Father? Eli, indeed, rebuked his sons with a rod, but he made his rod of roses and violets; he rebuked them for sins of presumption as if they had been but sins of infirmity; he rebuked them for sins of wilfulness as if they had been but sins of ignorance. And what was this but instead of striking them to stroke them, and instead of stopping them in their race to add rather a spur unto them? And was it not for this that God rebuked Eli in his anger, because Eli rebuked not his sons in his anger?[1] I deny not, O God, but that my sins deserve thine anger; or, rather, I acknowledge they justly provoke thine anger; but alas, O Lord, if thou shouldst enter into judgment with thy servants,[2] what flesh were able to stand before thee and not be consumed?[3] O vile sin of mine, enough to put patience itself into choler, able to anger a saint, nay, even the King of saints,—that if thou, O God, shouldst rebuke me in thine anger, if chasten me in thy heavy displeasure, I could not say but that thine anger were lenity and thy displeasure mildness.

But what boldness of language is this in speaking to God? Am I not worthy of rebuke for praying God not to rebuke me in his anger, as though I thought that God could be angry? For is not anger a passion of human infirmity, and will I make God subject to passions of infirmity? Is not anger a defect in reason? Is not God a perfection above reason? and can there be defect in perfection? Can there be passion in him that is *purus actus* [a pure act]? But is it not that anger in God is not a passion, but an action; not a defect, but an effect? for then is God said to be angry when he puts his judgments in execution, when his rebukings tend not to conversion but to confusion, when his mercy attempers not the rigour of his justice. Oh, then, rebuke me, O God, but not in thine anger; rebuke me as thou didst the Ninevites, who at thy rebuking repented and were converted;[4] but rebuke me not as thou didst Pharaoh, who hardened his heart[5] at thy rebuking, and was confounded. If thou, O God, shouldst rebuke me in thine anger, I should more have an eye to thy rod than give an

---

[1] 1 Sam. iii. 13. [2] Ps. cxliii. 2. [3] Cf. Nah. i. 6. [4] Jonah iii. 4—10.
[5] Ex. viii. 15, *et alibi*.

ear to thy lesson; I should be more terrified with thine anger than edified with thy rebuking, and should be made incapable of thy doctrine with the terror of thy teaching; for I, alas, am as a nail under the workman's hammer, better driven in with gentle strokes than with hard blows. Oh, therefore, rebuke me not, O God, if thou be angry; or, if thou rebuke me, be not angry. Two such sharp notes as anger and rebuking are, can never make any pleasing music if they meet together. Anger in rebuking makes the water troubled and thick, that should be drunk clear; makes the air sultry and hot, that should be breathed in cold—extremely (both of them) unwholesome for the body; and seeing thou intendest my health, and seekest not to make me sick, let not anger inflame thy rebuking, O God, that so the air of it I may take in the cooler, that so the water of it I may drink the clearer. I, alas, am as a narrow-mouthed vessel in the hand of the drawer, better filled with softly pouring in than with pouring in hastily, which commonly spills more than it fills; and seeing thy rebuking is too precious a liquor to be spilt, oh pour it in with the softly hand of patience, and not with the hasty hand of anger, that so it may the sooner fill and the better enter without spilling into this narrow-mouthed vessel of my empty soul. Thy rebuking, O God, is to me as thunder, but thine anger is as lightning; and is it not enough that thou terrify my soul with the thunder of thy rebuking, but thou wilt also set this flax of my flesh on fire with the lightning of thine anger?[1] Thy rebuking of itself is a precious balm, but mixed with anger turns to a corrosive. O keep thy corrosives, O God, for such hardened hearts as Pharaoh's was; apply to me only the simple balm of thy rebuking, and let it not have any mixture at all of thy corroding anger in it. What though I have offended thee with sins of anger, must thou needs take revenge in the same kind thou art offended? And if needs thou must do so, why mayst thou not, then, take revenge of my sins in thy good pleasure, seeing I have offended thee as much with sins of pleasure? Thou didst

---

[1] Isa. i. 31.

walk in Paradise with our first parents in the cool of the day,[1] when the heat of the sun was over, and this made thy presence as cheerful as glorious. Vouchsafe, O God, to deal so with me; rebuke me in the cool of thy Spirit, when the heat of thine anger is overpast, for else, alas, it may be glorious, but can never be comfortable.[2]

But if rebuking me in thine anger be so bitter a potion, what is it then to chasten me in thine indignation? for where the worst of thy rebuking in anger is but threatening of punishment, the best of thy chastening in indignation is inflicting of punishment; and though a strong heart may perhaps endure such threatenings, yet no strength of heart is able to bear such inflictings. It is terror enough to hear thee but chide; but to feel thee strike, and that with strokes of indignation, what power of any creature is able to endure it? I ask not, thou wouldst not chasten me; this were to ask, thou wouldst not love me; for whom thou lovest thou chastenest;[3] and would I lose thy love for any chastening? O gracious God, chasten me in what manner, with what measure thou pleasest; chasten me as thou didst Lazarus, by making him die for hunger at Dives' gate;[4] chasten me as thou didst Job, by making him lie with sores upon the dunghill;[5] chasten me as thou didst Daniel, by making him be cast into the lions' den;[6] but then chasten me in love, and not in indignation; for thy chastening in love, though it pain yet it heals; though it bruise, yet it comforts; thy rod and thy staff they comfort me;[7] but thy chastening in indignation is pain without hope, is bruising in despair, or, rather, not a pain, but a torment; not a bruising, but a breaking; that no misery can be comparable to this chastening, to be chastened in thine indignation.

Chastening and love may well be matched together; they are like to Jacob and Rachel; though there be seven years of service more, yet Rachel will be had at last;[8] but chastening and indignation are as badly matched as may be, for chastening inclines to conversion, and indignation is wholly bent upon confusion. Oh, therefore, match thy chastening

---

[1] Gen iii. 8.   [2] Strengthening.   [3] Heb. xii. 6.   [4] Luke xvi. 20—22.   [5] Job ii. 7, 8.   [6] Dan. vi. 16.   [7] Ps. xxiii. 4.   [8] Gen. xxix. 27, 28.

with love, and not with indignation, that so at least I may come at last to enjoy my Rachel,—that is, thy favour. Chastening and love may lodge both together in the bowels[1] of a father, but indignation comes not where bowels are; and how then, O God, canst thou chasten me in indignation, but thou must as it were disembowel thyself and utterly abandon the name of a Father? and shall anything make thee to leave that name? I know, O God, it is a name so dear unto thee that I hope I shall commit no such sin; and suffer me not, O God, to commit any such sin as shall ever be able to make thee abandon it. Indeed here, where we call thee Lord, indignation may appear, and be bold to show itself; but when we come to name thee Father, indignation must be gone, and never presume to come in place. If thy chastening be intended for reforming or for polishing, what wouldst thou do with indignation, that tends to abolishing? And if thou chasten whom thou lovest, and then destroy whom thou chastenest, what difference will there be between thy indignation and thy mercy? Oh, let not thy chastening, which is ordained to be a rod for thy children, be made a knife to slaughter thy children. Consider, O God, I am but a pot made of brittle clay,[2] that if thy hand hold not a temper in striking I shall soon be broken and beaten in pieces, and then thy workmanship will be defaced. And shall it ever be said of thee that with one hand thou makest and with the other hand destroyest? Remember, O God, whose title it is to be a destroyer;[3] thy title is to be a Creator; and shall I find no more favour at the hands of a Creator[4] than I might look to find at the hands of a destroyer?

Alas, my soul! I know full well it were a grievous case for me if God should let his chastening and his indignation join together and assail me with them both at once, but how shall I do to keep them asunder? Have I any Moses to stand for me in the gap?[5] Blessed be thy glorious name,

---

[1] Affection. [2] Isa. xlv. 9. [3] Rev. ix. 11: "The angel of the bottomless pit, whose name in the Hebrew tongue *is* Abaddon, but in the Greek tongue hath *his* name Apollyon" (or Destroyer). [4] 1 Pet. iv. 19: "Let them ... commit their souls *to him* ... as to a faithful Creator." [5] Num. xvi. 48.

O God! I have indeed a greater than Moses, even him whom thou didst chasten in thy heavy displeasure; to the end thou mightst not chasten me in thy heavy displeasure; for his agony of crying My God, my God, why hast thou forsaken me?[1] gives me boldness to cry, and confidence in crying, My God, my God, have mercy upon me. This I know will help when all other helps fail. But what have I in myself to plead why God should not chasten me in his heavy displeasure? Can I say I have not deserved it? or can I say I have not even provoked him to do it? Alas, O God, I have nothing in thee to fly to, but only thy mercy; nothing in myself to plead,[2] but only my weakness. *Have mercy upon me, O God,[3] for I am weak* [**ver. 2**].

But is this not a weak plea, to allege weakness for a plea? weak indeed with men who commonly tread hardest upon the weakest, and are ever going over where the hedge is lowest; but no weak plea with God, whose mercy is ever ready upon all occasions, and then most when there is most need; and seeing there is greatest need where there is greatest weakness, therefore no plea with God so strong as this, Have mercy upon me, O God, for I am weak.

But why should David pray for mercy to help his weakness? for what can mercy do? Mercy can but pity his weakness; it is strength that must relieve it. But is it not that mercy, I may say, is as the steward of God's house, and hath the command of all he hath; that if wisdom be wanting for direction, mercy can procure it; if justice be wanting for defence, mercy can obtain it; if strength be wanting for support, mercy can command it; and therefore no plea so perfect to be urged with God as this, Have mercy upon me O God, for I am weak.

But why should David make his weakness a motive to God for mercy? for is not weakness an effect of sin? and can God love the effect when he hates the cause? But it is not the weakness in David that God loves, but the acknowledging of his weakness; for what is this but the true humility? and who knows not in how high account such humility is

---

[1] Matt. xxvii. 46.   [2] Rom. vii. 18.   [3] " LORD " (A.V.)

with God, seeing it is indeed of this wonderful condition, that though nothing be so low, yet nothing reacheth so high, and therefore no motive so fit to move God as this: Have mercy upon me, O God, for I am weak. Mercy, indeed, looks down upon no object so directly as upon weakness, and weakness looks up to no object so directly as to mercy; and therefore they cannot choose but meet, and, meeting, not choose but embrace each other: mercy, weakness as her client; weakness, mercy as her patron; that no plea can be with God so strong as this, Have mercy upon me, O God, for I am weak. Let thy indignation, O God, be laid upon Pharaoh, and such as trust in their strength, for upon them thou mayst get thee honour;[1] but, alas, what honour can be gotten by pouring thy indignation upon so weak a creature as I am? Thy honour shall be as much to support my weakness by thy mercy as to abate their pride by thine indignation.

But what though David be weak, is every weakness sufficient cause to run to God about? Might he not take restoratives and cordials, and such other comfortable things, and so help his weakness without going to God? O my soul, what comfort is in a cordial, if it be not of God's making? What strength in a restorative, if it be not of God's giving? No, O Lord, thy mercy is the only restorative that can help my weakness, the true *aqua cælestis* [water of heaven] to comfort my spirits.

I know, O God, thou sweetly disposest all things both in weight and measure; thou considerest man that he is but dust;[2] thou knowest me, that I am a worm, and no man;[3] and can it then be thou shouldst have no consideration of my weakness? Wilt thou not proportion thy burden to the bearer? Wilt thou load a gnat as thou wouldst load a camel? Oh, have mercy upon me, O God, and consider my weakness, for I am weak.

But why should David make his weakness a cause for God to spare him? For how came he by his weakness? Was it not by his own disorder? And then, if his weakness be

---

[1] Exod. xiv. 18. [2] Ps. ciii. 14. [3] Ps. xxii. 6.

one of his faults, hath not God just cause to strike him the harder for his weakness? It seems, indeed, that David cannot deny but that he deserves it, and therefore lays not his plea in the court of God's justice, but of his mercy; for his mercy, he knoweth, hath bowels of compassion,[1] and will not always be ruled by rigour; but, finding contrition, will have a regard of weakness. And, indeed, seeing the end of God's chastening is but to piece up my breaches, why should he strike so hard to break me in pieces.

But are there not some men that feign themselves to be poor when yet they be rich, because they would pay but a little tribute? And may not David be such a one, feign himself to be weak when perhaps he was strong, because he would have God to spare him in his chastening? But never have such a thought of David, for hear him what he says farther: Heal me, *for my bones are troubled;*[2] and surely, if his bones be troubled, he may well be allowed to say he is weak. For if there be any strength in our bodies, it is in our bones: they are both ablest to withstand harm, and farthest removed out of harm's way; that before any trouble can come to them, it must pass the skin, the flesh, the membranes, and all other parts; that if once the bones come to be troubled, we may justly say, *Res rediit ad triarios* [there has arisen a need for the reserves], the matter is come to the height of extremity. And, therefore, David finding trouble in his bones, had just cause to complain of weakness, and to say, Heal me, O God, for my bones are troubled. Distempers and infirmities are ever more hard or easy to be cured, as they are seated in parts more hard or easy to be wrought upon; and therefore distempers in the spirits are of all other the easiest to be cured, more hard in the humours, but in the solid parts hardest of all, for then they grow to be hectic;[3] and such, in all account, are scarce held curable; and seeing of all the solid parts the bones are the most solid, and therefore diseases in them the hardest to be cured, David had just cause to call to God for help, and to say, Heal me, O God, for my bones are troubled.

---

[1] 1 John iii. 17.   [2] "Vexed" (A.V.)   [3] Fevered.

If the beams of a house be unsound and shaken, how is it possible the house should stand? and as little is it possible that this body of mine should be saved from ruin, if my bones which are the beams of it be out of order and troubled.

But if the trouble of the bones be so incurable, is it not presumption in David to say, Heal me, O God, for my bones are troubled; being, as if he should say, Cure me, O God, for I am past all cure; and so tempt God with desiring him to do a work that is impossible? But is it not that David knows to whom he speaks? He knows he speaks not to Galen or to Hippocrates:[1] he knows he speaks not to Æsculapius or to Apollo;[2] but he speaks to him that is a transcendent to all these: one to whom not only nothing is impossible, but to whom all impossible things are nothing. It were indeed an unreasonable request in the eye of nature, but very reasonable in the eye of faith, seeing faith indeed is then most reasonable when most it is above all reason, which therefore made Abraham the father of the faithful,[3] because, contrary to hope, he believed in hope that God would make him such a father. And, indeed, most properly then it grows to be a cure for God, when in man's judgment it is grown incurable, as Christ would not go to heal Lazarus until he was dead,[4] and had been four days buried,[5] thereby perhaps to prepare belief for his own resurrection, seeing it might well be believed he could rise himself the third day, who had raised another after four days. Never therefore fear, my soul, to say with David, Heal me, for my bones are troubled; for the time will come when he shall heal thee, not only when thy bones be troubled, but when they be mouldered away into dust and powder; for even then he will gather them together again, and make them stand up, and serve for beams to this body of thine, as now they do.

But how can the bones be troubled, seeing they have no sense? for it is the flesh and the membranes that feel the pain; the bones feel none. Oh, then, consider how great

---

[1] Celebrated ancient physicians, who taught the healing art to men.   [2] Apollo, god of medicine, father of Æsculapius.   [3] Gal. iii. 9: "Faithful Abraham."   [4] John xi. 14.   [5] John xi. 17.

my trouble is, which strikes a sense of pain into my very parts that are not sensible.

And now it would be comfort indeed to have my bones healed, if when they were healed I might then be at quiet; but, alas, what comfort is it now to be healed of their trouble when God's chastening hand pursues me still, and lays more and greater troubles upon me continually? For though the trouble of the bones be the height of trouble, yet it is but the trouble of the body; my soul all this while hath been at quiet, but now *my soul itself is troubled also*[1] [**ver. 3**], and so extremely troubled that I feel it, and feel it sensibly, in all the parts of my soul; I feel it in my memory when I remember the grievous sins which I have committed; I feel it in my understanding when I consider thy glorious majesty, whom I have offended; I feel it in my will when I think upon the terror of thy displeasure which I have incurred. If the trouble were but in this or that part only, I might yet find comfort in the other; but now that every part of my soul, now that all my whole soul is troubled, and extremely troubled, alas, now I may truly say, Was ever sorrow like my sorrow, was ever trouble like this of mine?

But can the soul be troubled? Is it not a spiritual substance? And are not all earthly things too gross to trouble that which is a spirit? They should be so indeed, and they would be so indeed, if the soul had her right. But, alas, while we live here the soul is but an inmate to the body, and therefore the body crows over it as being upon its own dunghill, and makes us all of kin to Martha, troubled about many things[2] when but one is needful. And yet these be not of the things that trouble the noble soul, not the soul of David. In matters, indeed, between the world and us, the soul is forced to look down upon the earth as upon that which sustains it; and if it find a want there, it finds withal a trouble indeed; but a trouble to the body only; or if to the soul, but in the body's behalf, which is not much. That which properly troubles the soul is the proper trouble of the soul, and is only in matters between God and us; and in matters

---

[1] "My soul is also sore vexed" (A.V.)   [2] Luke x. 40, 41.

of this nature it looks up to heaven, for there indeed is the soul's freehold; and if that inheritance be once questioned, then the soul finds itself in trouble presently, and so extremely troubled, that where the trouble of the body is but the body of trouble, this trouble of the soul is, I may say, the soul of trouble. And is not this inheritance questioned if God fall once to rebuke me in his anger? for seeing the inheritance is but a mere gift proceeding from his favour,[1] how can I expect it if I be in his displeasure? When I was in my greatest weakness, yet my bones afforded me at least some strength; and when my bones were troubled, yet my soul was able to take care of their curing; but now that my soul itself is troubled, alas, O God, who is there but thyself only of whom I can hope for any comfort? And therefore, *O Lord, how long?* How long wilt thou let me lie languishing in my weakness? How long wilt thou suffer me to struggle with oppression? How long wilt thou see the extremity of my misery, and not relieve me? Thou, indeed, inhabitest eternity,[2] and no time to thee is either short or long;[3] but I, alas, am a subject of times, and nothing so much tyrannizeth over me as this tyrant time, and specially when it joins with misery; for then, as a thousand years are with thee but as a day,[4] so a day with me is as a thousand years; measure me not therefore by thy standard of eternity, but measure me by the standard of time. And then, O Lord, how long? How long shall thy chastening hand lie heavy upon me?[5] How long wilt thou pour upon me the vials of thine indignation?[6] How long shall my soul be kept from her true inheritance, which is to bear a part in the comfort of angels? My soul is a free spirit, and is with nothing so much delighted as with liberty; with nothing so much vexed as with thraldom; and in thraldom, alas, in miserable thraldom is my soul detained; and therefore, O Lord, how long? How long shall my soul be restrained of her liberty? How long shall I lie groaning in the dungeon of captivity? How long shall no date be set to give a period to my thraldom? My

---

[1] 2 Thess. ii. 16: "Our Father, which . . . . hath given *us* everlasting consolation and good hope through grace." [2] Isa. lvii. 15. [3] Ps. xc. 4. [4] 2 Pet. iii. 8. [5] Ps. xxxii. 4. [6] Rev. xvi. 1; xxi. 9.

soul, I may say, is all heart, and therefore every trouble it
feels must needs go to the heart; yet none so deep as this,
that I am forced to cry to thee out of the deep,[1] and cannot
yet ascend out of this vale of misery;[2] and therefore, O
Lord, how long? How long shall I live in the death of this
fear, the fear of death? How long shall I desire to be
dissolved,[3] that being reunited again I may never more be
dissolved? How long shall my immortal soul be kept from
the possession of her immortality, from the immortality of
her possession? If the saints in heaven, who now tread
time under their feet, do yet continue this question still, to
ask how long,—How long, O Lord, holy and true, wilt thou
not avenge our blood on them that live in the earth?[4]—is
it marvel that I who live under the tyranny of time should
begin this question, to ask how long? How long, O Lord,
merciful and just, wilt thou not avenge me on the world and
Satan for the wrongs they have done me? How long shall
I be kept from saying, "O death, where is thy sting? O grave,
where is thy victory?"[5] How long shall the angel with the
flaming sword keep me from entering again into Paradise?[6]
Where is the morning of joy I promised to myself when I
said, Sorrow may be in the evening, but joy cometh in the
morning?[7] For how many evenings, how many tedious
nights of sorrow have I endured, and yet can see no morning
of joy, no dawning of morning toward?[8] Where is the
truth of that aphorism, *Dolor si gravis brevis* [sorrow when
grievous is short], for what dolor so grievous as this of my
soul, and yet, O Lord, how long? How long shall I stand
complaining, and say my soul is troubled? Is it not that I
shall never cease to say my soul is troubled, till he return
again who once said for me that his soul was troubled?[9]
For, alas, his soul should never have been troubled, but to
take away, amongst others, the trouble of mine, seeing he is

---

[1] Ps. cxxx. 1. [2] Probably referring to the valley of Achor (*trouble*); see Jos. vii. 24, and Hos. ii. 15. [3] Phil. i. 23: "Having a desire to depart" (Desiderium habens dissolvi.—*Vulgate*). [4] Rev. vi. 10: "How long, O Lord, holy and true, dost thou not judge and avenge our blood on them that dwell on the earth?" [5] 1 Cor. xv. 55. [6] Gen. iii. 24: "And he placed at the east of the garden of Eden cherubims, and a flaming sword which turned every way, to keep the way of the tree of life." [7] Ps. xxx. 5: "Weeping may endure for a night, but joy *cometh* in the morning." [8] Approaching. [9] John xii. 27.

the sacrifice for all our sins,[1] and "with his stripes we are healed."[2] And now, therefore, O Lord, how long? How long wilt thou turn away thy face[3] and not show me again the light of thy countenance?[4] How long wilt thou absent thyself from me, and not afford me the joy of thy presence? How long wilt thou be going still farther from me, and not so much as once offer to return? *Oh, return* at last, and *deliver my soul, save me for thy mercy's sake* [**ver. 4**]; for alas, O Lord, all my troubles are come upon me because thou wentest from me; all my grievance is long of thine absence, for as long as thou wert with me, and that I had thy presence, my soul was at quiet, my bones were at rest, and I enjoyed then a sweet and pleasing calm over all my parts; but as soon as thou departest from me, and didst but turn away thy face, my calm was presently turned into a tempest, a violent tempest of thunder and lightning—thunder of thy rebuking, and lightning of thine anger; that if thou stay not thy hand from chastening, and return the sooner, I shall never be able to hold out living, to taste of thy mercy. St. Peter was never so near drowning when he cried out to Christ, Lord, save me, or else I perish,[5] as David is now near sinking in the pit of perdition, if God return not speedily and deliver his soul. But what speak I of David, as though it were not my own case? And if my danger be as great, shall not my prayer be as earnest? or can I find a better way of saving than thy returning? No, O Lord; for if thou return, I am sure thou wilt not, I know thou canst not, leave thy mercy behind; and mercy, when it comes, I know it cannot, I am sure it will not, ever suffer it to be perdition; for though my soul were at the pit's brink, and ready to fall in, yet even then would mercy put forth her hand and save me.

Thou requirest me to return to thee; and alas, O Lord, how can I, if thou return not to me first? Can I come to thee unless thou draw me?[6] and canst thou draw me to thee if thou withdraw thyself from me? I know thou returnest

---

[1] Ps. liii. 10: "Thou shalt make his soul an offering for sin." [2] Isa. liii. 5.
[3] Ps. lxxxix. 46: "How long, LORD? wilt thou hide thyself for ever?" [4] Ps. iv. 6.
[5] Matt. xiv. 30. [6] John vi. 44.

continually to dispose and order the economy of thy creatures; but this returning is in thy providence, and is not that which I desire. I know thou returnest often to visit and judge the sins of the world, as thou didst at Sodom ;[1] but this returning is in thy justice, and therefore neither is this returning for my turn. But thou hast a returning in grace and favour, when thou returnest to me to make me return to thee—a returning from thine anger to thy patience, from thine indignation to thy lovingkindness ; and this is the returning which I so earnestly desire and sue for.

But, O my soul, before God return in this manner to thee, thou must look to hear him expostulate with thee in this manner: Alas, my creature, what hast thou done to bring these troubles upon thyself? Did I not make thee at first a sound body, and did I not give it a strong constitution? and how happens it now that thy bones should be troubled? Did I not breathe into it a perfect soul, and gave it endowments after mine own image? and how comes it now to be so quite out of order, and so clean bereft of all my graces? Thou wilt perhaps answer, It is true, O Lord, my bones are troubled; and how can they choose, seeing thou tookest one of them away from me[2] which thou gavest me at first? My soul also is troubled; and how can it choose, seeing thou didst suffer the serpent in Paradise to disturb and trouble it?[3] But may not God then justly reply, I took one of thy bones from thee indeed, but it was to make thee a helper. I let in the serpent into Paradise indeed, but it was to try thee for thy better perfecting ; and when I saw thee so foolishly hurt thyself with thy helper, and so easily won from me by a tempter, had I not just cause to leave thee to them for whom thou leftest me? And now, forlorn wretch, what hast thou to say, unless thou have leave to say, Return, O Lord, and deliver my soul; save me for thy mercy's sake?

But what more necessity is there of God's returning to deliver his soul than there was before to heal his bones? and in that case he spake not a word of returning, and why

---

[1] Gen. xviii. 21. [2] Gen. ii. 18, 21. [3] Gen. iii.

should he more importune it now? Is it not that many diseases may be well enough cured only by relation of symptoms, though the physician come not where the patient is? and of this sort it seems was the healing of his bones. But to deliver his soul is of another nature, and requires perhaps a feeling the pulse, perhaps an inspection of the patient; and therefore no remedy here but the physician must himself be present.

But is it enough to make suit to God, in general terms, to pray him to deliver my soul, and not tell him from what it is he must deliver it? Can any man think that God will return upon so uncertain an occasion? Alas, O Lord, it is not unknown to thee that my soul wants no clothes, and therefore it is not to deliver it from nakedness; my soul needs no meat, and therefore it is not to deliver it from hunger; my soul is never old, and therefore it is not to deliver it from the racks of time. But it is, indeed, to deliver it from trouble; and what it is that can trouble my soul thou knowest, for my soul is thy servant, depending wholly upon thy favour, and, having offended thee, desires to be delivered from all fear of thine anger. My soul was at first a free spirit, but is now become a bond-slave to sin, and therefore desires to be delivered from this bondage. My soul is itself immortal, but is troubled here with a mortal body, and therefore desires to be delivered from this body of death;[1] and in effect it is all but sin, and the train that sin draws after it, from which I desire my soul should be delivered. And, therefore, return, O Lord, and deliver my soul; save me for thy mercy's sake.

But, O my soul, with what reason canst thou expect that God should ever return to thee; for who would be willing to come to one in trouble, as thou art, lest he pay for his coming with drawing a trouble upon himself? And if he should return and come unto thee, wouldst thou be so satisfied? wouldst thou not presently be importuning him for further favours? He must help thee in thy troubles, he must help thee out of thy troubles, or thou wouldst

---

[1] Rom. vii. 24.

never be at quiet. And is it a small matter to deliver a soul out of trouble? Do souls used to be troubled for trifles? and were he not better then to endure thy importunity for his returning, than, being returned, to be troubled with importunity for thy deliverance? But, O my soul, be not frighted with these vain objections; for is God like man, that he should be afraid of being troubled? Is he not the God of mercy; and can it be a trouble to his mercy to do the works of mercy? Is it not his delight to be, is it not his title to be called, is it not his glory to be counted a deliverer?[1] And is any deliverance so fit for his mercy, so worthy of his mercy, as deliverance of souls? Alas, O Lord, it is a small work for thee to return, but thou shalt do an infinite work by thy returning; for thou shalt deliver my soul out of trouble, my grieved soul out of grievous troubles. And wilt thou not afford me so much kindness to do so small a matter for effecting of so great a matter? Oh return, O God, and deliver my soul, that, as thou art called a deliverer, so I may call thee my deliverer, and may sing with Moses, Thou, O God, art my strength and my song, for thou hast been my deliverance.[2]

But why should this be made so great a matter? For though in saying, Return, O Lord, and deliver my soul, I seem to require of God two several works, one to return and another to deliver me, yet they are in truth but both as one; at least, no more differing than the cause and the effect, seeing his very returning is itself a deliverance. The only turning his face towards me makes me to see the light of his countenance;[3] and no sooner doth that light shine upon my soul, but all the clouds that darkened it are presently dispelled; all the troubles that vexed my bones are instantly healed. But though deliverance be an effect of God's returning, yet it must be when he returns in a good mood, and not in a rebuking or in a chastening disposition; for if his anger continue still, were it not better for me he

---

[1] 2 Sam. xxii. 2; Ps. xviii. 2, xl. 17, lxx. 5, cxliv. 2, etc.   [2] Exod. xv. 2: "The LORD *is* my strength and song, he is become my salvation."   [3] Ps. lxix. 16, 17: "Turn unto me according to the multitude of thy tender mercies. And hide not thy face from thy servant."

should tarry away? and why, then, am I so importunate with him to return, before I know in what terms I stand with him, and whether he be angry still or no? But it is even for this that I importune his returning, that I may be assured his anger is past; for as long as he is angry, he never comes where I am; to do that were a greater favour than his anger can afford; but as soon as his anger is a little over, he is apt of himself to return unto me; for his delight is with the children of men,[1] and specially with those that call upon him; and when he returns, his anger being over, he useth to do as the dove did, that, when the waters were a little abated, returned into the ark and brought the olive branch with her in her mouth;[2] so God returning, when the waters of his displeasure are a little abated, brings the olive branch of peace and deliverance along with him.

But say, my soul, that God should return and should deliver thee, wouldst thou then be quiet, and not trouble him with any more suits? should this be the last request thou wouldst make? Alas, no! I have one suit more to make; and thou, O God, that gavest Abraham leave to importune thee with one suit after another,[3] vouchsafe me this favour, to make this suit also, and this indeed shall be the last I will ever make: Save me for thy mercy's sake. For as thy returning would be to small purpose if thou didst not deliver me, so thy deliverance will be to small purpose if thou do not also save me. To deliver me, and then leave me to be seized upon again, would make thee but *Auctor imperfecti operis*—leave thy work imperfect, which cannot agree with the perfection of thy most perfect workmanship. And now, O God, if thou take pleasure in conjunctions, be pleased to take pleasure in this conjunction—not to join thy rebuking and thy anger together, not to join thy chastening and thy indignation together, but to join thy deliverance and salvation together; for those conjunctions separate us from thee, this conjunction unites us to thee; those bring us to shipwreck, this brings us into the haven; deliverance avoids the rocks, salvation sets safe on shore. And is not this that which David means when in another place he saith,

---

[1] Ps. viii. 31. [2] Gen. viii. 11. [3] Gen. xviii. 23—32.

With thee, O God, there is plenteous redemption?[1] It is redemption, indeed, if thou but only deliver my soul; but it is not plenteous redemption unless, besides delivering, thou also save me. O then be pleased in thy plenteous redemption to grant me this conjunction of deliverance and salvation, that I may return thee the conjunction of praise and thanksgiving, and may sing and say, O LORD, I will praise thee: though thou wast angry with me, yet thine anger is turned away. Behold, God is my salvation; I will trust, and not be afraid.[2]

But how can God return to deliver me and to save me if he return not a deliverer and a Saviour? and when will this be? O my soul, in how much better state art thou than David was! for he only expected when it should be, but thou art assured when it was. For then was God manifested to return a deliverer and a Saviour, when the angel brought this tidings to the shepherds: This day is born to you a Saviour,[3] of whom also a voice from heaven testified, This is my well-beloved Son, in whom I am well pleased.[4] Oh, then, return to me in this Saviour in whom thou art well pleased, that so I shall be sure, for so I shall be sure thou wilt not chasten me in thy displeasure.

As there have been many particular deluges and floods, yet but one general, so there have been many particular deliverers and saviours, yet but one general; and from this general Saviour it is that I desire and expect salvation; for though his being a general Saviour may make him be thought less careful of me, having so many others to care for besides, yet have no fear of that, my soul, seeing he is as much a Saviour to me as if he were a Saviour to none but me; and this general Saviour will save me generally, not only from temporal but from spiritual enemies; not only from trouble of bones, but from trouble of soul; not only from miseries here on earth, but even from miseries when earth itself shall be no more. O happy salvation, when this Saviour shall come and save me! but how may I do to get him to come? for he comes not but upon some motive. If I had all the gold of Ophir, I would willingly give it all to get him to come and save me; but, alas! I neither have it to give, nor

---

[1] Ps. cxxx. 7.   [2] Isa. xii. 1, 2.   [3] Luke ii. 11.   [4] Matt. iii. 17.

doth he care to have it: if anything win him to do it, it must be *for his mercy's sake,* and for his mercy's sake he will do it, if ever he will do it.

But is not this strange? My weakness was the motive before to move God to mercy; and must his mercy now be itself the motive to move him to save me? yet so it is; for when God's mercy finds no motive from us, rather than fail of moving, it becomes a motive to itself; and happy it is for us that so it is, for else we might often be without it when most we need it; or, rather, always be without it, seeing we always need it. Indeed, this motive, for his mercy's sake, is the *primum mobile* [first mover] of all motives to God for showing his favour. He had never delivered the Israelites out of Egypt but for his mercy's sake; he had never saved Noah in the ark but for his mercy's sake; but, above all, he had never sent his Son to save the world but for his mercy's sake. And how then can I doubt, and not rather be confident, that for his mercy's sake he will also deliver my soul and save me? Never, therefore, my soul, look after any further motives; for upon this motive will I set up my rest. His mercy shall be both my anchor and my harbour; it shall be both my armour and my fortress; it shall be both my ransom and my garland; it shall be both my deliverance and my salvation.

And now, O God, thou seest the manifold troubles I am in; thou seest how weak I am; thou seest how my bones are troubled; thou seest how my soul is troubled; and what now can thy chastening hand have more of me but only to take away my life? and even my life I would willingly make a sacrifice to appease thy displeasure. But, alas! O Lord, what good can it be to thee to have me die? Can I praise thee in the dust? but can I praise thee when I am turned to dust? *Is there remembrance of thee in death? or is there hallowing of thy name in the grave?*[1] [**ver. 5.**] As long as I have breath in my body I can praise thy name; unworthily, indeed, but yet I can praise it. As long as I am numbered among the living I can show myself thy servant; an unpro-

---

[1] Ps. vi. 5: "For in death *there is* no remembrance of thee: in the grave who shall give thee thanks?" (Auth. Ver.)

fitable one indeed, but yet a servant; but if my soul and body be dissolved once, alas! then all my service of praising thee is at an end. I cannot then do it, though I would; but I cannot then will it, though I should; my soul will want her instruments with which thy praises should be sounded. O vile death, I hate thee for nothing so much as for thy hindering me in this service! O cruel grave, I abhor thee so much for nothing as for thy stopping my mouth for this praising! O merciful God, if I could but remember thee in death, I would never be loath to die. If I could but praise thee in the grave, I would willingly go to it of myself, and never be carried to it by force; but, alas, death is forgetful, the grave is dumb; and therefore deliver my soul, O God, save me for thy mercy's sake.

It is not life that is so dear unto me, but that in life I may praise thee that art so dear unto me. It is not death that is so frightful to me, but this affrights me in death, that being dead I cannot remember thee. It is not the grave that is so loathsome to me, but that in the grave I am forced to forget thee. If death will spare me but to praise thee, let death come and never spare me. If the grave will but let me be sensible of thee, the grave shall come and be welcome to me; but, alas, death hath no mercy, the grave hath no sense; and therefore return, O Lord, and deliver my soul, save me for thy mercy's sake.

Who knows not that death is a mortal enemy to all natural memory, and therefore makes all men at last to end in a lethargy; and what hope then of remembering thee in death? Who knows not that the grave never opens its mouth to let out anything, but still to take in; and what means then of praising thee in the grave? If I could but get death to learn the art of memory, or if I could but hear the grave to say once it had enough,[1] I could then like to have some dealing with death, some traffic with the grave; but, alas, death's lethargy is incurable, the grave's mouth is insatiable; and therefore return, O Lord, and deliver my soul, save me for thy mercy's sake.

---

[1] Prov. xxx. 15, 16.

But doth David's prayer tend to this, that he may not see death? Is this the intent of his request that he may not descend into the pit? Doth he pray to be as Enoch [1] or Elijah,[2] taken from the earth without returning into earth? Alas, he knows this to be either altogether impossible or altogether unlikely, and therefore no likely request to be made by so wise a man. This therefore is certainly the intent of his prayer, that God will not so chasten him in his indignation as to leave him in the hands of death; but that as death receives him from life and delivers him to the grave, so the grave, receiving him from death, may deliver him again to life, that as Christ commanded his apostles to shake off the dust from their feet when they came into any unworthy house, and to come away,[3] so he, coming into this unworthy house of death, the dungeon of the grave, may be able to shake off the dust from his feet, and by the power of him that said, Lazarus, come forth![4] have his soul and body reunited again; and so united be admitted into the choir of saints and angels, eternally to sing the eternal Hallelujah. For as the departing of the soul from the body is the death of the body, so the dividing of the body from the soul is a kind of death to the soul; that it is not as it would be, nor fully enjoys itself until it can meet with the body, and be united to it again. For though it find the body here but a base cottage, or rather a loathsome prison, yet it shall find it there a glorious palace, or rather a holy temple consecrated to God; and therefore, until this be had, it will not fully be accomplished that is here prayed for: Return, O God, and deliver my soul, save me for thy mercy's sake.

The remembrance of this, that I cannot remember thee in death, makes me forgetful of myself in life; and because I cannot praise thee, nor pray to thee, in the grave, it makes me to sigh and weep to thee in my bed, and what I want in continuance to supply with violence. For *I am weary with my sighing;*[5] *all the night make I my bed to swim, I water my couch with my tears* [**ver. 6**]. Oh, let my remembering thee

---

[1] Heb. xi. 5. [2] 2 Kings ii. 11. [3] Matt. x. 14. [4] John xi. 43. [5] "I am weary with my groaning." (Auth. Ver.)

in life supply the place of my forgetting thee in death; and when I lie in my grave senseless and silent, be pleased to remember how I have lain in my bed sighing and weeping. My sins, as being disordinate passions,[1] make me undergo a passive penance, and this hath been my weakness, my trouble of bones, and my trouble of soul; but being also disordinate actions, they make me liable also to do active penance; and what is this but my fighting and my weeping? And though I cannot act sorrow so well as sin, yet my bed and my couch can be witnesses of my sorrow as well as of my sin. Mine eyes indeed chiefly have done the penance, because mine eyes first began the offence.[2] If mine eyes had not set me first on fire, mine eyes had not shed such showers of tears; but now how could burning be quenched but with water? how burning rising from mine eyes, but with water falling from mine eyes? But yet why should my bed suffer, for my bed had no hand in the fault of mine eyes? But, alas, how could my bed but prove a *deodand*,[3] which so apparently,[4] I may say, did *movere ad mortem* [move to (cause) death]? Though my bed were not principal in the act, yet my bed was accessory to the fact, as receiving unlawful and stolen pleasures.

But though my sins indeed be my greatest enemies, yet there are personal enemies that have their malignity also, which though I cannot say they trouble me as ill, yet I may truly say they trouble me as well as these; for *mine eye is consumed because of grief, and is waxen old because of all mine enemies* [**ver. 7**]. You may say, perhaps, that my sighs were feigned, and that my tears were counterfeit; but the consumption of mine eye is a witness of my sorrow, without exception, that if my passive penance before were not cause sufficient, at least my active penance now gives me just cause to say, Was ever sorrow like my sorrow?[5] was ever grief like this of mine? And all this penance I suffer and do because of

---

[1] Disorderly emotions. [2] 2 Sam. xi. 2. [3] In Exod. xxi. 28—32, it was enacted that an ox, that killed a man or woman, should be stoned. By an extension of this principle it was at one time usual in this country that the instrument of a homicide, whether malicious or accidental, should be confiscated under the name *Deodand* (forfeit to God). [4] Evidently. [5] Lam. i. 12.

mine enemies, for how could I choose but sigh and weep, to see the vile, the execrable dealing of mine enemies that persecute me in their hearts,[1] and yet speak peace with their mouths;[2] that lay snares to entrap me,[3] and yet bear me in hand it shall be for my good; that prejudice my cause as if it would never succeed, and prejudicate my prayers as if they would never be heard?[4]

But what means David by this? Will not his weeping make his enemies rejoice the more? will not the seeing him thus dejected make them the more insulting over him? will they not be ready to say, Is this he that encountered a lion and a bear?[5] he that entered combat with a giant, the terror of a whole army?[6] and now to fall a-crying, one cannot tell for what? But David is a better husband of his tears than to spend them idly; he knows for what he spends them—because of his enemies, indeed, but not for fear of his enemies. They are neither tears of fear,—for whom should he fear that hath God on his side? nor tears of vainglory,—for why then should he shed them in the night, when none can see them? nor tears of joy,—for how then should they make him look old, which is an effect of grief? but they are tears of supplication and tears of compassion. First of supplication, that God will either convert them or confound them; and, not converting, then tears of compassion, to think of their confusion. For such is the tenderness of a godly eye, that it hath tears to shed even for enemies. And when these two waters, the tears of supplication and the tears of compassion, meet together, what marvel if they make a flood in David's bed, seeing the concourse of like waters[7] made the great deluge in the whole world? for what are his tears of supplication but as the waters that rose from the springs of the earth, and what are his tears of compassion but as the waters that fell from the cataracts of heaven? Or is it not perhaps that David makes his enemies here a figure

---

[1] Ps. cxl. 2: "Which imagine mischiefs in *their* heart." [2] Ps. xxviii. 3: "Which speak peace to their neighbours, but mischief *is* in their hearts." [3] Ps. xxxviii. 12. [4] Ps. iii. 2: "Many *there be* which say of my soul, *There is* no help for him in God." [5] 1 Sam. xvii. 34, 35. [6] 1 Sam. xvii. 23, 24, 45. [7] Gen. vii. 11: "The same day were all the fountains of the great deep broken up, and the windows of heaven were opened."

of his sins, which are indeed his greatest enemies? as also that he makes his own passion a figure of Christ's compassion, which was indeed one of his passions? for then he wept over Jerusalem in compassion of their confusion,[1] when with tears of supplication he could not prevail with them in compassing their conversion. When they would not hear him how often he would have gathered them together as a hen gathereth her chickens,[2] with tears of supplication; then they hear him say, There shall not be a stone left upon another which shall not be cast down,[3] with tears of compassion.

I grieve not so much that mine eye is waxen old, though it be waxen old with grief, as I grieve to see that my enemies have no eyes at all,—at least, no eyes but of malice, who rejoice at my afflictions, and make themselves as merry with my weeping eyes as the Philistines made themselves with Samson's blinded eyes.[4] I grieve to see their destruction draw near, and they laugh at my grieving, and at the oldness and alteration which grief hath brought upon me. And was it not so with my Saviour Christ, which made the Jews say, Thou art not yet fifty years old,[5] as though he looked like one near fifty, when he was indeed not much above thirty.

But seeing with all my sighing and grieving I cannot reclaim them, I here disclaim them: *Depart from me, all ye workers of iniquity;* [**ver. 8**] away from me, all ye that are wolves in sheep's clothing.[6] I put not away poor penitent sinners, that do penance for their sins as I have done, and may rather be said to suffer sin than to do it, as being more of infirmity than of will; I put away them that make iniquity their work, and think it a penance when they be not committing of sin,—them that are journeymen to the trade, or rather masters in the mystery,[7] them that vilify my sighs and say they are but suitors *in formâ pauperis* [in the character of a needy person], and therefore that God scorns them that reproach my tears, and say they are but dumb solicitors, and therefore God cannot hear them. But see how much

---

[1] Luke xix. 41, 42. [2] Luke xiii. 34. [3] Luke xix. 44. [4] Jud. xvi. 23—25. [5] John viii. 57. [6] Matt. vii. 15. [7] Craft or profession.

they are deceived; for now, contrary to their hopes, and more to their wishes, *the Lord hath heard the voice of my tears;* hath heard it, and therefore does not scorn it; the voice of my tears, and therefore my tears are not dumb; and where all other voices may be doubted, whether God will hear them or no, the voice of tears hath God's care, I may say, at command; at least, is never denied access unto his hearing. And this is but my first and lowest degree of comfort, for a higher than this, *He hath heard my request.*[1]

[**ver. 9.**] But what! hath God no masters of requests about him, but is master of requests himself? Indeed, when he would know the sins of Sodom,[2] he took not information from the angels, but came down himself to see; and should he in person see sins, and not in person hear prayers? And to show himself to be his own master of requests indeed, he hath taken my petition into his hands, that I cannot now doubt of having my request granted, seeing the Prince that must grant it is himself the master of requests to present it; and what is it to receive a supplication into his hands but to receive the suppliant into his favour?

If he only heard the voice of my tears, I might doubt lest he thought them but like the tears of Esau,[3] and so should slight them; or if he only heard my request, I might fear lest he thought it but like the request of the mother of Zebedee's sons, and so reject it;[4] but now that he hath taken my supplication into his hands, now I may be sure he means to do something in it, seeing he never takes anything in hand which he brings not to a happy and successful period, against all opposition. The voice of my tears brought God to cast his eye upon me;[5] my request brought him to bow his ear unto me; but the taking my supplication into his hand hath brought him to compassionate my estate; and seeing his compassion is active, and his pity relieving, my tears of sorrow may now be turned into tears of joy,[6] my lamentations into songs of thanksgiving. The lamentable

---

[1] "The LORD hath heard my supplication: the LORD will receive my prayer" (Auth. Ver.)   [2] Gen. xviii. 20, 21.   [3] Heb. xii. 17: "He found no place of repentance, though he sought it carefully with tears."   [4] Matt. xx. 20—23.   [5] Ps. lxxxvi. 1: "Bow down thine ear, O LORD, hear me: for I *am* poor and needy."
[6] Jer. xxxi. 13: "I will turn their mourning into joy."

accent of my language made God first to look upon me; the pitiful nature of my suit made him next to listen to me; but the justness of my cause in hand made him lastly to take my petition into his hand, which is in effect to grant it out of hand.

Indeed, God is with no music so much delighted as with that of voices; with no voices so much as with those of tears; with no tears so much as with those of the heart, and such were mine, though sent forth by the eyes. And now whose eyes would not be moved at so strange a sight, to hear eyes speak? whose ears would not be moved at so strange a hearing, to see tears be a suitor? whose hands would refuse so strange a writing, where eyes, I may say, are the pen, tears the ink, and sighs the paper? Pardon my curiosity, O God, in imagining wonders, while I meditate of thee in whom are nothing but wonders.

And what remains now but that my sorrows remove their lodging, and sojourn with my enemies, as they have done with me? [**ver. 10.**][1] What remains but that my sighs be turned upon mine enemies' breasts, my tears upon their eyes, and that the pit they digged for me they may fall into themselves,[2] and that with the violence of falling suddenly? As for me, I shall live to see mine enemies turn their backs and be ashamed;[3] I shall live to see them hide their faces, and be confounded; but before all, and above all, I shall live to magnify thy glorious name, O God,[4] who art blessed for ever.

But is David's charity come to this, to be turned into cursings and imprecations? Indeed, no otherwise than God to the serpent, when he said, Cursed art thou above all cattle;[5] for when men are grown into that reprobate sense that they are more like to limbs of Satan than to creatures after the image of God, then it is lawful in God's cause to take God's course, and to turn them over to shame and confusion.

---

[1] Ps. vi. 10: "Let all mine enemies be ashamed and sore vexed: let them return *and* be ashamed suddenly." [2] Ps. lxxvi. 6: "They have digged a pit before me, into the midst whereof they have fallen themselves." [3] Ps. xxxv. 4: "Let them be turned back and brought to confusion that desire my hurt." [4] Ps. cxviii. 17: "I shall not die, but live, and declare the works of the LORD." [5] Gen. iii. 14.

Blessed *is he whose* transgression *is* forgiven, *whose* sin *is* covered. 2. Blessed *is* the man unto whom the LORD imputeth not iniquity, and in whose spirit *there is* no guile. 3. When I kept silence, my bones waxed old through my roaring all the day long. 4. For day and night thy hand was heavy upon me : my moisture is turned into the drought of summer. Selah. 5. I acknowledged my sin unto thee, and mine iniquity have I not hid. I said, I will confess my transgressions unto the LORD ; and thou forgavest the iniquity of my sin. Selah. 6. For this shall every one that is godly pray unto thee in a time when thou mayest be found : surely in the floods of great waters they shall not come nigh unto him. 7. Thou *art* my hiding place ; thou shalt preserve me from trouble; thou shalt compass me about with songs of deliverance. Selah. 8. I will instruct thee and teach thee in the way which thou shalt go : I will guide thee with mine eye. 9. Be ye not as the horse, *or* as the mule, *which* have no understanding : whose mouth must be held in with bit and bridle, lest they come near unto thee. 10. Many sorrows *shall be* to the wicked : but he that trusteth in the LORD, mercy shall compass him about. 11. Be glad in the LORD, and rejoice, ye righteous : and shout for joy, all *ye that are* upright in heart.—PSALM xxxii. (Auth. Ver.)

MEDITATIONS AND DISQUISITIONS

UPON

THE THIRTY-SECOND PSALM.

BLESSEDNESS was cried in the first Psalm,[1] but was there held so dear, that few or none have ever been able to go to the price. Now in this Psalm it is cried again, and at a low rate; and if it be not taken now, it is not like hereafter to be ever had so cheap again; for where before it must have cost an absolute declining from sin, and a perfect delighting in the law of God, with a continual exercising in it day and night,[2] now, if we can but get our iniquities to be remitted, and our sins to be covered, it will serve the turn, and be accepted.[3]

But is this so much an easier rate? For though the purchasing of blessedness were before a great work to be done, yet it was a work that might be done by ourselves, where the purchasing it this way must be the work of another; and were it not better to have it by a way in our own power than by a way in another's will? But, O my soul, is it in man to direct his own way?[4] Is it in man's power to perform the work that is required? Hath he not long since put out the light that should have guided him in it? hath he not long ago cut off the lock[5] that should have been his strength to perform it? Oh, therefore, blessed be he that affords us blessedness at this rate; for though it be in another's will to grant it, yet consider

---

[1] Ps. i. 1. [2] Ps. i. 2. [3] Blessed *is he whose* transgression *is* forgiven, *whose* sin *is* covered. [4] Jer. x. 23: "*It is* not in man that walketh to direct his steps." [5] Judg. xvi. 19.

whose will it is—even his that is more ready to forgive than we are ready to ask forgiveness, and is rather a suitor to us to take a pardon[1] than stays for us to be suitors to have a pardon.

But may it not be thought, because blessedness is set here at a lower rate, that it is not so good a blessedness as the other? And then what is gotten by the bargain? A lower price, indeed, but meaner ware. But this cannot be, for blessedness admits no degrees of comparison: as blessed they that have their sins forgiven, as they (if any such were) that have no sins to forgive. For though blessedness be a positive thing, yet it is a superlative thing; and if there want anything of being a superlative, there must needs want something of being a blessedness. Blessed then are they that have their sins forgiven, for to be forgiven is as much as never to have been guilty; and to say, Blessed are they whose iniquities are forgiven, is all one as to say, Blessed are they that never sinned. When our sins are once forgiven, we are then at peace with God,[2] with whom, until they were forgiven, we were at enmity; and if no misery be comparable to this, to have God's displeasure, then no blessedness can be comparable to this, to have his favour;[3] and his favour we shall be sure to have, if he forgive us our sins, and, therefore, Blessed are they whose iniquities are forgiven.

But is all the way as smooth as this? Is there not a rub in the way here? For to say, Blessed are they whose iniquities are forgiven, is very plausible; but to say, Blessed are they whose sins are covered, seems to mar all; for what if my sins be so great that they cannot be covered, must I therefore be forced to lose my blessedness? It is true indeed, though my sins be in number as the sands of the sea, yet the sea is great enough to cover them all. But, alas, the sea covers not sins, though it cover the sinners; and what blessedness can there be in such a covering? If I go to the world to cover them, and indeed the world is wide, and no doubt a great coverer of sins; but,

---

[1] Cf. 2 Cor. v. 20: "As though God did beseech *you* by us," etc. [2] Rom. v, 1.
[3] Rom. v. 10.

alas, the world's covering is but hypocrisy, and what were this but to cover one sin with another, a lesser with a greater? and so I should be covering them still, and never cover them, but lay them more open in the sight of God than they were before. If I go to the heavens to cover them, and indeed the heavens are large, *Et tegit omnia cœlum* [and the sky covers all]; but, alas, the heavens are full of lights, and will sooner discover that which is hidden than cover anything that lies open to view. Yet I may hope to get the cherubim to cover them, for they have broad wings, and of wonderful extent;[1] but, alas, the cherubim have use enough of their wings to cover their own faces;[2] they cannot with all their wings so much as cover the least of all my sins. And what hope, then, to have my sins covered, when neither the sea, nor the world, neither the heavens, nor the cherubims that are above the heavens, be able to cover them? Yet they must be covered, or there can be no blessedness. And how am I then in any better case for attaining of blessedness than I was before? Two ways propounded for attaining it, and both impossible. There, the price not possible to be paid; here, the bargain not possible to be performed. But, O thou that sittest in the heavens,[3] O thou that ridest between the cherubims,[4] blessed be thy glorious name,[5] for thou camest thyself from heaven on purpose to cover them. Thou broughtest that with thee from heaven which only is able to cover them; for what can cover sins but righteousness? what cover infinite sins but infinite righteousness? and where is any infinite righteousness to be found but in him only that is infiniteness itself? Be comforted, therefore, my soul, for now it is not a hope, it is an assurance, that my sins at last shall come to be covered; it is not a hope, it is an assurance, that I shall come at last to this blessedness in covert.

There are some, perhaps, will grant that blessedness may consist in covering indeed, but not in covering of sins.

---

[1] Ezek. xxviii. 14: "Thou *art* the anointed cherub that covereth." [2] Isa. vi. 2: "With twain he covered his face." [3] Ps. lxviii. 4: "Extol him that rideth upon the heavens." [4] Ps. lxxx. 1: "Thou that dwellest *between* the cherubims." [5] Ps. lxxii. 19.

They think rather in covering their tables with rich plate and dainty dishes, or in covering their houses with slates of gold, *aurea domus Neronis* [Nero's golden palace], or in covering their backs with silk and soft raiment, such as Christ saith are in kings' houses;[1] but Nebuchadnezzar will come in for one,[2] Dives[3] for another, and Haman for a third,[4] and give clear evidence that all these are deceived, and that David only tells us the truth. They, they only are the blessed men whose sins are covered.

But what needs all this scanning and discussing, for what more mystery is there in saying, Blessed are they whose iniquities are forgiven, and whose sins are covered, than if it were said, Blessed are they from whose iniquities thou turnest away thy face, and whose offences thou blottest out?[5] Or (because the Scripture hath plenty of expressions of this kind) than if it were said, Blessed are they whose iniquities thou castest behind thy back,[6] and whose sins thou removest from thee as far as the east is from the west;[7] for to what tends this variety of expression, but either for illustration, or, at most, for vehemence of asseveration that our sins are pardoned? But if it be conceived to be not so much a divers expressing of the same way as an expressing of a divers way to blessedness, then, indeed, as being more mystical, it will be more misty for discerning clearly what the meaning of David is. Is it, then, that forgiving our sins is the work of God's mercy, for it is mercy's work only to forgive; covering our sins the work of his love, for love covers the multitude of sins,[8] *not imputing our sins* [**ver. 2**],[9] the work of his will, as he saith, I will have mercy on whom I will have mercy,[10] that so we may have here a threefold cord of God's goodness to rely upon for our blessedness? Or is it that remission is necessary for sins of commission, covering necessary for sins of omission; but not imputing may serve for sins of transmission, that is, for sins original, transmitted to us from our first parents? Or is it that

---

[1] Matt. xi. 8.   [2] Dan. iv. 31—33.   [3] Luke xvi. 22, 23.   [4] Esth. vii. 10.   [5] Ps. li. 9: "Hide thy face from my sins, and blot out all mine iniquities."   [6] Isa. xxxviii. 17.   [7] Ps. ciii. 12.   [8] 1 Pet. iv. 8: "Charity shall cover the multitude of sins" (Gk. ἀγάπη).   [9] Blessed *is* the man unto whom the LORD imputeth not iniquity, and in whose spirit *there is* no guile.   [10] Rom. ix. 15.

forgiving is mentioned as the work of God the Father, whose work properly it is to forgive, as he saith, I am he that blotteth out transgressions?[1] Covering is mentioned as the proper work of God the Son, as with whose righteousness our sins are covered, and therefore St. Paul saith, Put ye on the Lord Christ Jesus.[2] Not imputing is mentioned as the work of the Holy Ghost, who, being all love, compassionates our infirmities;[3] and so all the Persons in the Deity have a hand (as it is fit they should) in this great work of procuring to us our blessedness that, as at the making of man at first, so at the making of man blessed at last, they may all join together, and say, *Faciamus hominem ad imaginem nostram* [Let us make man in our image].[4]

As long as iniquities are unforgiven, the conscience lies, as it were, on a rack, tortured and tormented day and night; but as soon as there comes a pardon, it is presently taken off the rack and laid at ease; and is not this a blessedness? As long as our sins remain uncovered, God turns away his face and frowns upon us; but as soon as our sins be covered, he shows us again the light of his countenance;[5] and is not this a blessedness? As long as our sins are imputed to us, we are in the state of Adam when he was cast out of Paradise; but as soon as we are freed from this imputation, we presently hear Christ say, This day thou shalt be with me in Paradise;[6] and is not this again a blessedness? And is it not now that David expresseth it in three ways, to show that by it a godly man is not only blessed, but thrice blessed?

But seeing forgiving and covering and not imputing of sins are all but privative things, how can they make a blessedness, which is a positive thing? They may take away misery, but can never make a blessedness. But is not the very taking away of misery in this case a blessedness; for seeing we were ordained by God at first to a blessed estate, and nothing bars us from that estate but sin, are we not by the removing this bar either left in this estate, or at least restored to it again? O gracious God, grant me for-

---

[1] Isa. xliii. 25. [2] Rom. xiii. 14. [3] Rom. viii. 26: "helpeth our infirmities."
[4] Gen. i. 26. [5] Ps. lxxx. 3, 7, 19. [6] Luke xxiii. 43.

giveness of mine iniquities and the covering of my sins, and let me never come at heaven, if I make not of these privatives a Jacob's ladder to climb up to heaven.[1] Neither yet is remission of sins a mere privative, but it hath in it an influence of grace also, which brings with it a shower of blessings, turns Ebal into Gerizim,[2] and of the thief upon the cross makes a saint in Paradise.[3]

Hitherto David's doctrine we may well subscribe to, but what means he by this, And in whose spirit there is no guile?[4] For if there be no guile in his spirit, what needs either covering or forgiving? But is it not, as Christ said of Nathaniel, Behold a true Israelite, in whom there is no guile? and yet who doubts but in Nathaniel there was sin? It seems therefore meant that though covering and forgiving be all God's work, yet there is a condition required in him whose sins are to be forgiven; and this is the condition, that there be no guile in his spirit, but that his repentance be sincere and unfeigned, and without hypocrisy. And it is as if he had said, Blessed is he whom God justifies, and justifying sanctifies;[5] for having said, Blessed is he to whom the Lord imputeth no sin, which is our justification, it presently follows, And in whose spirit there is no guile, which is our sanctification. Or is it here annexed with a conjunction, perhaps to show that sanctification doth not so much follow, as it is annexed; and from the same breath of God's spirit riseth together with justification? Or is it therefore added lest we should think blessedness to be in such sort God's gift, as that there should be nothing required in us towards the attaining it; which yet is so in us that it is not of us, but must come from God to us? for, alas, else what spirit of ours could be without guile if it were not influenced by that spirit which is the truth itself?

It seems this is a doctrine in favour plainly of plain dealing; but is this a world for plain dealing to thrive in? and if no thriving, what blessedness? But is it not said of Jacob that he was a plain man?[6] and yet would any man

---

[1] Gen. xxviii. 12: "The top of it reached to heaven."   [2] Deut. xi. 29.   [3] Luke xxiii. 43.   [4] John i. 47: "Behold an Israelite indeed," etc.   [5] Rom. viii. 30: "Whom he justified, them he also glorified."   [6] Gen. xxv. 27.

desire to thrive better than he did, who went over Jordan with nothing but his staff, and returned back with multitudes of cattle?[1] Never therefore fear thriving by plain dealing, for God that requires plainness in thy dealing with him, will no doubt bless it in thy dealing with others; and they that make themselves rich by guile will but find themselves beguiled in the end, when God blows upon them,[2] and that they find that guile in their fortunes which they so greedily entertained in their spirits.

But why am I so earnest against guile in the spirit? Do I not herein speak against myself? [**ver. 3**];[3] for was there not guile in my spirit when I held my peace for confessing my sins, and yet cried out for sense of my pain, as though I would have made God believe it was for sense of my sin? but God knows I was silent in that, and that silence is now cause of my roaring; for if I had spoken and confessed my sin at first, I might have been heard in a lower voice; but having deferred my repentance so long, what marvel if God be gone so far out of hearing that a lower voice than roaring will never be heard? Every sin we commit makes God to turn away his face and depart from us; and the longer time the sin is unrepented, the longer time he hath to go from us the farther; and the slower we are in repenting, the more he hastens his pace; and have we not need then to cry the louder to make him to hear us, that by long deferring our repentance is gone so far from us? Oh, the foolishness of men that defer repentance! for to defer the repenting of sins is a greater sin than the sins to be repented; and have we not need then of the louder voice to obtain forgiveness when to our former sins to be repented is added this great sin of deferring our repentance? O foolish tongue, how often hast thou spoken when it nothing concerned thee! and wouldst thou not speak now when it concerned thee so much? How often hast thou spoken at the urging of impatience, and wouldst thou not speak now at the entreaty of repentance? But why then is it said, *Non*

---

[1] Gen. xxxii. 10.   [2] Isa. xl. 24: "He shall also blow upon them, and they shall wither."   [3] Ps. xxxii. 3: "When I kept silence, my bones waxed old through my roaring all the day long."

ulli tacuisse nocet, as if to hold one's peace did never hurt any? Silence, indeed, never hurts any by sins of commission, but by sins of omission often; silence is never guilty of idle words, yet guilty often of idleness, in letting slip opportunity. And therefore Solomon's counsel seems much the sounder, There is a time to speak, and a time to hold one's peace;[1] and if there be a time for each of them, then each of them in their due time is good; out of time is bad. It is as great a fault to be silent when it is fit to speak as it is to speak when it is fit to be silent; and if any time be fit for speaking, unfit for silence, this is the time when sins are to be confessed, and when our iniquities are to be acknowledged and made known to God. Now therefore am I justly punished for my silence; for seeing I held my peace when it was fit to speak, now my speaking will not serve, but I am fain to roar; seeing I would not spend a few hours in prayer at first, now I am fain to lie crying and praying all the day long. Alas, to what a miserable state had I brought myself that could neither make use of my silence nor of my crying out; for if I held my peace, I concealed my sin, and the sore still festered more and more;[2] and if I cried out, it spent my spirits, and the very pain did age's work for it in my bones, and made them old while my body was young. The truth is, I felt myself in pain, but knew not what I ailed. I knew all was not well with me, but knew not well why it was so. Now, after much searching and examining the cause, I find what it was: it was even sin that lay all this while in my bosom, as a fire raked up in the embers of security, and burnt me to the very bone; but finding it to be sin, I was ashamed to confess it; and so between shame of revealing and danger of not revealing I lived a long time as a man distracted, holding my peace for very shame, and crying out for very pain. And alas, O Lord, how could I choose when it was *thy hand* that lay *heavy upon me* [**ver. 4**];[3] thy hand of which it is said that with it thou dost terrible things;[4] and that which is, in terror, the most terrible, when

---

[1] Eccles. iii. 7: "A time to keep silence, and a time to speak." [2] Ps. lxxvii. 2: "My sore ran in the night, and ceased not." [3] Ps. xxxii. 4: "For day and night thy hand was heavy upon me: my moisture is turned into the drought of summer." [4] Ps. xlv. 4: "Thy righthand shall teach thee terrible things."

thou once beginnest thou never givest over; thine anger is not as an ague, but as a fever; comes not by fits, but is a continual fit without either remission or intermission; and what marvel, then, if in this torrid zone of affliction my almond tree flourish[1] before the time, and my strong men bow themselves[2] under the burden? As a flower that is parched with the sun and is ready to fall from the stalk that upheld it, and as earth that is overdried with the heat and is ready to crumble into dust and powder, such, O Lord, was I, while neither wind nor so much as a breath of thy favour blew upon me; while neither shower nor so much as the dew of thy grace instilled into me;[3] and in this maze of distress whither could I think to turn myself for help? I thought sometimes that time would help me, but alas! time was no friend of mine; for the longer time I stayed the more my sore festered and rankled within me. Then I thought that place might help me; but, alas, I turned me from side to side, and could neither find rest in resting nor ease in motion. Then I thought of friends; but, alas, my friends were my fortune's, and not mine; they bore me fair in hand while the weather was fair, but as soon as a storm came they shrunk in the wetting. So I bethought me at last of a way which the world would rather think a precipice than a way, and yet, perplexed as I was, I thought best to venture it. *I said, I will confess my sins to God*[4] [**ver. 5**]. A dangerous way, I vow, to go for help to him whom I had offended; to look his hand should raise me up that had cast me down: yet see the event, or rather wonder at the wonderfulness of God's goodness: I confessed my sin to God, and he forgave me the iniquity of my sin. Oh, let every sinful soul take this from me: There is no such way in the torment of sin as to confess it to God. For it is not with God as it is with men. God's ways are not as men's ways;[5] if we confess a debt to men, no way but we must pay it; but in a debt to

---

[1] Eccl. xii. 5. [2] Eccl. xii. 3. [3] Hagg. i. 10, 11: "The heaven over you is stayed from dew, and the earth is stayed *from* her fruit. And I called for a drought upon the land," etc. [4] Ver. 5: "I acknowledged my sin unto thee, and mine iniquity have I not hid. I said, I will confess my transgressions unto the LORD, and thou forgavest the iniquity of my sin.' [5] Isa. lv. 8.

God, the very confessing it is a payment,[1] and it is instead of ability that we acknowledge ourselves to be unable.

And indeed, O my soul! what danger can there be in confessing thy sins to God, who knows them already better than thyself? Thou informest him of nothing he knew not before; thou dost but discharge thy conscience, and prostrate thyself at the foot of his mercy; and he is the Lion of the tribe of Judah,[2] and who knows not that it is the noble nature of the lion to spare anything that prostrates itself before him? If Adam had confessed his sin to God, would God have cast him out of Paradise?[3] If Eve had confessed her sin to God, should she have had such throes in her child-bearing?[4] Oh, then, let every Adam that would recover Paradise, let every Eve that would have ease in her labour, confess their sins to God, for they may be confident a true confession shall never return either unregarded or unrewarded; that where it was said before, Blessed are they whose iniquities are forgiven and whose sins are covered, we may now alter the style, and say, Blessed are they whose iniquities are confessed and whose sins are discovered; for if we confess them, God is just, and will forgive them;[5] if we discover them, God is merciful, and will cover them; that as it was said of Abraham he believed, and it was counted to him for righteousness,[6] so it shall be said of us we confess our iniquities, and it is imputed to us for innocency.

But is there nothing required to forgiveness of sins but only the confessing of them? Alas! confession is but a part of repentance; God's pardons are always entire, and is it likely that he will grant a whole pardon for only a piece of repentance? Indeed, so great is God's forwardness in showing of mercy, so great his favour towards penitent sinners, that as he useth the figure, I may say, of anticipation in his grace to them, so he accepts of the figure synecdoche in their performance to him. Though confession be but a part of repentance, yet if it be a true part he accepts

---

[1] 1 John i. 9: "If we confess our sins, he is faithful and just to forgive us *our* sins."
[2] Rev. v. 5.   [3] Gen. iii. 12, 24.   [4] Gen. iii. 13, 16.   [5] 1 John i. 9.   [6] Rom. iv. 3.

it for the whole, and puts a penitent in possession of a full pardon upon his first payment. But then it must not be a bare confession, such as the earth was in the beginning, *vacua et informis* [void and without form],[1] of which it was not said, *et vidit Deus quod erat bonum* [and God saw that it was good],[2] as the confession of Pharaoh and Judas was, but it must be *confessio informata* [a confession not factitious], a confession of one in whose spirit is no guile ;[3] a confession not only *gravida* [pregnant], but *parturiens*, in labour, which is contrition, such as the publican's was, who in confessing struck his breast. And yet this is not all, but it must be a confession made to God.[4] Pharaoh indeed confessed, but it was but to Moses ;[5] and Judas confessed, but it was but to the rulers,[6]—neither of them to God, as David doth here. And yet neither is this all, but it must be a confession with professing to confess, as it is here : I said, I will confess my sin to God [the LORD], and this kind of confession is so acceptable to God that, next to a martyr, he loves a confessor.

For this shall every one that is godly pray unto thee in a time when thou mayest be found; [**ver. 6**] for what favour can a prayer look to find that is made to one that is not to be found? But are there, then, critical times for finding of God, as there are for taking of physic, or for setting of figures in astrology? Is not God everywhere, and therefore to be found in any place? eternal, and may be found at any time? O my soul, it is neither time nor place that is any considerable circumstance for finding of God; but if thou wouldst know the true place to find him, indeed thou must look [for] him in thy heart; if the truest time, thou must observe thy repentance, for in a penitent heart are all the considerable circumstances for finding of God, either for time or place. Look [for] him there, and then thou shalt find him ; look [for] him then, and there thou shalt find him. O then, my soul, if my heart be the true place for finding of God, had I not need to look [for] him there betimes? for how long am I sure I shall keep my heart? I may be sure not

---

[1] Gen. i. 2. [2] Gen. i. 4, 10, 12, etc. (Vulgate, "Quod esset bonum.") [3] John i. 47. [4] Luke xviii. 13. [5] Exod. ix. 27. [6] Matt. xxvii. 4.

long, seeing it is always upon going, and makes all the haste it can to be gone; and if it should be gone before I find God in it, alas, my soul, there would be no finding him there for thee for ever; and as the heart is the true place, so what may we say is the true time when God may be found? What, no doubt, but the present time? for seeing in God there is neither time past nor time to come, how should we look to find him where he is not? For this, therefore, shall every one that is godly pray to God while he may be found,—that is, presently, and at this very instant,—and not defer repentance to the time to come, in which God is not found, no more than it is found in God.

God, no doubt, may be found at all times, but we are not at all times in case to find him; for how should we find him when we have no eyes to look [for] him? And am I sure I shall have eyes always? God knows, I am sure I shall not, for I find them to grow dimmer every day than other, and this dimness ere long must needs end in darkness. Oh, then, my soul, make haste to find God before the crystal of thine eyes be broken; for if thou tarry till then, there will be no finding him; and if not find him, no asking him forgiveness; and if not ask it, not have it; and not having forgiveness there will be no blessedness. For this shall every one that is godly pray to God while he may be found—that is, before his lights be put out, and before he go to dwell at the city of worms, in the dungeon of darkness. There is indeed no finding of God without repentance, and no repentance without faith, which, because it shall cease in the life to come, we must therefore find him now, or shall not at all, either here or hereafter.

But if no more but repentance be required for finding of God, what hinders but he may be found at any time, seeing what hinders but I may repent at any time? O my soul, who tells thee so? for hast thou the heart to break thy heart at any time? and if thou hast not, then canst thou not repent at any time, for true repentance is a breaking of the heart. Thou mayest perhaps quench the Spirit[1] when thou

---

[1] 1 Thess. v. 19: "Quench not the Spirit."

pleasest, but canst thou set it a-burning when thou pleasest? If thou canst not, then canst thou not repent when thou pleasest; for a true repentance is never without a burning ardour of God's Spirit.

But is there indeed any time when God may not be found? Is he like to some princes, who shut themselves up in state at times, and are not then to be spoken withal, or seen? O great God, thou art not like man, and therefore not found after their manner—found when only their persons are found; but to find thee is to find thee gracious, without which as good lost thou wert as found; and gracious can none find thee but only the penitent, and therefore for this shall every one that is godly pray unto thee, so that through the grace of a true repentance he may find thee gracious.

When a sin is committed, a shower of God's anger rains presently down upon the sinner, and continues raining till there be repentance; and if the repentance be deferred long, it may rain down anger so long till it make a flood, and then there will be no going near to God for water, but rather the water will go near to be a cause of drowning, for it is not every one's case to have an ark to save himself in from the flood of God's anger; he only may be confident to be saved that, like Noah, begins to make his ark betimes,[1] and returns to God with a speedy repentance.

But why is it said every one that is godly, and not, rather, every one that is wise, seeing it is wisdom, and not godliness, that can discern the fitness of times and seasons? Is it not that wisdom and godliness in spiritual matters are terms convertible: no true wisdom without godliness, no godliness without true wisdom; but therefore rather said godly than wise, because indeed there is no other godliness, though there be other wisdom.

And now, O my soul, consider the blessedness of a true repentance, and what a conversion it makes in a penitent heart. I could never think before but that the world was the safest sanctuary, the flesh the best paradise; but now I can say, Thou, O God, art my refuge from tribulation[2] [ver. 7],

---

[1] Gen. vi. 14. [2] Ver. 7: "Thou *art* my hiding place; thou shalt preserve me from trouble; thou shalt compass me about with songs of deliverance."

thou my jubilee against all persecutions: the place from which I hid myself before is now become the place to hide me in, and that which I fled from before as my only terror I now fly to as my only succour. Before I repented, I thought that to go to God was to run upon a rock; but now I find it is to go into the haven. Before, I thought still upon that saying, A man shall leave father and mother, and cleave to his wife;[1] but now I find that *adhærere Deo bonum est*, there is no blessedness but in cleaving to God. Before I repented, I aspired to nothing but to sit at Dives' table,[2] and to fare deliciously every day. I took pleasure in nothing but in wearing soft raiment, in mirth and jollity; but now I find that all the dishes I fed on there were poison. I find there is no wearing like to sackcloth, no sweet powder like to ashes, and say to laughter, Thou art mad.[3] Thou, O Christ, art the true food that nourisheth to eternal life;[4] thou the true garment[5] that gives me entrance to the marriage of the Lamb, and makest me to hear the melody of heaven in the choir of angels. Before I repented, I said to the world, Egypt, thou art my staff;[6] and to the flesh, Delilah,[7] thou art my joy; but now I can say, Thou, O God, art my refuge in all tribulations;[8] thou the joy of my heart against all my persecutors.

But, O the vanity of the world, have I lived to hear that glorious acclamation, Saul hath killed his thousand, and David his ten thousand,[9] and is my glory come now to this, that I am glad of a place to hide me in? Indeed, *sic transit gloria mundi* [so passes the glory of the world]. But, O my body, never do thou trouble thyself for the matter, for thou art sure enough of a place to hide thee, seeing a span or two of earth will serve thy turn. It is thou, my soul, that makest me glad of a place to hide me, for thou indeed art not easily hidden; thou liest open to all assaults of Satan, to all temptations of the world, and that which is more than these, to the angry hand of God;

---

[1] Gen. ii. 24. [2] Luke xvi. 19. [3] Eccl. ii. 2: "I said of laughter, *It is* mad." [4] John vi. 33: "The bread of God is he which cometh down from heaven, and giveth life unto the world." [5] Matt. xxii. 11, 12. [6] Isa. xxxvi. 6: "Lo, thou trustest in the staff of this broken reed, on Egypt." [7] Judg. xvi. 4. [8] Ps. xlvi. 1: "A very present help in trouble." [9] 1 Sam. xviii. 7.

and from this it is chiefly I am glad of a place to hide me, though the world may think it strange I should go to God to hide me from God. But, O foolish world, it is not strange, for I go to God's mercy to hide me from his justice; for God forbid I should be of those that call to the mountains to cover them, and to the hills to hide them.[1] No, dear Jesus, thou art the mountain that must cover me, thou the sanctuary that I fly unto, to which, if Joab had fled, it had not been *Abner* [Benaiah] that could have drawn him forth.[2]

But had not David towers[3] and fortresses to defend him? and could he not be safe unless he were hidden? And say he were brought to a necessity of hiding himself, yet is he well advised to make choice of God for his place to hide him? The darkest places are fittest for hiding; and what hiding then could he look for of God, who is nothing but light?[4] O my soul, there is no hiding so excellent as to be hidden with light; for thither my enemies, who are children of darkness, can never come. When I am hidden with light, I can see my enemies, and they not see me,—not much unlike the advantage that God himself hath over us.[5] When I am hidden with light, there is more glory in the light than disparagement in the hiding; and have I not reason then to make choice of God, who dwells in light inaccessible,[6] for my place to hide me? Others' hiding can but keep me from the eyes of my enemies; it cannot keep me from the hands of my enemies. God's hiding can do both; for *thou, O God, shalt preserve me from trouble.* Though in others' hiding, enemies perhaps cannot, yet troubles at least may find me out; but when thou hidest me,[7] as enemies cannot, so troubles dare not, I shall be as free from the fear as from the sense of troubles. And yet, O God, if thou shouldst only preserve me from trouble, this were no more than I might enjoy if I were a senseless

---

[1] Hos. x. 8; Luke xxiii. 30.   [2] 1 Kings ii. 28, 34: "And Joab fled into the tabernacle of the LORD, and caught hold on the horns of the altar. . . . So Benaiah the son of Jehoiada went up, and fell upon him, and slew him."   [3] Song iv. 4: "Thy neck *is* like the tower of David, builded for an armoury," etc.   [4] 1 John i. 5: "God is light."   [5] Gen. xvi. 13: "Thou God seest me." John i. 18: "No man hath seen God at any time."   [6] 1 Tim. vi. 16: "Dwelling in the light which no man can approach unto."   [7] Ps. xxvii. 5: "In the time of trouble he shall hide me in his pavilion."

creature, for what trouble where there is no sense? But thy hiding will do more than this; it will *compass me about with songs of deliverance;* and this will give me a sense, and in that sense a delight of the happiness I enjoy by the benefit of thy hiding.

If thou shouldst deliver me but in part, I should in part be in bondage still; and what would my state be the better for this, seeing, in this case, all figures are synecdoches—a part here as much as the whole? To be a prisoner in part is to be a prisoner altogether; but when thou compasseth me about with deliverance, this leaves no place for synecdoches, but gives me a total and absolute freedom, and makes me obnoxious to no molestation. And yet if thou shouldst also compass me with deliverance, and so leave me, I might be still both insensible of it in myself and unthankful for it to thee, and so my state but little the better for this either; but when thou compasseth me about with songs of deliverance; this makes me a chorister in the choir—I might say of angels, but that their songs are all songs of jubilee,[1] and mine only of deliverance. O my soul, God is not a deliverer like a half-moon, bright in one part and dark in another; but he is a deliverer like the sun—his deliverance shines always the whole compass; and with his deliverance he delivers also songs of thankfulness to him, and in myself of joyfulness.

But what need is there of plurality of songs: may not one song serve; and if one may, what need many? One song perhaps may serve for one deliverance; but if there be many deliverances, must there not be many songs? And must there not be many deliverances when there are many bondages? And are there not many bondages when I incur a new bondage as often as I commit a new sin?[2] And yet another reason as great as this: for say that God's deliverance be but one, will that one deliverance require but one song? O my soul, it deserves, and therefore requires, I say not a plurality, but an infinity of songs; for there must be

---

[1] Jubilee, understood as a period of rejoicing in music, and so a time of rest, see Lev. xxv. 11, 12. It however includes the idea of deliverance and restoration, see context *loc. cit.*   [2] John viii. 34: "Whosoever committeth sin is the servant of sin."

some songs to express it, and others to extol it; some songs of *miserere*, and others of *magnificat;* some *de profundis*, and others *in excelsis;*[1] some songs of praise, and others of thanksgiving; and though there will be a time when all these songs shall be collected into one, and so collected make the great *Canticum Canticorum* [Song of Songs], yet till that time come there will be need of many songs; and seeing I shall need many, I hope, O God, thou wilt not see me want, and tie me to one song, but wilt compass me about with songs of deliverance.

But alas, O Lord, I am far as yet from being compassed with songs of deliverance; I have not so much as one song of deliverance to sing; for how should I sing of deliverance that am still in bondage? how sing at all that am still a-weeping? But I know thy goodness, O God; I know how much thou delightest in the music of thanksgiving; and therefore am assured the time will come, and (considering the haste thou makest) will come speedily, that thou wilt compass me about with songs of deliverance.

But have I been all this while right in the understanding of David's meaning, where he saith, Thou shalt compass me about with songs of deliverance; for are they songs that are sung for me, or songs that are sung by me? If sung for me, then they are men and angels[2] that sing them, as rejoicing for my deliverance. If sung by me, then it is I, O God, that sing them to thee, as giving thanks for my deliverance.[3] Songs of deliverance, of my deliverance, that I am delivered; or songs of deliverance, of thy deliverance, that thou hast delivered me: take them in either sense, and David is pleased; take them either way, and God is glorified. So there need be no question of this, yet of this there will be question, How I can be sure of repenting if I am not sure to repent when I list? And this question David seems to answer, putting the matter upon God, and therefore brings

---

[1] *Miserere*, a cry for mercy, a litany whose refrain is "Lord, have mercy upon me;" *Magnificat*, a song of praise like that of Mary, "My soul doth magnify the Lord" (Luke i. 46, etc.); *De profundis*, a psalm of the tempted and despairing, "Out of the depths have I cried unto thee, O Lord" (Ps. cxxx.); *In excelsis*, an anthem of exuberant joy, like the angel's song, "Glory to God in the highest," etc. (Luke ii. 14).
[2] Luke xv. 7, 10 [3] Isa. xii. 2, 3; cf. Ps. xl. 3, xcviii. 1.

God in as speaking thus : I will give thee understanding, and will instruct thee in the way that thou shalt walk : I will fix mine eye upon thee [1] [ver. 8]. And God's instructions are never in vain; for with the lessons he gives, he gives also an aptness to understand them; and with the aptness a capacity to perform them; and then having God for an instructor, by teaching thee the way, and for an overseer, by fixing his eye upon thee, how canst thou doubt of profiting in a learning where all the learning is but one lesson of repentance? Repentance, indeed, is but one lesson, but it is the hardest lesson in all the book; and we may see how hard it is by the great ado that is about it; for, first, God must give us understanding for it, and this will not be enough; then he must give us instruction in it, and neither will this be enough; then he must have a continual eye upon us to hold us to it, and all these together will be but little enough : alas, all these together will be too little, and not enough, if we be wanting to ourselves. Be not therefore, O my soul, like the vineyard of which God said, What could I do more to my vineyard than I did, and yet it hath brought forth nothing but wild grapes?[2] No, my soul, be not like to horse and mule that have no understanding[3] [ver. 9]; when thou art showed the right way, do not wilfully run another way ; when one comes to dress and comb thee, do not offer to bite and strike; do not cast thy riders, nor kick at thy rulers ; be not headstrong like the horse, nor lazy like the mule, for if thou use thyself like a horse and a mule, thou must look to be used like a horse and a mule—have a bridle put in thy mouth, and a snaffle in thy jaws; and if these will not serve, a spur and a rod too, to quicken and beat understanding into thee. For consider, O my soul, in what state thou standest; though thou have understanding, as being made *ad similitudinem Dei* [towards the likeness of God],[4] yet if thou use not understanding, thou makest thyself

---

[1] Ver. 8 : "I will instruct thee and teach thee in the way which thou shalt go : I will guide thee with mine eye." (Auth. Vers.) The citation in the text is from the Vulgate, " Intellectum tibi dabo, et instruam te in viâ hac, qua gradieris : firmabo super te oculos meos." [2] Isa. v. 4. [3] Ps. xxxii. 9 : " Be ye not as the horse, *or* as the mule, *which* have no understanding ; whose mouth must be held in with bit and bridle, lest they come near unto thee." [4] Vulg., Gen. i. 27.

ad similitudinem bruti [to the likeness of a beast], or rather so much worse than a beast as corruption makes worse than privation; for if a man shall do that by abusing reason which a horse doth by wanting reason, shall he not do it, not only with more shame, but with more violence, as making that an instrument of stubbornness which was given for a furtherance of obedience? Is it not a shameful thing that a man should be bridled and spurred as a horse? yet if he use not understanding, but will be like a horse, he must be so; for as understanding is the stern,[1] I may say, of a man, to direct him in his course, so a bridle is the stern of a horse to guide him in his way; and he that will not take into his heart his own stern of understanding, must be forced to take into his mouth the horse's stern of a bridle; for a stern he must have,—no remedy,[2] either his own stern or a horse's, either understanding or a bridle, that we may truly say there is not a more necessary trade in the world than a bridle-maker is, seeing without such a one there would be no living in the world for the multitude of unruly horses.

And thus when men grow so wicked and so void of understanding, to be like horse and mule, it may justly then be said, Many are the troubles of the wicked [**ver. 10**];[3] for there will be troubles of bridle, and troubles of snaffle, troubles of spur, and troubles of rod, from all which the godly are free. No bridle in their mouths, because they do that willingly which the foolish horse will not do but by constraint. No spur in their sides, because, with the assistance of God's grace, they use understanding, and run readily of themselves to the mark[4] that is before them.

But why, then, should David in another place say, Many are the troubles of the righteous? for by this it should seem there is nothing lost by being wicked, nothing gotten by being righteous, for whether wicked or righteous, there will be troubles still. It is true there will be troubles, but is there not a difference? The troubles of the godly are but only outward, but the troubles of the wicked are in-

---

[1] Rudder.   [2] Inevitably.   [3] "Many sorrows *shall be* to the wicked: but he that trusteth in the LORD, mercy shall compass him about." (Auth. Vers.)   [4] Phil. iii. 14: "I press toward the mark for the prize," etc.

ward rather; the troubles of the godly are but to exercise them, but the troubles of the wicked tend to ruin. The troubles of the wicked have a corrosive—I may say, a worm, within them; but the troubles of the godly have a cordial—I may say, a kernel, within them, a sweet kernel indeed that makes ample amends for all the hardness and fracture of their shell. The troubles of the wicked have no deliverer; but of the troubles of the godly it is said, The Lord shall deliver them out of all.[1] And all this long of God's mercy that compasseth them about. It is, no doubt, a strong fortress to the godly that the angels pitch their tents about them;[2] but it is a far stronger that God's mercy compasseth them about; for that which is but ministerial in the angels is primitive in God; and though the ministry of angels may be, yet God's mercy can never be, frustrate, and especially when it compasseth about, for then neither troubles on the right hand nor troubles on the left, neither tumours of prosperity nor gripings of adversity,—then, neither troubles before them nor troubles behind them, neither agonies of terror nor racks of persecution, shall ever come so near them as to touch them,—at least, not so prevail against them as to hurt them. That, notwithstanding all their troubles, it shall be justly said still, Be glad ye that are righteous, and rejoice in the Lord: shout for joy, all ye that are upright of hear [ver. 11].[3]

And may it not be as well said to the wicked, Be glad, and shout for joy? or, rather, have they not more cause for rejoicing than the godly? The wicked, indeed, may rejoice to see their full barns and their full bags; but, alas, what becomes of their joy when they hear it said, *Stulte, hac nocte repetent animam tuam* [Thou fool, this night shall they require thy soul]?[4] They may rejoice to sit with Belshazzar, at their full cups, in revelling and feasting; but, alas, what becomes of their rejoicing when they see it written upon the wall before them, Mene, Tekel, Peres?[5] All gladness of the world is often converted, always convertible,

---

[1] Ps. xxxiv. 19. [2] Ps. xxxiv. 7. [3] Ps. xxxii. 11: "Be glad in the LORD, and rejoice, ye righteous: and shout for joy, all *ye that are* upright in heart."
[4] Luke xii. 20. [5] Dan. v. 25—28.

into sorrow; only the gladness that is in God never suffers eclipse. A single kind of joy the wicked may have, but because their rejoicing is in the world, and not in God, they are far, God knows, from shouting for joy. None but the righteous rejoice in the Lord, and therefore none but the righteous can shout for joy. This David did when he danced before the ark,[1] and this Abraham did when, *exultavit ut videret diem Domini*, he leaped for joy to see the day of Christ.[2] Is there a shouting for joy at Olympic games, where but a garland is gotten, perhaps of bay, at most but of some fading matter; and shall there not be shouting for joy at the game of the great Olympus [heaven], where there will be a crown gotten of glory, that shall never wither nor fade away? O my soul, there will be the victory, that is only worthy of shouting for joy, which, as it is common to all the godly, is proper to only the godly, who being upright in heart, and having their conversation in heaven[3] already, they see, with clearer eyes than Abraham saw, Christ's day, the saints expecting them, the angels ready to receive them, and that which is more than the most that can be said or thought, God himself preparing for them their several mansions of beatitude;[4] [so] that we may justly conclude as we began: Blessed are those whose iniquities are forgiven, and whose sins are covered. Blessed is the man to whom the Lord imputeth no sin, and in whose spirit there is no guile.[5]

---

[1] 2 Sam. vi. 14—16.   [2] John viii. 56: "Abraham rejoiced to see my day, and he saw *it*, and was glad." Quoted from Vulgate, "exultavit ut videret diem meum."   [3] Phil. iii. 20.   [4] John xiv. 2: "I go to prepare a place for you."   [5] Ps. xxxii. 1, 2.

O LORD, rebuke me not in thy wrath: neither chasten me in thy hot displeasure. 2. For thine arrows stick fast in me, and thy hand presseth me sore. 3. *There is* no soundness in my flesh because of thine anger; neither *is there any* rest in my bones because of my sin. 4. For mine iniquities are gone over mine head: as an heavy burden they are too heavy for me. 5. My wounds stink *and* are corrupt because of my foolishness. 6. I am troubled; I am bowed down greatly; I go mourning all the day long. 7. For my loins are filled with a loathsome *disease:* and *there is* no soundness in my flesh. 8. I am feeble and sore broken: I have roared by reason of the disquietness of my heart. 9. Lord, all my desire *is* before thee; and my groaning is not hid from thee. 10. My heart panteth, my strength faileth me: as for the light of mine eyes, it also is gone from me. 11. My lovers and my friends stand aloof from my sore; and my kinsman stand afar off. 12. They also that seek after my life lay snares *for me:* and they that seek my hurt speak mischievous things, and imagine deceits all the day long. 13. But I, as a deaf *man*, heard not; and *I was* as a dumb man *that* openeth not his mouth. 14. Thus I was as a man that heareth not, and in whose mouth *are* no reproofs. 15. For in thee, O LORD, do I hope: thou wilt hear, O Lord my God. 16. For I said, *Hear me*, lest *otherwise* they should rejoice over me: when my foot slippeth, they magnify *themselves* against me. 17. For I *am* ready to halt, and my sorrow *is* continually before me. 18. For I will declare mine iniquity; I will be sorry for my sin. 19. But mine enemies *are* lively, *and* they are strong: and they that hate me wrongfully are multiplied. 20. They also that render evil for good are mine adversaries; because I follow *the thing that* good *is*. 21. Forsake me not, O LORD: O my God, be not far from me. 22. Make haste to help me, O Lord my salvation.—PSALM xxxviii. (Auth. Vers.)

MEDITATIONS AND DISQUISITIONS

UPON

THE THIRTY-EIGHTH PSALM.

BUT is it not an absurd request to require God not to rebuke me in his anger, as though I thought he would rebuke me if he were not angry? [**ver. 1.**][1] Is it not a senseless suit to pray to God not to chasten me in his displeasure, as though he would chasten me if he were not displeased? The frowardest natures that are will yet be quiet as long as they be pleased; and shall I have such a thought of the great yet gracious God, that he should be pleased, and yet not be quiet? But O my soul, is it all one to rebuke in his anger, and to rebuke when he is angry? He may rebuke when he is angry, and yet restrain and bridle in his anger; but to rebuke in his anger is to let loose the reins to his anger; and what is it to give the reins to his anger but to make it outrun his mercy? And then what a miserable case should I be in, to have his anger to assault me, and not his mercy ready to relieve me? to have his indignation fall upon me when his lovingkindness were not by to take it off? Oh, therefore, *rebuke me not in thine anger*, O God; but let thy rebuking stay for thy mercy; chasten me not in thy displeasure, but let thy lovingkindness have the keeping of thy rod.

But though the request be never so just, yet must it not needs be a wearisome thing to God to have us always come to him with the same petition, as though we would persecute him with importunity, and make him do that which he is

---

[1] Ps. xxxviii. 1: "O LORD, rebuke me not in thy wrath: neither chasten me in thy hot displeasure."

not willing to do?[1] For if he were willing to grant it, he would no doubt have done it before now, when in the sixth Psalm[2] we asked him as earnestly for it as we can do in this. But, O my soul, is importunity a fault? If it be, it is a fault I shall hardly be persuaded ever to leave. Did Christ count it a fault in the woman of Canaan, who would take no answer, but still cried after him till he granted her suit?[3] Did not Abraham importune God five [six] times about the sparing of Sodom?[4] and did not God grant as long as he importuned? and may we not think that if he had continued his importunity still, he might as well have gotten Sodom to be spared for one man's sake as he had done for ten? Is God like man, that the importunity of suitors should be a trouble to him? Can we think that God should be displeased with our importunity to him, when he is pleased to use importunity himself to us? Did not God call to Samuel three [four] times, one after another, when he bid him go to Eli with a message?[5] Was it not importunity which Christ used to Peter when thrice together he asked him, Simon, son of Jonas, lovest thou me?[6] Indeed, Peter seemed not well pleased with this importunity; but God never was, never will be, found to be displeased with it. Never, therefore, fear to be importunate with God, but fear rather thou canst never be importunate enough; for so highly is God pleased, or rather indeed delighted, with our importunity in praying, that he oftentimes denies the first suit of his servants because he would be importuned by a second, oftentimes the second because he would have a third. Indeed that which in suits to men is importunity, in suits to God is fervency and perseverance, and seems to resemble the nature of the Seraphim;[7] where single prayer but of ordinary angels, of whom as some fell, so this may fail, and often doth; the other never.

But though importunity be to God most pleasing always, yet to us it is then most necessary when the cheerful face

---

[1] See Luke xviii. 1—7 (the parable of the importunate widow.)   [2] Ps. vi. 1.
[3] Mark vii. 25—30.   [4] Gen. xviii. 24, 28, 29, 30, 31, 32.   [5] 1 Sam. iii. 4, 6, 8, 10, etc.   [6] John xxi. 15—17.   [7] Isa. vi. 2, 3: "Above it stood the seraphims. . . . And one cried unto another and said, Holy, holy, holy, *is* the LORD of hosts; the whole earth *is* full of his glory."

of God is turned into frowns, and when there is a justly conceived fear of the continuance of his anger. And have not I just cause to fear it, having the *arrows* of his anger *sticking so fast in me?* [**ver. 2.**][1] If he had meant to make me but a butt at which to shoot his arrows, he would quickly, I suppose, have taken them up again; but now that he leaves them sticking in me, what can I think but that he means to make me his quiver? and then I may look long enough before he come to pluck them out. They are arrows, indeed, that are feathered with swiftness and headed with sharpness; and to give them a force in flying, they are shot, I may say, out of his cross-bow,—I am sure, his bow of crosses; for no arrows can fly so fast, none pierce so deep, as the crosses and afflictions with which he hath surprised me. I may truly say surprised me, seeing when I thought myself most safe, and said, I shall never be moved,[2] even then these arrows of his anger lighted upon me, and stick so fast in my flesh, that no arm but his that shot them is ever able to draw them forth. O then, as thou hast stretched forth thine arm of anger, O God, to shoot these arrows at me, so stretch forth thine arm of mercy to draw them forth, that I may rather sing hymns than dirges unto thee; and that thou mayest show thy power as well in pardoning as thou hast done in condemning. I, alas, am as an anvil under two hammers—one of thine anger, another of my sin [**ver. 3**],[3] both of them beating incessantly upon me,—the hammer of thine anger beating upon my flesh, and making that unsound; the hammer of my sin beating upon my bones, and making them unquiet; although, indeed, both beat upon both, but thine anger more upon my flesh, as being more sensible; my sin more upon my bones, as being more obdurate. God's anger and sin are the two efficient causes of all misery; but the procatarctic cause[4] indeed is sin. God's anger, like the house that Samson pulled upon his own head, falls not upon us but when we pull it upon ourselves[5] by sin.

---

[1] Ps. xxxviii. 2: "For thine arrows stick fast in me, and thine hand presseth me sore." [2] Ps. x. 6; xxx. 6, etc. [3] Ps. xxxviii. 3: "*There is* no soundness in my flesh because of thine anger; neither *is there any* rest in my bones because of my sin." [4] The prime and originating cause, from προκατάρχομαι, *to begin first*. [5] Judg. xvi. 30.

I know by the unsoundness of my flesh that God is angry with me, for if it were not for his anger my flesh would be sound. But what soundness can be in it now, when God's angry hand lies beating upon it continually, and never ceaseth? I know by the unquietness of my bones that I have sin in my bosom, for if it were not for sin my bones would be quiet. But what quietness can be in them now when sin lies gnawing upon them incessantly with the worm[1] of remorse? One would think my bones were far enough removed, and closely enough hidden, from sin's doing them any hurt; yet see the searching nature, the venomous poison of sin, which pierceth through my flesh, and makes unquietness in my very bones.

I know my flesh is guilty of many faults, by which it justly deserves unsoundness. But what have my bones done? for they minister no fuel to the flames of my flesh's sensuality; and why then should they be troubled? But are not my bones supporters of my flesh, and are they not by this, at least, accessory to my flesh's faults? As accessories, then, they are subject to the same punishment the flesh itself is, which is the principal.

I cannot but wonder at this condition in myself. There is nothing I more loathe than sin, yet nothing I more willingly embrace; nothing that I more abhor, yet nothing I more readily entertain. What marvel, then, if there be unsoundness in my flesh, and unquietness in my bones, when I will needs be taking so turbulent a guest, so deadly a poison as sin is, into my bosom, and make an idol of that which I know so well to be a monster?

As a man that stands in the water as long as it comes but to his middle, or but up to his shoulders, endures and bears it safely enough, but when it comes once to go over his head, it then overwhelms, and presently strangles him, such, alas, am I. My sin a long time came, I may say, but up to my shoulders, and then I thought myself safe enough; now God knows I am over head and ears in sin [**ver. 4**],[2] and so overwhelmed with it that my breath is taken from me, and

---

[1] Isa. lxvi. 24; Mark ix. 48.　　[2] Ps. xxxviii. 4: "For mine iniquities are gone over mine head: as an heavy burden they are too heavy for me." (A.V.)

I have not so much as any breath of grace remaining in me. No strength is so great but it may be overburdened, though Samson went light away with the gates of *Azzah* [Gaza],[1] yet when a whole house fell upon him it crushed him to death. And such, alas, am I. I have had sin as a burden upon me ever since I was born, but bore them a long time as light as Samson did the gates of *Azzah;* but now that I have pulled a whole house of sin upon me, how can I choose but be crushed to death with so great a weight? And crushed, O my soul, thou shouldst be indeed, if God, for all his anger, did not take some pity on thee; and for all his displeasure, did not stay his hand from further chastening thee.

I know, O Lord, I have done most foolishly to let my sores run so long without seeking for help; for now my wounds stink and are corrupt[2] [**ver. 5**], in as ill a case as Lazarus' body was when it had been four days buried;[3] enough to make any man despair that did not know thee as I do; for do not I know that *nullum tempus occurrit tibi* [no time (no condition of things) withstands thee]? Do not I know thou hast as well wisdom to remedy my foolishness as power to cure my wounds? Could the grave hold Lazarus when thou didst but open thy mouth to call him forth?[4] No more can the corruption of my sores be any hindrance to their healing when thy pleasure is to have them be cured. Although therefore I have done my own discretion wrong to defer my care, yet I will not do thy power wrong to despair of thy cure; for how should I despair who know thee to be as powerful as thou art merciful, if I may not rather say to be as merciful as thou art powerful; each of them indeed an *abyssus*, and when *abyssus abyssum vocat* [deep calleth unto deep][5] what marvel if there follow marvels?

And as I do not despair, so neither do I presume; for I am troubled, *I am bowed down, and go mourning all the day long*[1] [**ver. 6**]. I am troubled no less with the grief of

---

[1] Judg. xvi. 1, 3. (The form Azzah is another transliteration of עַזָּה, and is used in Deut. ii. 23; 1 Kings iv. 24; and Jer. xxv. 20). [2] Ps. xxxviii. 5: "My wounds stink *and* are corrupt because of my foolishness." (A.V.) [3] John xi. 39. [4] John xi. 43 44. [5] Ps. xlii. 7.

thy displeasure than with the pain of my wounds, each of them alone just cause of mourning, but both of them together of mourning all the day long.

I have told heretofore how I spend my night: all the night I water my bed with tears.[2] Now I tell how I spend my day: all the day long in mourning. And can it be, O God, thou shouldst neither regard my weeping nor my mourning, neither my weeping all night nor my mourning all day?

If my flesh had continued as God made it, there had been in it both soundness and beauty; but, alas, my sin and his arrows, his arrows by reason of my sin, have so wounded it that it is nothing now but a very cistern of corruption; for all sin hath poison in it, and breeds diseases,—infinite diseases in the soul, loathsome diseases in the body. And what will not diseases do in these bodies of ours, whose spirits can be so erect, but will be dejected; whose limbs so strong, but will be bowed down; whose heart so cheerful, but will be made to mourn with the violence of diseases? And now therefore am I dejected, I am bowed down, I go mourning all the day long; and may I not say with the worst kind of mourning, the mourning perhaps of the chine, like horse and mule that have no understanding? For *my loins are filled with a loathsome disease* [**ver. 7**],[3] the very disease that made Elijah[4] and John Baptist[5] to wear girdles of beasts' skins about their loins, and they with wearing such girdles prevented in themselves the loathsomeness of this disease; but I, alas, never thought of any girdle, much less of beasts' skins, and therefore the disease is now grown so loathsome upon me that it hath filled my loins—so filled them, that it hath not so much as a spare room left to make a perfume in; so loathsome, that it makes me fit for no company but lazars, for no place but an hospital; for how should others endure the stench of my sores when I am not able to endure it myself? How much less, O God, canst thou endure it, whose pure sense is sensible even of that impurity which

---

[1] Ps. xxxviii. 6: "I am troubled; I am bowed down greatly; I go mourning all the day long." (A. V.)   [2] Ps. vi. 6: "All the night make I my bed to swim; I water my couch with my tears."   [3] Ps. xxxviii. 7: "For my loins are filled with a loathsome *disease:* and *there is* no soundness in my flesh."   [4] 2 Kings i. 8.   [5] Matt. iii. 4; Mark i. 6.

is to us insensible in the stars themselves?[1]   Thou, O God, didst vouchsafe this favour to our first parents to make them garments of beasts' skins to cover their nakedness,[2] and may we not be bold to think that the girdles of beasts' skins which Elijah and John Baptist wore about their loins were also of thy making? Oh then vouchsafe, O God, to give me such a girdle to wear about my loins, a girdle of continence and true mortification, which though it cannot now, as in Elijah and John Baptist it did, prevent the growth and loathsomeness of concupiscence in me, it may at least, as in Mary Magdalene, restrain it, and make me capable of being cured.

And as I have not despaired nor presumed, so neither have I murmured nor repined at thy chastisements [**ver. 8**] ;[3] I acknowledge myself most worthy to suffer them, but most unable to bear them. I am dejected no less in body than in spirit; and yet though I could not speak for weakness, I have roared for grief, and the unquietness of my heart hath supplied the feebleness of my tongue. Indeed, if I could have been a Boanerges, and have gotten a voice like thunder,[4] I should have used it now in speaking to thee, that if my importunity before could not, at least my loudness now might prevail with thee to procure thee to hear me; for *I am feeble and sore broken, I have roared through the unquietness of my heart.* All long of the unquietness of my heart, all long of my sin; for where sin is there will never be but unquietness of heart, and an unquiet heart will always produce these miserable effects, feebleness of body, dejectedness of mind, and roaring of voice.

But how can roaring stand with feebleness, which seems to require a strength of spirits? Is it not therefore a roaring, perhaps, not so much in loudness as in an inarticulate expressing? that having done actions more like a beast than a man, I am forced to use a voice not so much of a man as of a beast? Or is it, perhaps, a roaring in spirit, which the heart may send forth though the body be feeble, or rather

---

[1] Job xxv. 5.   [2] Gen. iii. 21.   [3] Ps. xxxviii. 8: "I am feeble and sore broken: I have roared by reason of the disquietness of my heart." (A.V.)   [4] Mark iii. 17.

then most when it is most feeble: not unlike the blaze of a candle, then greatest when going out? Howsoever it be, this is certain: the heart is that unhappy plot of ground which, receiving into it the accursed seed of sin, brings forth in the body and soul of man these miserable fruits; and how then can I be free from these weeds of the fruits, that have received into me so great a measure of the seed? Oh, vile sin! that I could as well avoid thee as I can see thee, or could as easily resist thee as I deadly hate thee: I should not then complain of either feebleness of body, or dejectedness of mind, or roaring of voice; but I should perfectly enjoy that happy quietness in all my parts which thou, O God, didst graciously bestow as a blessed dowry on our first parents at their creation. And now, O my soul, let me ask thee a question: Why art thou cast down, and why art thou disquieted within me? Hope thou in God, for I will yet praise him who is the health of my countenance and my God.[1] But what need was there of roaring? for what matter is it whether I speak to God in a soft voice or in a loud? seeing thou knowest, O God, the very thoughts of my heart, *and my groaning is not hid from thee*[2] [**ver. 9**]. Though I speak not, but only think to speak, yet thou knowest it; though I think not, but only groan to think, yet thou knowest it; and knowing these things, thou knowest, O God, that my grief is more for thy displeasure than for my wounds; less for the pain I feel of thine arrows sticking in me, than for the unkindness I take at thy shooting them at me. As the love with which thou givest is more dear to me than thy gifts, so the anger with which thou strikest is more grievous to me than thy rod; and alas, O Lord, how can I then choose but roar through the unquietness of my heart, when I want both thy gifts and thy love too, and yet feel thy rod and thine anger too? *All my desire, O Lord, is ever before thee, and my groaning is not hid from thee.* But what avails it me that my desire be all before thee, if it be not all for thee? what avails it me that my groaning be not hid from thee, if it be not made to thee? If I desire anything besides thee, that desire is from weakness, and then thou

---

[1] Ps. xlii. 5, 11; xliii. 5. [2] Ps. xxxviii. 9: "Lord, all my desire *is* before thee; and my groaning is not hid from thee." (A. V.)

regardest it not; if I groan to any but thee, that groaning is from vainness, and then thou seest it not; but now that my desire is only for thee, and my groaning only to thee, now I know thou both seest and regardest them, and I doubt not, O God, but me for them.

But alas, O Lord, this is not yet the whole chapter of my misery; for besides this, *My heart panteth, my strength faileth me; and as for the light of mine eyes, that also is gone from me* [**ver. 10**]. And what is my heart, but the foundation? what my strength, but the pillars? what mine eyes, but the windows of my building? If these, then, be ruined, how can my whole building choose but be demolished? My heart is not wont to pant but in some great agony; nor my strength to fail but in some great conflict; nor my sight to go from me but in some great disaster: how great then, alas, must my agony be, how hard my conflict, how grievous my disaster, when my heart, my strength, my sight, all fail me at once? Though my heart panted, yet if my strength continued I should have a support; or though my strength failed, yet if my sight continued I should have a guide; but when they all fail, and fail at once, alas, O Lord, how can I choose but fall, that have neither strength to support me nor eyes to guide me? Thou, O God, must say to my heart, Be of good cheer:[1] thou must say to my strength, I will be thy fortress:[2] thou must say to mine eyes, I will be thy light:[3] and then, and not till then, shall I ever have ease, or confidence, or consolation.

It is some comfort to men in misery when they have their friends about them, if not to relieve them, yet at least to pity them; for even pity is a comfort to men in misery; but so miserable am I, that I am left alone as one utterly forsaken, for even *my lovers and friends stand aloof from me,*[4] *and my kinsmen stand afar off* [**ver. 11**]. They are all pieces that recoil and fly back at the first voice of the powder. Yet it is not so much me they stand aloof from as my sore; for if it were not for my sore, I should have enough of their company easily

---

[1] John xvi. 33. [2] Ps. xviii. 2: "The LORD *is* my rock, and my fortress."
[3] Isa. lx. 20: "The LORD shall be thine everlasting light." [4] Ps. xxxviii 11: "From my sore," (A. V.)

enough; but they cannot abide sores; their eyes are too tender to endure to see them, and yet hard enough not to relieve them. Or is it they stand aloof—that is, so near as to show they are willing enough to see them, but yet so far off as to show they have no meaning to come and help them? But call you these lovers and friends,—men that flutter about us like flies in the summer of prosperity, but vanish and are gone in the winter of adversity? Are friends but painted flowers, only for show, and nothing at all for use? or if true flowers, yet only to make nosegays of, and never to make medicine of? Is there use of physicians but when there are sores, and when sores come will not they be gotten to come? Is there use of friends but in time of need, and when need comes will they then be gone? But alas, O Lord, was it not so with Christ himself?—company enough, friends enough, when there was no need; but as soon as Judas comes with a band of men, scarce a man found that will be gotten to tarry;[1] and if they used the Master so, can I that am a servant look to be better used?[2]

But say you call them friends, yet how can you call them lovers? for it is the nature of love to be readiest at hand when there be troubles at hand. Doth not the elm, a lover of the vine, support the vine, when itself would sink down and fall to the ground? Doth not the vine stick close to the elm, and if the elm chance to fall, chooseth rather to fall with it than to forsake it? And shall nature do this in trees, and shall not reason, shall not virtue, do it much more in men? or shall trees be reckoned the reasonable creatures, and men be cashiered out of the number? But this is the world: they are called lovers and friends of their faces no otherwise than baboons may be called men, for when a day of trial comes they are often found as far from friendship and true love as baboons from reason and true understanding. And such were my lovers and friends (always excepting Jonathan[3]); but I looked for better at my kinsmen's hands, for there is in them a propinquity of

---

[1] Matt. xxvi. 56: "Then all the disciples forsook him and fled."   [2] Matt. x. 24, 25.   [3] 1 Sam. xviii. 1: "The soul of Jonathan was knit with the soul of David, and Jonathan loved him with his own soul."

nature, and nature will hardly be kept from working; yet such is my unfortunateness, that in my behalf even nature herself grows idle, and I find as little comfort from my kinsmen as from my other lovers and friends; and to say truly, rather less, for where my lovers and friends stand but aloof, my kinsmen stand afar off; neither of them near, indeed, but yet my kinsmen the farthest off. My lovers and friends stand but aloof from my sore, as taking it perhaps for a *noli me tangere* [touch me not]; but my kinsmen stand afar off, as taking it for no less than the very plague. My lovers and friends stand aloof from my sore, as expecting perhaps a time of recovery when they may come on again: but my kinsmen stand afar off, as never intending to hearken more after me. My lovers and friends stand aloof from my sore, as fearing more my sore than me; but my kinsmen stand afar off, as fearing me no less than my sore; and where my lovers and friends by standing aloof do but violate the law of a contracted friendship, my kinsmen by standing afar off violate even the law of natural affection. And is not this a grievous thing, that the law of reason, the law of friendship, the law of nature shall all be broken, rather than I shall be relieved, or find assistance? And now, O my soul, seeing thy lovers and friends and kinsmen prove all unloyal, unfaithful, and unnatural, in whom, alas, canst thou hope for help?—in whom, O Lord, but only in thee? for thou art a lover incomparably more loyal than either the vine to the elm, or the elm to the vine. Thou art a friend infinitely more faithful than either Jonathan to David, or David to Jonathan. Thou art a kinsman, but rather a father, unspeakably more tender of thy children than either Boaz of Ruth,[1] or Abraham of his one and only son Isaac.[2]

But though to be thus forsaken, rejected, and even abhorred by lovers, and friends, and kinsmen be misery enough, and more than enough, for one man to bear, yet this is not all the misery I bear; but *they also that seek after my life lay snares for me, and they that seek my hurt speak mischievous things, and imagine deceit[s] all the day long*

---

[1] Ruth ii. 8, etc. [2] Gen. xxii. 2.

[ver. 12]. It is not enough that my friends and kinsmen will do me no good, but there are others that will do me hurt; and it is not enough that they wish my hurt, but they seek to do it—they hunt after me[1] as after a prey. And it is no small hurt they seek to do me; but they lay snares for my life: nothing but my life will serve them. And they do it not so much by open violence, which might perhaps be withstood, but they do it by fraud and deceit, which is not easy to be avoided; for, first, they speak mischievous things, they raise scandals, and work the world to an ill opinion of me, and then they lie devising of ways how to entrap me; and they spend not an hour or two about it, but they imagine deceit all the day long. And, alas, O Lord, is this a world to have safety in scandals, where, if some be ready to devise them, others are as ready to believe them? If there be a Jezebel to plot a false accusation, are there not elders to put it in execution?[2] and do I not in this still run in the same line with my Lord Christ Jesus? for did not the Scribes and Pharisees first devise mischievous things against him,[3] and then the high-priests and rulers believe what they devised, and execute what they believed?[4] And what, O Lord, do I all this while? Do I stand upon my guard, and have an eye to their practices? Do I seek to repel their violence by force, or to frustrate their fraud with circumspection? Do I clear their scandals with apologies, or do I answer their clamours with vociferations? God knows, none of all these. I neither use arms offensive nor defensive; all my doing is suffering, and all the apology I make for myself is silence; for *as a deaf man I heard not, and as a dumb man I opened not my mouth*[5] [ver. 13]. For why should I hear when I meant not to speak, and why should I speak when I knew beforehand I should not be heard? I knew by contesting I should but provoke them, and make them more guilty that were guilty

---

[1] 1 Sam. xxiv. 11: "Thou (Saul) huntest my soul to take it." [2] 1 Kings xxi. 8, etc. [3] Luke vi. 7: "The scribes and Pharisees watched him . . . that they might find an accusation against him." [4] Luke xxiv. 20: "The chief priests and our rulers delivered him to be condemned to death, and have crucified him." [5] Ps. xxxviii. 13: "But I, as a deaf *man*, heard not: and *I was* as a dumb man *that* openeth not his mouth."

too much before. I therefore thought it better myself to be silent than to set them a-roaring, and make them grow outrageous. No doubt, a great wisdom in David to know that to be deaf and dumb was in this case his best course; but yet a far greater virtue that, knowing it, he was able to do it. O how happy should we be if we could always do that which we know is best to be done;[1] and if our wills were as ready to act as our reason is able to enact, we should then decline[2] many rocks we now run upon; we should then avoid many errors we now run into. To be deaf and dumb are, indeed, great inabilities and defects when they be natural; but when they be voluntary, and I may say artificial, they are then great abilities, or rather perfections. They are two stems upon which do grow the excellent virtues of patience and charity, which, though David showed in himself in a great measure at the railing of Shimei,[3] yet he could never so properly speak them of himself as in the person of Christ, for of him, indeed, the sacred story relates, that being railed upon and reviled,[4] buffeted and beaten by the base multitude,[5] yet, as a sheep led to the slaughter, he opened not his mouth, but was deaf and dumb even to death.[6]

O grievous alteration! transcendent indignity! He that restored cripples to health, and raised the dead to life, now to be deprived himself of the chief faculties of life, both active and passive! He that made the deaf to hear, and the dumb to speak, now himself neither to speak nor hear! A grievous case, no doubt, to be so; and yet, no doubt, a just cause it should be so; for if he had heard, he should have heard but blasphemies; and if he had spoken, he must have spoken but reproofs [7] [ver. 14]. And seeing blasphemies were too profane for his sacred ears to hear, and reproofs too harsh for his mild tongue to utter, what marvel if he that made the ear did himself not hear? what marvel if he that was the Word itself did not speak a word?

And as my deafness and dumbness have not proceeded

---

[1] John xiii. 17. [2] Turn aside from. [3] 2 Sam. xvi. 7—12. [4] 1 Peter ii. 23.
[5] Luke xxiii. 62—65. [6] Isa. liii. 7. [7] Ps. xxxviii. 14: "Thus I was as a man that heareth not, and in whose mouth *are* no reproofs."

from imbecility, but from patience, so neither have they proceeded from fear, but from reverence; for why should I speak when my hope is in thee, O God, that thou wilt speak? why should I hear when thou wilt hear for me?[1] [**ver. 15.**] For alas, O Lord, when I hear, they speak what they list, as either thinking I cannot control them, or not caring whether I can or no; but when thou hearest, they are glad to take heed what they say; for thou hast scales to weigh their words, and, if [thou] find them light, power to censure them. Why then should I offer to hear or speak, when I know ere long I shall have a hearing before thee, where thou shalt be their judge, and wilt be my advocate? And have I not reason till then to consecrate my ears and tongue to thee? It is true, injurious language is a provocation able to make a dumb man to speak, and I may say able to loosen the tongue of Crœsus's dumb son; but he that so provoked should fall a-speaking[2] were very like to fall in speaking, for it is a slippery argument to be spoken in; and if in speaking I should slip never so little, oh what a joy it would be to my enemies! they would never desire better sport, they would magnify themselves against me[3] [**ver. 16**]: I should be their blind Samson to make them merry,[4] I should serve them for a stock of derision. Oh, therefore, suffer me not, O God, to suffer these indignities; but do thou hear for me, do thou speak for me; *for I*, alas, *am ready to halt, and my sorrow is continually before me* [**ver. 17**], that if my slipping and falling be a cause to make mine enemies rejoice, they may be sure of joy enough; for how can I choose but often fall, that am of myself so ready to halt, and specially when my sorrow is always before me, that makes me I cannot see my way before me; for what doth more blind the eyes and take away the sight than sorrow? Was it not sorrow that hindered Mary Magdalene from discerning Christ when she saw him at the sepulchre?[5] And, besides, my halting is the worst kind of

---

[1] Ps. xxxviii. 15: "For in thee, O LORD, do I hope: thou wilt hear, O Lord my God." [2] The son of Crœsus, long dumb, is said to have been so moved by seeing an attempt to assassinate his father, as to call out, "Man! kill not Crœsus," and, thus, by securing assistance, to save his parent's life (Herod i. 86). [3] Ps. xxxviii. 16: "For I said, *Hear me*, lest *otherwise* they should rejoice over me; when my foot slippeth they magnify *themselves* against me." [4] Judg. xvi. 25. [5] John xx. 14, 15.

halting that is, for I come not to it, as Jacob came to his, by wrestling with an angel, which brought a blessing with it; but I come to it as Mephibosheth[1] did, by the imbecility or inequality of my parts: for having two feet to go upon, my reason and my will, how can I choose but halt when my will is so much longer than my reason? And then, if to the aptness of my falling by reason of my halting, there be added the inadvertency of the way by reason of my sorrow, how can I choose but even trip at every step I take?—that if mine enemies rejoice at my fallings, they are very like to have their fill of rejoicing; for if a just man fall seven times a day, how often, alas, am I like to fall that halt, I may rightly say, downright in sin? But let mine enemies rejoice to see me fall as much as they please, this shall not hinder me from seeking to rise; and seeing there is no rising from sin but by confessing it, *I will* therefore *declare mine iniquity, I will be sorry for my sin* [**ver. 18**]. I will declare mine iniquity, that my enemies may see I can speak to God though I was dumb to them; and I will be sorry for my sin, to make them see how little I envy their rejoicing that can take pleasure in my own sorrowing; for to declare mine iniquities without sorrowing for my sin might rather be thought an ostentation than a penitence, and rather show me proud of my sin than ashamed of it. I will therefore be sorry for my sin, that my sorrow may testify for me that my declaration now is out of contrition, as my declaration shall testify that my dumbness before was out of compassion. But though I scorn mine enemies' deriding, yet I am not insensible of mine own disgrace, and therefore hope that my speaking now shall supply my dumbness before, and make thee, O God, to take my cause into thine own hearing, and either convert mine enemies or else confound them. This, indeed, is my hope, though I see as yet but small fruit of my hope; *for mine enemies are lively and* [they are] *strong, and they that hate me* without a cause[2] *are multiplied* [**ver. 19**]. I looked

---

[1] 2 Sam. iv. 4: "And Jonathan, Saul's son, had a son *that was* lame of *his* feet. He was five years old when the tidings came of Saul and Jonathan out of Jezreel, and his nurse took him up and fled; and it came to pass, as she made haste to flee, that he fell, and became lame. And his name *was* Mephibosheth."   [2] Ps. xxxviii. 19: "Wrongfully." (A.V.)

for abatement of their rejoicing, and they continue lively still for abatement of their power, and they continue as strong as ever for abatement of their number, and they are rather multiplied and increase. But though it be an easy matter for them to be lively, being so strong as they are, and to be strong being so many as they are, yet how easy is it for thee, O God, by thy spirit of life to strike a dump[1] into their liveliness, by thy almightiness to suppress their strength, by thy infiniteness to confound their number; and why, then, should I be afraid what mine enemies can do unto me?[2] Why should I be frighted with an arm of flesh?[3] But that which is most strange of all, they hate me without a cause[4] [ver. 20]; as if one should say, Their hatred to me is miraculous; an effect without a cause; for what cause of hatred where such motives of love?[5] I seek to do them good, I follow the thing that is good, and yet they hate me. And yet this is no wonder, for is it not said, *Qui male agit, odit lucem* (They that do evil hate the light)? and if hate the light, how can they choose but hate the children of light? That it appears to be cause enough to the wicked to hate the godly, if they discern in them but any sparks of godliness; and then if this be the case, that I must either be wicked myself or else be hated of the wicked, I shall never stand long in making my choice, seeing I shall never certainly buy their love so dear. But since they are generations of vipers, and render me evil for good, at least, O Lord, do not thou forsake me; be not thou far from me[6] [ver. 21]; for as long as thou art on my side, and stayest by me, what though the waters roar, and the mountains shake with the swelling thereof?[7] What though the bulls of Bashan compass me, and the strong bulls be set me round,[8] seeing thou art able to deliver me from their fury, and from the hands of all that hate me?

But, O my soul, thou mayest call long enough to God

---

[1] A heavy sadness. [2] Ps. lvi. 11: "I will not be afraid what man can do unto me." [3] 2 Chron. xxxii. 8: "With him *is* an arm of flesh; but with us *is* the LORD our God to help us, and to fight our battles." [4] Ps. xxxv. 19. [5] Ps. xxxviii. 20: "They also that render evil for good are mine adversaries; because I follow *the thing that* good *is*. [6] Ps. xxxviii. 21: "Forsake me not, O LORD: O my God, be not far from me." [7] Ps. xlvi. 3. [8] Ps. xxii. 12: "Many bulls have compassed me: strong *bulls* of Bashan have beset me round."

not to be far from thee, and all in vain if thou be far from him. Take heed, therefore, it be not found in thee which he sometimes said, This people draweth near me with their lips, but their hearts are far from me;[1] for if thou be near him only with thy lips, such nearness will do thee small good. It is not the neighbourhood of lips that he cares for, but if thou wilt have him not to be far from thee, thou must be careful that thy heart be not far from him. And yet neither is this enough, O God, that thou be not far from me, if thou stand but only looking on, and makest not haste to help me.[2] Thy slowness may be as prejudicial to me as thy being far off; for, alas, mine enemies are ready to devour me,[3] and they that seek after my soul make haste. Do thou, therefore, O God, make haste also, and be not slower than mine enemies; neither let thy love be outrun by their hatred. But, O my soul, why shouldst thou require God to make such haste, as though thou wouldst, as it were, surprise him on a sudden? Alas, is God like man, that he should stand in need of time to consider? Are there *secunda cogitationes* [second thoughts] with him, as there are with men? Is there anything that can be sudden or unlooked-for to him? Although, therefore, he be slow to anger,[4] yet he is never slow to mercy; but for showing of mercy he hath the wings of a dove, and rides upon the wind.[5] And seeing, O God, thou art able, and canst do it, O show thyself willing also, and be forward to do it; make haste to help me, O Lord my salvation. Make haste to help me, that thou mayest be Lord of my salvation, lest I fall into mine enemies' hands that would be lords of my destruction; or, rather, make haste to help me, O Lord, thou that art my salvation; for until thou come, I am, alas, a servant of sin, and a bond-slave to Satan, that would be my destruction.

---

[1] Isa. xxix. 13: "Forasmuch as this people draw near *me* with their mouth, and with their lips do honour me, but have removed their heart far from me."   [2] Ps. xxxviii. 22: "Make haste to help me, O Lord, my salvation."   [3] Ps. lvi. 2: "Mine enemies would daily swallow *me* up."   [4] Neh. ix. 17.   [5] Ps. xviii. 10.

MEDITATIONS AND DISQVISITIONS

UPON

The one and fiftieth Pfalme of *DAVID*.

Miserere mei Deus.

By Sr. RICHARD BAKER, *Knight*.

LONDON,
Printed by *Iohn Dawson*, for *Francis Eglesfield*, and are to be fold at the Marigold, in *Pauls* Church-yard. 1639.

To the
RIGHT HONOURABLE
EDWARD, EARL OF DORSET,
OF HIS MAJESTY'S MOST HONOURABLE PRIVY COUNCIL, LORD CHAMBERLAIN TO THE QUEEN, AND KNIGHT OF THE MOST NOBLE ORDER OF THE GARTER.

MOST HONOURED LORD,—I know you neither like nor have leisure to look upon trifles, but I know also you account not discourses of piety in the number of trifles. This makes me bold to present your Lordship with this short treatise of Meditations; that, being short, it may not divert you long; being pious, not divert you at all. I so much honour your Lordship for your public virtues, so much am bound to you for your private, that I cannot forbear to present you with something as a testimony of my service in both; and a richer present I could not think of than meditations upon this psalm of David, which is indeed the masterpiece of his repentance, as his repentance the masterpiece of all his virtues. The jewel itself is from David, only the case from me; and though the jewel deserve a more illustrious case, and your person a more illustrious present, yet there is colour to hope I may be pardoned in both, seeing the jewel's splendour gives a lustre to any case, and your nobleness to any present. And though it might be presented with a better hand, yet it cannot with a better heart, seeing he presents it that is

Your Lordship's humble and devoted servant,
RICHARD BAKER.

Have mercy upon me, O God, according to thy lovingkindness: according unto the multitude of thy tender mercies blot out my transgressions. 2. Wash me throughly from mine iniquity, and cleanse me from my sin. 3. For I acknowledge my transgressions: and my sin *is* ever before me. 4. Against thee, thee only, have I sinned, and done *this* evil in thy sight: that thou mightest be justified when thou speakest, *and* be clear when thou judgest. 5. Behold, I was shapen in iniquity; and in sin did my mother conceive me. 6. Behold, thou desirest truth in the inward parts: and in the hidden *part* thou shalt make me to know wisdom. 7. Purge me with hyssop, and I shall be clean: wash me, and I shall be whiter than snow. 8. Make me to hear joy and gladness; *that* the bones *which* thou hast broken may rejoice. 9. Hide thy face from my sins, and blot out all mine iniquities. 10. Create in me a clean heart, O God; and renew a right spirit within me. 11. Cast me not away from thy presence; and take not thy holy Spirit from me. 12. Restore unto me the joy of thy salvation; and uphold me *with thy* free Spirit. 13. *Then* will I teach transgressors thy ways; and sinners shall be converted unto thee. 14. Deliver me from bloodguiltiness, O God, thou God of my salvation: *and* my tongue shall sing aloud of thy righteousness. 15. O LORD, open thou my lips; and my mouth shall shew forth thy praise. 16. For thou desirest not sacrifice; else would I give *it:* thou delightest not in burnt offering. 17. The sacrifices of God *are* a broken spirit: a broken and a contrite heart, O God, thou wilt not despise. 18. Do good in thy good pleasure unto Zion: build thou the walls of Jerusalem. 19. Then shalt thou be pleased with the sacrifices of righteousness, with burnt offering and whole burnt offering: then shall they offer bullocks upon thine altar.—PSALM li. (Auth. Vers.)

MEDITATIONS AND DISQUISITIONS

UPON THE

FIFTY-FIRST PSALM OF DAVID.

O LORD our God, how excellent is thy name in all the world![1] Thy glorious majesty is excellent, but that brings nothing to me; thy justice is excellent, but that brings me to nothing; it is thy mercy that must do me good;[2] and therefore thy other excellences I adore, but this I invocate. To invocate thy justice I dare not; thy glory, I cannot; but thy mercy, I both dare and can. For why should I not dare, when fear gives me boldness? How should I not be able, when weakness gives me strength? Why should I not dare, when thou invitest me to it? How should I not be able, when thou drawest me to it? Dost thou invite me, and shall I not come? Dost thou draw me, and shall I draw back? Can there be a patron so powerful as thou? Can there be a suppliant so dejected as myself? Of whom, then, is it fitter to ask for mercy than of thee, O God, who art the God of mercy? and for whom is it fitter to ask for mercy than for me who am a creature of misery? If I were not so miserable, thou couldst not be to me so merciful; and have I not reason, then, to ask that of thee which thou couldst not have so much occasion to manifest to me as by me? If it were not for sin, there should be no misery; and if no misery, no exercise for thy mercy; and wilt thou let it stand idle where it hath so

---

[1] Ps. viii. 1: "O LORD our Lord, how excellent *is* thy name in all the earth."
[2] Ps. li. 1: "Have mercy upon me, O God, according to thy lovingkindness: according unto the multitude of thy tender mercies blot out my transgressions."

foul sins for so fair fields to walk in? Hast thou mercy, and wilt thou not show it? or wilt thou show it to others and not to me? To say I have deserved it were to make it no mercy, for if I deserved it, it were justice, and not mercy. Is not thy mercy over all thy works?[1] and am not I the work of thy hands? The more mercy thou showest, the more is thine honour; and wilt thou not do that which is most for thine honour? Thou didst show mercy to Adam, who was the first sinner; and thou didst show mercy to the thief on the cross, who was the longest sinner; and wilt thou not show mercy to me, who am not the first, and hope not to be the longest? Hast thou showed mercy to so many that thou hast not mercy left for me also? If thy mercy were finite, and could be exhausted, it were no charity to ask it, lest others might want it; but seeing it is infinite, and can never be spent, why should I be sparing to ask it, or thou to bestow it? Thy mercy is infinite, or none at all, for all thou art is infinite; and wilt thou by showing thy mercy less, show thyself to be merciless? If thy mercy be infinite, it must extend to all; and how extends it to all if not to me? Thou hast as much mercy for me as if thou hadst none to have mercy on but me; and can it be thou shouldst have so much for me, and let me have none of it? Can my daily infirmities alien thy love? This were to think thou didst not love me but for my goodness; and, alas, what goodness is there? What goodness ever was there in me that thou shouldst love me? Can thy love aliened[2] turn away thy mercy? This were to think thy mercy did reach no further than thy love; and so, because I know thou lovest not sin, I might justly fear thou wouldst never have mercy upon sinners. But, O gracious God, thou lovest for thy love's sake, and thou hast mercy for thy mercy's sake; and seeing thy love, which is thyself, can never leave thee, it makes me assured thy mercy, which is thy nature, will never leave me. If I refused thy mercy, thou mightst justly withhold it; but now, behold, I hold my breast open to receive it; or if I did not ask thy mercy, thou mightst forbear to show it; but now,

---

[1] Ps. cxlv. 9: "His tender mercies *are* over all his works."   [2] Alienated.

behold, I beg it upon my knees. I am none of Zebedee's sons, that ask to sit at thy right hand and at thy left;[1] I desire not exaltation, but absolution; it is not thy bounty I ask, but only thy mercy: Have mercy upon me, O God, according to thy lovingkindness, and according to the multitude of thy tender mercies do away mine offences.

It may be thought severity in God to cast Adam out of Paradise for only one sin; but was Adam's sin but only one?—but one, perhaps, in action, but a million in affection. For say it was pride—hath not pride more branches than a tree hath? Say it was gluttony—hath not gluttony more dishes than Dives[2] had? Say it was curiosity—hath not curiosity more eyes than Argus had? Say it was disobedience—hath not disobedience more faults than Absalom had?[3] For how else could Manasseh's sins come to be more than the sands of the sea, if it be not that a sin, though but in thought, may justly be thought a million of sins? And as it is said in the Gospel that a man was possessed with an unclean spirit, but that unclean spirit was a legion,[4] so we may say of every sin it is but one sin, but that one sin is a legion. Here, therefore, O my soul, take heed thou mistake not thyself in casting up the audit of thy sins, and think thou hast perhaps but one or two sins to answer for to God, when in God's sight every sin thou committest is a legion; and for a legion of sins thou must make thy account—thou shalt make account. And now, seeing my sins are in number so many, and so great in measure, have I not reason to ask for mercies of equal proportion? Although, therefore, I ask not thy bounty, but thy mercy, yet the bounty of thy mercy I ask: to ask less than would serve, would prejudice my wants, and not relieve them; and how then can I ask less than a multitude of great mercies, to do away my offences, who have a multitude of great[5] offences to be done away?

But hath God then a multitude of mercies, whereof some be greater, and some be lesser? Is not his mercy, as himself is, only one and *simplicissimus?* No doubt, it is so in itself; one and single as himself, but yet in relation to us,

---

[1] Matt. xx. 21. [2] Luke xvi. 19. [3] 2 Sam. xiii., *seqq.* [4] Mark v. 9.
[5] Ps. xxv. 11: "Pardon mine iniquity, for it *is* great."

and to our understanding, it is said to be as it is applied; to every sin a mercy, to great sins great mercies, to a multitude of sins a multitude of mercies.

But is not this a disorder in praying, to pray for that for which we should rather give thanks? to pray for a multitude of great mercies, as though we had them not already, when we should rather give thanks for them which we have so continually? for is it not God's great mercy to us all that we be not all consumed?[1] and this great mercy multiplied unto us, when thousands fall on our right hand, and ten thousands on our left, yet we in the midst of these dangers are kept safe from danger?[2] Is it not his great mercy that he gives riches and plenty, and this mercy multiplied unto us, when so many are pined away with penury, yet our land floweth with milk and honey?[3] Is it not his great mercy that the light of the Gospel shines upon us, and this mercy multiplied unto us, when so many live in darkness, and in the shadow of death?[4] These indeed are great mercies; yet they are but the mercies of his patience, or of his general goodness and bounty; and of these mercies we may justly be afraid, as it is said, There is mercy with thee, that thou mayest be feared;[5] but it is the mercies of his special love that I desire; and of these mercies there can be no fear; for love casteth out fear.[6] The mercies of his patience, and of his bounty, are not his tender mercies; we may have them, perhaps, and to our hurt, as long life; but to heap up wrath against the day of wrath: riches and honours but to make our camel the greater, and the unfitter to pass through a needle's eye;[7] the light of the Gospel, but to make us the more guilty, and subject to be beaten with more stripes;[8] but his tender mercies are the mercies of his love, and can never be had but for our good; for love covers the multitude of sins;[9] and this covering of our sins is the recovering again of Paradise, and suffers not the angel with the flaming sword to find

---

[1] Lam. iii. 22. [2] Ps. xci. 7: "A thousand shall fall at thy side, and ten thousand at thy right hand; *but* it shall not come nigh thee." [3] Exod. iii. 8, 17, *et alibi*.
[4] Isa. ix. 2. [5] Ps. cxxx. 4: "*There is* forgiveness with thee, that thou mayest be feared." [6] 1 John iv. 18: "Perfect love casteth out fear." [7] Matt. xix. 24.
[8] Luke xii. 47, 48. [9] 1 Pet. iv. 8: "Charity shall cover the multitude of sins."

anything in us, to keep us out.¹ Oh, therefore, however it pleaseth thee, O God, to deal with me, in the mercies of thy patience, by length of days, or in the mercies of thy bounty, by riches and honours, be pleased at least to grant me the mercies of thy love to cover my sins, and according to the multitude of thy tender mercies do away mine offences. It was a great mercy, even of thy love, that with great miracles thou didst bring the Israelites out of Egypt;² but that thou didst endure to be grieved with that generation forty years together, and yet bring them at last into the land of Canaan,³ this was a multitude of great mercies. And yet more than this, it was a great mercy that thou didst suffer our first parents, after their great sin, to live, and to propagate their sinful race; but that thou didst send thine only Son to expiate their sin, and to make satisfaction for it, with infinite indignities, in life and death—this was a multitude of great and tender mercies. And now that I have the multitude of God's tender mercies at the height, what would I have to do? Even to do away mine offences, for this is a work for a multitude of mercies, and of mercy only. Thy power, O God, is almighty, and yet cannot; thy justice most perfect, and yet will not; thy wisdom infinite, and yet knows not how to do away offences without thy mercy; but thy mercy alone, and of itself, both can, and may, and will; and therefore thy mercy is the sanctuary that I fly unto; and seeing thou delightest in showing of mercy,⁴ Behold, I show thee a large field here, wherein thou mayest show it—a multitude of my great sins for a multitude of thy great mercies. And because sins are pollutions, and no way to do away pollutions so well as by washing, therefore *wash me throughly from mine iniquity, and cleanse me from my sins* [sin]. [**ver. 2.**]

I must confess I was at first afraid of thy washing, for thou didst once wash the whole world, and then thou didst wash away the sinners, but not the sins; and if thou shouldst

---

¹ Gen. iii. 24: "Cherubims . . . to keep the way of the tree of life."   ² Exod. xx. 2.   ³ Heb. iii. 9—11: "When your fathers tempted me, proved me, and saw my works forty years. Wherefore I was grieved with that generation, and said, They do alway err in *their* heart, and they have not known my ways. So I sware in my wrath, They shall not enter into my rest."   ⁴ Micah vii. 18.

wash me so, it were as good for me to be unwashed; but I consider that washing was in thy justice; the washing I desire is in thy mercy; and I should not have dared to pray thee to wash me, if I had not prayed thee first to have mercy upon me, for it is thy washing in mercy only that washes clean; thy washing in justice, washeth clean away.

But why is David so preposterous[1] in making his suit,—to pray God to wash away his sins, before he makes his confession, and tells what his sins be?—as a man that should require his physician to cure his disease without telling what he ails, and what his disease is. But is it not that the ardour and burning heat which David felt of his sins, made him, as it were, to leap into the water at the very first, crying out to be washed, quite forgetting all order, through the violence of his ardour; much like to St. Peter, who through heat of desire to be instantly with Christ, whom he saw upon the water, never stayed, but girt his coat about him, and leapt into the water, clothes and all.[2] Or is it that David might well require to be cured of his disease without telling it, being come to a Physician who knew his disease better than himself? Or is it, indeed, that to tell our disease is part of our curing; to confess our sins, is an act of our washing, and therefore no preposterous course in David to pray for washing before confessing, seeing no confessing is truly found which hath not its beginning, and is not proceeding from God's washing?

But how can we answer this to God? He saith unto us by Isaiah, Wash you, make you clean;[3] meaning, it seems, we should wash ourselves; and now we come to him to wash us, as though we should say, If you will have us be washed, you must come and do it yourself. Indeed, both must be done: God must wash us, and we must wash ourselves. But God's washing is not like our washing: God's washing is by the fire of his Spirit, our washing is by the water of contrition; God's washing is by pardoning, our washing by repenting. Peter washed himself when, having denied his

---

[1] Preposterous, having the wrong end forward, topsy-turvy, unnatural (Bailey's Dict.)   [2] John xxi. 7.   [3] Isa. i. 16.

Master, he went out and wept bitterly.[1] Christ washed him when he prayed for him that his faith might not fail.[2] David washed himself when, for grief of his sins, he watered his bed with tears;[3] God washed him when he sent him word by the prophet Nathan that his sin was forgiven.[4] And, indeed, if God wash us not with his water of pardon, the water of our own tears will do no great good. It may wet, but not wash, or wash, but not cleanse, if God put not our tears into his bottle,[5] which only can give them the power of cleansing. For Esau had a flood of tears to wash himself withal, but God never put them into his bottle; they were tears for his punishment, but not for his sins;[6] and, therefore, they might wet perhaps, but they never cleansed. Oh, then, put my tears into thy bottle, O God, for they are tears for my sins, and not for my punishment; and then wash me with them, and I shall be clean.[7] My tears, God knows, are of themselves too cold, unless they be warmed by the fire of God's Spirit; but if we bring the water, and God bring the fire, then, indeed, a fit lexative[8] will be made to make us clean. Oh, then, warm the cold tears of my repentance with the fire of thy Spirit, O God, and then wash me with them, that my repentance itself, being first cleansed, may be made effectual to cleanse me from my sin. Our own washing is of itself imperfect, and makes us never a whit the cleaner, because we mistake the water, as Pilate did, who washed his hands from Christ's blood[9] where he should have washed them in Christ's blood; but thy washing, O God, is never without cleansing; for thou canst not mistake the water, who art the water thyself; and not in a cistern, but the fountain itself.[10] We wash ourselves, commonly, but as the Pharisees wash their cups, only the outside;[11] and this makes us but hypocrites. But thy washing, O God, is always inward, for thou searchest the hearts and reins;[12] and this is the washing that makes the

---

[1] Matt. xxvi. 75. [2] Luke xxii. 32. [3] Ps. vi. 6. [4] 2 Sam. xii. 13: "And David said unto Nathan, I have sinned against the LORD. And Nathan said unto David, The LORD hath also put away thy sin." [5] Ps. lvi. 8. [6] Heb. xii. 17: "He found no place of repentance, though he sought it carefully with tears." [7] Cf. Ps. li. 7. [8] *Sic* in text. The meaning is clear. [9] Matt. xxvii. 24. [10] Jer. ii. 13. [11] Matt. xxiii. 25. [12] Ps. vii. 9: "The righteous God trieth the heart and reins."

true Israelite, in whom there is no guile.[1] When Naaman was cured of his leprosy by washing in Jordan,[2] did God then wash him, or did Naaman wash himself? Indeed both: Naaman washed himself by obedience and confidence in God's power; God washed him by giving power to the water and confidence to Naaman. But this power was but a personal estate to Jordan; it hath no such power in cleansing of me. The water that must cleanse me is the water that flowed out of my Saviour's side; and in confidence of the power of that water, I humbly prostrate myself before thee, O God, and say, Wash me throughly from my iniquities, and cleanse me from my sins.

But why should David speak so superfluously—use two words when one would serve? for if we be cleansed, what matter is it whether it be by washing or no? Yet David had great reason for using both words, for he requires not that God would cleanse him by miracle, but by the ordinary way of cleansing, and this was washing; he names, therefore, washing as the means, and cleansing as the end; he names washing as the work a-doing, and cleansing as the work done; he names washing as considering the agent, and cleansing as applying it to the patient; and, indeed, as in the figure of the law there was not, so in the verity of the gospel there is not, any ordinary means of cleansing but only by washing; and therefore out of Christ our Saviour's side there flowed water and blood,—water to wash us, and blood to cleanse us; water to make the laver of our regeneration in baptism, and blood to make the laver of our expiation in Christ's sacrifice. But though the words seem here to be thus distinguished, yet otherwhere[3] they are oftentimes promiscuously used, and as well cleansing as washing referred to this water, as well washing as cleansing referred to this blood.

But what means David to say, Wash me from mine iniquity, and cleanse me from my sin, as though he would be washed from one thing and cleansed from another, and not be cleansed from that for which he is washed? But

---

[1] John i. 47.   [2] 2 Kings v. 14.   [3] Elsewhere.

is it not that iniquity and sin, though called by divers names, are both the same thing, but called iniquity, as being a transgression of the law,—called sin, as being an offence against God? Or is it that in sin there is both a stain and a guilt, and he prays to be washed from the stain and cleansed from the guilt? Or is it indeed that he useth divers words to show that he asks forgiveness for all his sins, by what name or title soever they be called?

But is not this an indignity to the great majesty of God? We put our meanest servants to wash our clothes, and will we put God to so mean an office, to be a launderer[1] of sins? Yet see the humility of majesty, a humility even to ecstasy; he descends yet lower, not only to wash our sins, but to take our sins upon him. It seems St. Peter, indeed, was in this error, to think it an indignity, and therefore would not by any means suffer that Christ should wash him until he heard Christ say, Unless I wash thee, thou canst have no part in me; and then he cried, Not my feet only, but my hands and my head; and is not this my case also, that unless God wash me I can have no part in him?[2] And will I lose my part in God for want of washing? Oh, therefore, my soul, prepare thyself for this washing; put off thy clothes, and strip thyself stark naked; keep not so much as fig-leaves about thee,[3] either to hide thy sins by contumacy, or to cover them by hypocrisy, or to slight them by indulgency; but lay them all open and bare before the face of God, that whilst nothing is interposed between God's water and thy sins, it may without impediment have full liberty to work upon thee.

But what though God do wash us, are we sure his washing will always cleanse us? Why is it, then, that he saith, I have purged thee, and thou wast not purged;[4] for may he not as well say, I have washed thee, and thou wast not cleansed? and if not cleansed, as good not washed. Oh, therefore, not wash me only, but cleanse me from my sins, that as in washing thou showest thy love, so by cleansing thou mayest show thy power, seeing it is an office which as none will be willing to undertake but he whose love is

---

[1] Masc. form of *laundress*.   [2] John xiii. 6—8.   [3] Gen. iii. 7.   [4] Ezek. xxiv. 13

unspeakable, so none can be able to discharge but he whose power is ineffable. For can washing be without touching? and would any man foul his fingers to touch so foul a thing as my sin, if he did not love exceedingly? Can cleansing me be without doing a miracle? For seeing it cannot more truly be said that I have sin than that I am sin, what is it now to cleanse me but even *laterem lavare* [to wash a brick[1]], which was never counted less than either a labour lost or a miracle wrought; and can any do miracles but he whose power is unlimited? Oh, then, wash me from mine iniquity, that I may praise thee for thy love; and cleanse me from my sin, that I may magnify thee for thy power, which, as I shall do both if once I be cleansed, so I am able to do neither until I be washed. For, alas, O Lord, what am I but as a filthy rag[2] before thee? Who am I but the man by the highway side, lying bound and wounded?[3] no means at all left me to wash, much less to cleanse, myself. They must be both thine own, thine only work, O God, both to wash me by thy preventing grace, and by thy assisting grace to cleanse me. Oh, then, cleanse me from my sins, O God; let not the foulness of my sins make thee unwilling to wash me; let not the reluctancy of my flesh make thee unable to cleanse me, but make thy work of washing me to prosper in thy hand. Oh, wash me, but not as Simon Magus was washed,[4] who came fouler out of the water[5] than he went in; but as the eunuch was washed, who came so clean out of the water that he was ready to run through fire and water for thy name's sake,[6] and by his washing was made a fit minister for the washing of others.[7] And now, O great God, since it hath pleased thee to descend to so low a work as washing me, O wash me throughly; not rinse me only, as though I were but lightly stained, and had but some small spots upon me, but wash me throughly, as having a leprosy that overspreads me,[8] a foulness that is deeply engrained in me—so deeply, O God, that nothing but a washing by thine own hand can fetch it out.

---

[1] A Latin proverbial phrase expressive of "labour lost." [2] Isa. lxiv. 6: "All our righteousnesses *are* as filthy rags." [3] Luke x. 30: "A certain *man* . . . fell among thieves, which stripped him of his raiment, and wounded *him*, and departed, leaving *him* half dead." [4] Acts viii. 13. [5] Acts viii. 18—23. [6] Acts viii. 38, 39: ". . . and he went on his way rejoicing." [7] Tradition ascribes to this eunuch the founding of the church in Ethiopia. [8] Lev. xiv. 8, 9.

And yet, stay,—why should I put God to this trouble of washing me at all, seeing I have an easier way of cleansing, taught me by the centurion in the Gospel, Speak the word, only, and I shall be clean?[1] or, if this be still too much, an easier way yet taught me by another, *Si vis, potes me mundare*, If thou wilt, thou canst make me clean?[2] O gracious God, whether it be by washing, or by speaking the word, or by thy will only to have it so, whatsoever be the means, let this at least be the effect, that though I be not made bright, which is more than I can be, yet I may be made clean, which is no more than I must be; for I am not of the Pharisee's mind, to think myself clean enough already; but I know mine iniquity, and my sin is ever before me[3] [**ver. 3**]; although, perhaps, it be a knowledge I were better be without; for Christ knew no sin,[4] which we may be sure he should have done if it had been worth the knowing. Christ, indeed, knew no sin in himself, but he knew sin in itself; he knew no sin by committing it, but he knew sin by understanding it. My misery is not that I know sin, but that I know my sin, that I have sin of mine own to know. Christ knew no sin, because he could not say I know my sin; but I know my sin because I cannot say I know not sin. And yet who will believe that a man knows sin that will be meddling with it? We say there are no miracles nowadays in the world; and can there be a greater wonder than this, that a man should know sin and yet commit it? should know the foulness of sin, and yet lie wallowing in it? should know the horror of sin, and yet run headlong into it? But is it not that we are all in this the children of Adam? Our eyes are not opened till we have eaten of the forbidden fruit;[5] we know not sin truly till we have committed it; we see not the foulness till we feel the guiltiness; and this makes me say now, which I could not so well say till now, I know mine iniquities, and my sin is ever before me; for they were strangers to me before, and I knew not their conditions; but now I find what they are, and am sick

---

[1] Matt. viii. 8: "Speak the word only, and my servant shall be healed."   [2] Matt. viii. 2.   [3] Ps. li. 3: "For I acknowledge my transgressions, and my sin *is* ever before me." (A.V.)   [4] 2 Cor. v. 21.   [5] Gen. iii. 7.

of their company. They were, indeed, pleasing to me in the doing, but are now most loathsome being done. They stood behind me at first as servants waiting upon me; but are now ever before me as tormentors seizing upon me; that if ever I loved them before, I hate them now a thousand times more.

But why should David make it so great a matter to say, I know my sin, as though a man could commit a sin and not know it? as though Adam could eat of the forbidden fruit, and not know he had eaten it? Adam, indeed, knew his eating, yet he knew not his sinning; he knew his nakedness, but he knew not his guiltiness. If, when he answered God, I know my nakedness,[1] he had said, I know my sin, he might, perhaps, have tarried in Paradise still; that we may see how hard a thing it is to say, I know my sin, which cost Adam no less than Paradise before he could say it. And how much easier came David to be able to say, I know my sin; for do we think he could say it as soon as he had committed it? No, nor almost a whole year after,[2] that, as we may say of Adam, it cost him a great place, so we may say of David, it cost him a long time to learn to say, I know my sin.

But how can David say, I know my sins, and yet in another place say, Forgive me my secret sins?[3] For if he knew them, how be they secret? and if they be secret, how doth he know them? Indeed, both David and every one of us hath sin enough to serve both turns; not only because sin is of a greater size in God's sight than it is in ours, and therefore leaves much for him to see which to us is secret, but because also there are many actions in our life which we so lightly pass over as if we thought them no sins—perhaps thought them virtues, when yet in God's sight they are grievous sins. David had committed a great sin, which he could not choose but know to be a sin, and therefore might justly say, I know my sin; but that his sin had caused God's name to be blasphemed,[4] this was a sin he knew not

---

[1] Gen. iii. 10. [2] 2 Sam. xi. 4, 27; xii. 13. [3] Ps. xix. 12: "Cleanse thou me from secret *faults*." [4] 2 Sam. xii. 14: "By this deed thou hast given great occasion to the enemies of the LORD to blaspheme."

till God himself did tell him; and from hence he might justly suspect he had cause enough in other sins to say, Forgive me my secret sins. St. James saith, "In many things we offend all;"[1] this we all know, and [it] gives us all just cause to say, I know my sin; but what those many things are in which we offend, and what those offences be which in many things we commit, this many times we know not, and gives us as just cause to say, Forgive me my secret sins.

But alas, my soul, I must not stay here only to know my sin and keep it to myself, as though I thought it a jewel which none might know of for fear of losing it; but in this I acknowledge the great favour of God, that as I know my sin, so I acknowledge my sin; for far be it from me I should be found of Saul's disposition, to think to make God believe that I saved the fat of the sheep for sacrifice,[2] when I saved them for mine own profit: this hiding a sin is a greater sin than the sin it hides, for it is an affront to God's omnisciency. Adam's fig-leaves proved as hurtful to him as the forbidden fruit; for nothing lays our sins so open to God as our seeking to hide them; and although it be oftentimes dangerous to acknowledge a fault to a civil magistrate, who without our acknowledging could not know it, yet there can be no danger to acknowledge our sins to God, who knows them already, whether we acknowledge them or no. Our acknowledging them to him is not a discovery, but the first degree of recovery; and seeing I am now travelling to repentance, how is it possible I should ever come at it if I acknowledge not my sins, which is the first step to it? and therefore, howsoever I am guilty of many great and heinous sins, yet of this sin of hiding my sin thou canst clear me, O God; for I acknowledge mine iniquity, and my sin is ever before me.[3]

But yet what good will the knowing or the acknowledging my sin do me, if I let it slip from my heart as soon as it is off my tongue?—if, having once acknowledged it, I cast it behind me, and think no more of it? Behold, therefore, O God, I set it before me, and am always beholding it. It is

---

[1] James iii. 2.   [2] 1 Sam. xv. 15: "And Saul said . . . the people spared the best of the sheep and of the oxen, to sacrifice unto the LORD thy God." (cf. ver. 9.)   [3] Ps. li. 3: "For I acknowledge my transgressions, and my sin is ever before me." (A.V.)

ever before me in meditation, for I cannot but be thinking still how foolish I have been to procure thy displeasure, though it had been *regni causâ*, for the gaining of a kingdom; how much more to provoke thine anger for the pleasing only of some idle fancy? It is ever before me in remorse, for it is ever running[1] as a sore in my mind, that against thee only have I sinned, against whom only I should not have sinned; much like the fault of our first parents, who seem to have eaten of that fruit only of which fruit only they should not have eaten. It is ever before me in prospect; for, looking earnestly upon sin, I can see nothing in it that should make any man to love it. It is deformed and crooked, it is foul and ill-favoured, it is unsound and diseased, it is old and wrinkled; that I wonder at myself how I was ever gotten but once to embrace it; yet I see withal it paints and makes a fair show; it perfumes and makes a sweet smell; it is in profession an angel of light,[2] and carries apples in its hand, of the tree of good and evil, that would entice any man.[3] It is ever before me in terror: waking, methinks I hear the Judge pronouncing sentence of condemnation against me; sleeping, I am frighted with dreams no less fearful. If a leaf do but wag, methinks it threatens me; if a bird do but chirp, it seems to accuse me. I am frighted with light, and jealous of darkness. For how can I choose but fear lest all thy creatures have set themselves against me, who have so unnaturally, so unloyally, so ungratefully set myself against thee? For against thee, against thee only have I sinned[4] [ver. 4], not against heaven,[5] not against earth, not against angels, not against men; for to these I never vowed allegiance, nor stand engaged; but against thee only; against thee, my Father, and so have sinned in disobedience; against thee, my sovereign Lord, and so have sinned in rebellion; against thee, my Benefactor, and so have sinned in ungratefulness; that whilst no grace hath

---

[1] Ps. lxxvii. 2: "My sore ran in the night and ceased not." [2] 2 Cor. xi. 14: "Satan himself is transformed into an angel of light." [3] Gen. iii. 6: "The woman saw that the tree *was* good for food, and that it *was* pleasant to the eyes," etc. [4] Ps. li. 4: "Against thee, thee only, have I sinned, and done *this* evil in thy sight: that thou mightest be justified when thou speakest, *and* be clear when thou judgest." (A.V.) [5] Yet in Luke xv. 21, "the son said unto him, Father, I have sinned against heaven," etc.

been found wanting in thee that might have kept me from sinning, no grace hath been found in me to keep me from sin.

But is there not matter here to make us at a stand? For to say, Against thee I have sinned, is most just and fit; but to say, Against thee only I have sinned, seems something hard. It had perhaps been a fit speech in the mouth of our first parent Adam; he might justly have said to God, Against thee only have I sinned, who never sinned against any other; but for us to say it, who commit sins daily against our neighbours, and specially for David to say it, who committed two notorious sins against his neighbour and faithful friend Uriah,[1] what unfitter speech could possibly be devised? But is it not that these actions of David were great wrongs indeed, and enormous iniquities against Uriah; but can we properly say they were sins against Uriah? For what is sin but a transgression of God's law?[2] And how then can sin be committed against any but against him only whose law we transgress? Or is it that it may justly be said, Against thee only have I sinned, because against others perhaps in a base tenure, yet only against God *in capite*?[3] Or is it that David might justly say to God, Against thee only have I sinned, because from others he might appeal, as being a king, and having no superior, but no appealing from God, who is King of kings, and supreme Lord over all? Or is it that we may justly say, Against thee only I have sinned, seeing Christ hath taken, and still takes, all our sins upon him, and every sin we commit is as a new burden laid upon his back, and upon his back only? Or is it, lastly, that I justly say, Against thee only have I sinned, because in thy sight only I have done it? For from others I could hide it, and did conceal it. But what can be hidden from thy all-seeing eye? And yet, if this had been the worst, that I had sinned only against thee, though this had been bad enough, and infinitely too much, yet it might perhaps have

---

[1] 2 Sam. xi. [2] 1 John iii. 4: "Sin is the transgression of the law." [3] Base tenants are those holding in villenage (as serfs); accordingly, " sin in a base tenure" is an offence against one's own immediate lord, while a sin against God *in capite* is an offence against Him as supreme Lord to whom our best, our "knight's service" is due.

admitted reconcilement; but to do this evil in thy sight, as if I should say I would do it, though thou stand thyself and look on, and as it were in defiance, what sin so formidable? what sin can be thought of so unpardonable? A sin of infirmity may admit apology; a sin of ignorance may find out excuse; but a sin of defiance can have no defence. But hath not David a defence for it here, and that a very just one? For in saying, Against thee only I have sinned, that thou mightst be justified in thy saying, doth he not speak as though he had sinned to do God a pleasure? therefore sinned that God might be justified? And what can be more said for justifying of a sin than to say it was done for justifying of God? But far is it from David to have any such meaning; his words import not a lessening, but an aggravating of his sin, as spoken rather thus, because a judge may justly be taxed of injustice, if he lay a greater punishment upon the offender than the offence deserves; therefore to clear thee, O God, from all possibility of erring in this kind, I acknowledge my sins to be so heinous, my offences so grievous, that thou canst never be unmerciful in punishing, though thy punishing should be never so unmerciful;—for how can a judge pass the bounds of equity where the delinquent hath passed all bounds of iniquity? and what error can there be in thy being severe when the greatness of my fault is a justification of severity?—that thou canst not lay so heavy a doom upon me which I have not deserved; thou canst not pronounce so hard a sentence against me which I am not worthy of. If thou judge me to torture, it is but mildness; if to die the death, it is but my due; if to die everlastingly, I cannot say it were unjust. Yet in judgment, O Lord, remember mercy; consider not how foul I am become, but how I am become foul; for though my sin be great, yet I was not the beginner of it; for behold I was born in iniquity, and in sin hath my mother conceived me [1] [ver. 5]. And seeing my birth did not amend my conception, how should my growth amend my birth? Did not sin, at least the author of sin, hear thy voice when thou saidst, Increase

---

[1] Ps. li. 5: " Behold I was shapen in iniquity, and in sin did my mother conceive me." (A.V.)

and multiply?[1] which, though not spoken to him, yet, as an intruder, he claims to have a part; and seeing all parts of my soul and body have increased and grown greater since my birth, will not he look that sin also shall have a share in growing as well as they? Doth anything grow so fast as a weed? and is there any so very a weed as sin? hath it not been growing ever since I was born? and can so fast growing, in so long growing, make less than a monster? And am I a fit champion to encounter monsters? Indeed I encountered a bear, and slew him; a lion, and killed him; a giant, and overcame him;[2] but these were no monsters, at least no monsters to be compared with sin. O the monstrousness of sin! far harder to be vanquished than all the monsters that ever nature made; for I could vanquish a bear, a lion, a giant, the greatest of nature's monsters, but with all my forces have not been able to vanquish this monster sin.

But why am I partial towards my parents, and charge my poor mother with conceiving me in sin, but let my father pass without blame? Or is it that to say I was born in sin is as much as to say I was begotten in sin, and so my father hath a share of sin in begetting me, as well as my mother in conceiving me? Indeed, if Eve had only sinned, and not Adam, it might have been said we were conceived in sin, but not, perhaps, that we were begotten in sin; or if Adam had only sinned, and not Eve, it might have been said we were begotten in sin, but not, perhaps, that we were conceived in sin; but now that Adam and Eve have both of them sinned, it is justly said, I was begotten in iniquity, and in sin hath my mother conceived me; and so we are all of us sinners now of the whole blood, both by father and mother, and no inheritance so sure to us from them as this of sin, and in this inheritance we are all great husbands: whatsoever becomes of Naboth's vineyard, we commonly make sure work to improve this, and we seldom leave till we can leave more of it to our children than we received from our parents; and seeing no diseases are so incurable as those which come *ex traduce* [by derivation] from either of

---

[1] Gen. i. 28: "Be fruitful and multiply." [2] 1 Sam. xvii. 34, 50.

our parents, how incurable must sin needs be, which is *ex traduce*, from them both? If I were only born in sin, then all the time I lived in the little world of my mother's womb I must have been without sin, and so might hope thou wouldst at least have some respect to that time of innocency I lived there; but now that not only I was born in sin, but my mother also conceived me in sin, now I was a sinner as soon as a creature, and not one minute's time of innocency to plead for myself. And now, alas! O Lord, what couldst thou ever look for at my hands but only sin? The leopard cannot change her spots,[1] no more can I that am conceived in sin conceive anything but only sin. It is natural to me, and nature will have her course. But though it be natural to me to sin, yet it is not natural to me to sin so grievously as I have done, for then every one should be as great a sinner as myself; but now that I must say with St. Paul, Of all great sinners, I am the greatest,[2] this is an estate of sin, which I have not by inheritance, but by purchase; and I cannot blame nature, but myself, for this; all the help is, that though I might be ashamed to do it, yet I am not ashamed to confess it; and is not a sincere confessing, in the balance of thy mercy, O God, of even weight with the not doing? and therefore, although the sin I confess be great, and, being great, must needs be greatly displeasing to thee, yet this confessing my sin to be great cannot be displeasing, for Thou lovest truth in the inward affections[3] [**ver. 6**], and this my confession comes from thence; for there is a truth in words when it is without lying, as St. Paul saith, I speak the truth, I lie not.[4] But this truth reacheth not home to confessing of sins; and there is a truth in deeds, when it is without deceit, as Christ said of Nathaniel, Behold a true Israelite, in whom there is no guile;[5] but neither doth this truth reach home to confessing of sins; but there is a truth in heart when it is in sincerity, as it is said here, Thou lovest truth in the inward affections; and this is the truth that carries home the con-

---

[1] Jer. xiii. 23.　[2] 1 Tim. i. 15: "Sinners, of whom I am chief."　[3] Ps. li. 6: "Because thou desirest truth in the inward parts: and in the hidden *part* thou shalt make me to know wisdom." (A.V.)　[4] Rom. ix. 1.　[5] John i. 47.

fessing of sins to its full period; for though thou lovest all truth, and everywhere, yet the truth of the inward affections thou affectest most inwardly, for this is properly within thine own survey, seeing thou only art καρδιογνώστης, the trier and searcher of the heart and reins. Truth of words may have for its motive vain-glory and praise of men; truth of deeds, awe of the law; but truth in the inward affections can have no motive, but only the love of truth, which therefore must needs be pleasing to thee, who art thyself both Love and Truth.

Where thou lovest truth, thou teachest wisdom; and because thou lovest truth in the inward affections, thou teachest wisdom in the secret of the heart; and who can come to teach it there but only thou? Superficial and external wisdom is the gift oft-times of nature, sometimes of art; but this wisdom in the secret of the heart is only God's advowson: none can give it, none bestow it, but God himself, and he alone. Wherefore, O God, though I have not hated that which thou hatest, the committing of sin, yet, seeing I have loved that which thou lovest, the truth of heart, thou hast taught me wisdom in the secret of my heart: though thou didst not give me the grace to prevent sin, yet thou hast taught me the wisdom to repent sin, a wisdom which none can have unless he be taught, and none can teach but only thyself; a wisdom which cannot be had but in the heart, and nowhere in the heart but in the secret of the heart. A man may have the wisdom to see his sin by the outward eye of the heart; and he may have the wisdom to understand his sin by the common sense of the heart; but he cannot have the wisdom to repent his sin, but only in the secret and innermost of his heart. And we need not wonder that God only is the Schoolmaster of this wisdom, seeing the wisdom of the world is not capable of it; it is a secret hidden from carnal eyes. It is as hard a matter to feel the power of repentance in the soul, as to believe the resurrection from the dead in the body; both great secrets, but this perhaps the greater, as being indeed the resurrection of the soul. There are wisdoms of divers sorts in the heart of man: the voluptuous man hath a wisdom to accomplish his desires; the worldly man hath a wisdom to gather riches; the politician hath a wisdom to compass his ends; but all these wisdoms are but floating in the heart, or rather but hovering about the heart, as the crow about the ark; they enter not into the secret of it, nor bring into the heart, as the dove into the ark, the olive-branch of peace. For when the mind bethinks itself, and dives into its own bottom, it finds no place for these distended and swelling wisdoms, which, indeed, the secret of the heart hath not room enough to receive :[1] only the contracted wisdoms of humility and repentance can find harbour and entertainment there.

But though a little room will serve humility, yet, little as it is, it must be clean ; and what one clean corner have I in my whole heart to give humility or repentance entertainment? Oh, therefore, *Purge me with hyssop, and I shall be clean: wash me, and I shall be whiter than snow* [**ver. 7**]. But did not the washing I had before make me clean ? and what need then of any more cleansing? It seems that washing was but only a preparative to purging, to make it work the better ; at least it went not so far as the secret of the heart. And seeing the foulness of my sin hath pierced my heart to the very bottom, no remedy now but I must be purged if I will be cleansed.

But do I well to prescribe to God with what he shall purge me, as though I knew all God's medicines as well as himself? and, which is worse, I to prescribe, and he to minister? But excuse me, O my soul ; it is not I that prescribe it to God ; it is God that prescribes it to me ; for hyssop is his own receipt, and one of the ingredients prescribed by himself to make the water of separation for curing the leprosy.[2] But why then with hyssop, and not with hellebore or scammony rather ? For how else happens it that God's purging should not work, as he saith himself, I have purged thee, and thou wast not purged,[3] but that he gives purges of too weak operation ? for hyssop, God knows,

---

[1] Mal. iii. 10: "Prove me now herewith, saith the LORD of hosts, if I will not open the windows of heaven, and pour you out a blessing, that *there shall not be room* enough to *receive it.*'   [2] Lev. xiv. 4: "Then shall the priest command to take for him that is to be cleansed two birds alive *and* clean, and cedar wood, and scarlet, and hyssop."   [3] Ezek. xxiv. 13.

is but a weak purger; it scarce reacheth to amend the errors of the first digestion;[1] and how then is it possible it should ever be able to purge away my sins, which have tainted my blood, and are grown, as it were, a part of my very substance? But is it not that God's arm is of a strange strength, and can put force into the weakest instruments, and therefore can do more with hyssop than all the world besides can do with hellebore? But it is indeed the great love, or rather indulgence of God, that he will never use hellebore where hyssop will serve; never use roughness and severity where lenity and mildness may be effectual. Reserve, then, O God, thy hellebore and thy scammony for more stubborn and reluctant humours; purge me with hyssop only, and I shall be clean. I must confess I was glad at heart when I first heard hyssop spoken of, to think I should be purged so gently, and with a thing that may so easily be had; for hyssop grows in every garden; and then I thought I might go fetch it thence and purge myself; but now I perceive this is not the hyssop of which Solomon writ, when he writ from the cedar to the hyssop, but this hyssop is rather the herb grace,[2] which never grew in garden but in that of Paradise, and which none can fetch thence unless God himself deliver it. The truth is, this hyssop was sometime a cedar; the highest of all trees became the lowest of all shrubs, only to be made this hyssop for us; for Christ indeed is the true hyssop, and his blood the juice of hyssop, that only can purge away my sins, that I need not now fear the weakness of God's purge, seeing this hyssop far exceeds, not only hellebore and scammony, but all the strongest drugs that ever the earth brought forth. Purge me, then, O God, with this true hyssop, and I shall be truly clean: wash me, and I shall be whiter than snow. But how is this possible? All

---

[1] Errors affecting the stomach, for digestion is "the decoction of the aliment in the stomach, or the dissolution of it, by which it is turned into chyle;" whereas "chymus" is defined as "any kind of juice; that especially of meat after the second digestion; this, mixing itself with the blood, runs through veins, repairing the waste of every part."—(Bailey's Dict.)   [2] 1 Kings iv. 33: "From the cedar that *is* in Lebanon, even unto the hyssop that springeth out of the wall." See Hamlet iv. 5: "There's *rue* for you; and here's some for me: we may call it herb of grace o' Sundays: you may wear your *rue* with a difference." For the word is equivocal, and means either repentance or the medicinal herb.

the dyers upon earth cannot dye a red into a white; and how then is it possible that my sins, which are as red as scarlet, should ever be made as white as snow?[1] Indeed, such retrogradation is no work of human art; it must be only his doing who brought the sun ten degrees back in the dial of Ahaz;[2] for God hath a nitre[3] of grace that can bring not only the redness of scarlet sins, but even the blackness of deadly sins, into its native purity and whiteness again.

But say it be possible, yet what need is there of so great a whiteness as to be whiter than snow? seeing snow is not as *paries dealbatus*, a painted wall, white without and foul within; but it is white, *intus et in cute*, within and without, throughout and all over; and what eye so curious[4] but such a whiteness may content? yet such a whiteness will not serve, for I may be as white as snow, and yet continue a leper still; as it is said of Gehazi that he went out from Elisha a leper as white as snow.[5] It must be therefore whiter than snow; and such a whiteness it is that God's washing works upon us, makes within us; for no snow is so white in the eyes of men as a soul cleansed from sin is in the sight of God. And yet a whiter whiteness than this too; for being purged from sin we shall *induere stolam albam*,[6] put on the white robe; and this is a whiteness as much whiter than snow as angelical whiteness is more than elementar.[7]

But may we not conceive rather that in saying, Purge me with hyssop, it is not meant *purgando* [by medical purgation], but *aspergendo* [by sprinkling or lustration], that so there may be two degrees expressed of using the juice of this hyssop,—one, when it is but a sprinkling only, yet enough to take away the foulness of sin; another, when it is a full and thorough washing, which, besides the cleanness, adds also a beauty, and that to admiration? Indeed, the least drop of Christ's blood, the true juice of this hyssop, makes fit to stand in the congregation of the righteous; but a full bath of it gives a high degree in the hierarchy of

---

[1] Isa. i. 18. [2] 2 Kings xx. 11. [3] Natron, an impure soda-carbonate, of great cleansing power; cf. Jer. ii. 22. [4] Inquiring and exacting. [5] 2 Kings v. 27. [6] Rev. iii. 5: "He that overcometh, the same shall be clothed in white raiment." [7] Elemental.

saints and angels. Howsoever, we may plainly see a great difference between the washing that was spoken of before and the washing that is spoken of here ; as great a difference as between cleanness and whiteness ; for that washing was to cleanse us, but this washing is to whiten us. Of that it was said, Wash me, and I shall be clean ; but of this it is said, Wash me, and I shall be whiter than snow ; and therefore upon this it presently follows, and very justly, *Make me to hear* [of] *joy and gladness ; that the bones which thou hast broken may rejoice* [**ver. 8**]. For white is the emblem of joy ; and where the emblem of whiteness is once had, the motto[1] of joy and gladness will not long be behind. But we must be whited first ; for while the blackness of sin remains in the soul, there can be no emblem of whiteness engraven upon it ; but if once we be whited by God's washing, and have the emblem upon us, this motto, we may be sure, will be added to the emblem. He will make us hear of joy and gladness. And the like may be seen in the kindly order of God's physic—first a purge, and then a cordial. Having purged us with hyssop, he will make us to hear of joy and gladness ; but we must be purged first ; for while the peccant[3] humours remain in the soul there is no place fit for the cordial of joy ; but if the humours be purged by the hyssop of repentance, then the heart will be lightened and the spirits refreshed, and the cordial of joy and gladness will have its full operation.

But had David ever any return of this petition? Did God ever hear it, or grant it? Oh, the wonderful graciousness of God ! He heard it, and granted it ; made a return, and that presently, and by a sure mouth—the mouth of the prophet Nathan. Behold, God hath forgiven thy sin ;[2] for this, no doubt, was the joy which David here makes suit to hear of, for what joy of what jubilee can make the broken bones rejoice, but this only, that we be at peace with God through the remission of our sins? David was happy that had a Nathan by whom to hear it ; but by whom may we

---

[1] A word or short sentence put to an emblem or device, on the coat of arms of nobility and gentry. (Bailey's Dict.) [3] Injurious. [2] 2 Sam. xii. 13 : "The Lord also hath put away thy sin."

hope to hear it? Indeed, [we are] as happy in this as David; for though we have not the same Nathan *in individuo* [in person], yet we may truly say we have him *in specie* [in equivalent form]; and the same message of joy which that Nathan told to David, our Nathans tell us, when they say, He pardoneth and absolveth all them which truly repent, and unfeignedly believe his holy gospel;[1] which though we hear, perhaps, as words of course, yet it is the very same joy which David here makes such earnest suit to hear of.

But why should David pray to God to make him hear of joy and gladness, and not rather do as his son Solomon did afterward, gather gold and silver, get him men-singers and women-singers,[2] and so make joy and gladness to himself? Alas, my soul! these are joys to be repented of, and not joys to repentance; for but for such delights as these, I had never fallen into these sorrows; they have been my snares, and cannot now be comforts: it is not all the delights and pleasures of the world that can ease one pang of a penitent heart. The sorrows are spiritual, and must have spiritual joys. Thou, O God, hast caused the sorrows, and thou only canst minister the comforts.

Qui vulnera fecit,
Solus Achilleo tollere more potest.
[He only can, Achilles-like, heal, who caused the wounds.]

But say, O my soul, how came thy bones to be broken? Hath this been the work of God's hyssop? Is the breaking of bones the gentle purging that was talked of? What could hellebore or scammony have done more? And yet thou canst not wonder so much at the force of God's purging to break thy bones, as thou mayest wonder at the force of his cordial to make thy broken bones rejoice; and that which thou mayest wonder at more, the same hyssop is both the cordial and the purge. Wonderful indeed, that the same thing should both break the bones and make the broken bones rejoice; yet so it is, for this hyssop is not only

---

[1] Quotation from the "Absolution" in the Book of Common Prayer.   [2] Eccl. ii. 8.

a cleanser, but a knitter and binder together; and as by the force of cleansing it breaks the bones, so by the virtue of knitting together it makes the broken bones rejoice; for what greater joy to broken bones than to be knit together and made whole again? It was not I, God knows, that broke my bones; I could never have had the heart to do it. It is thou, O God, didst break them, and that in mercy; for thou knewest that unless my bones were broken, my sin that is bred in the bone could never be thoroughly purged away. And now, O God, if I be not purged enough already, purge me yet more, and purge me still, until I be made more white than snow; but then make me to hear of joy and gladness, for without this cordial I shall faint in my purging, and shall never be able to go through with thy course of physic, for my bones are already broken, and I have scarce any blood left me in my veins; but if thou give me this cordial of joy and gladness, my strength will return, and my broken bones will be made whole again.

But why is it said, Make me to hear of joy and gladness; and not said rather, Make me to feel joy and gladness? For were it not better to feel joy than only to hear of joy? But, indeed, we cannot feel this joy unless we hear it first; and if once we hear it, it is then our own fault if we do not feel it. For what is this joy but that of which the angels brought tidings to the shepherds, Behold I bring you tidings of great joy: this day is born to you a Saviour,[1] one that shall make whole again all broken bones, seeing he is one of whom there shall not a bone be broken.[2] But what is this to us, that his bones be not broken, if ours be? Great good to us, if we be purged with this hyssop, for then we shall be united and knit unto him, made flesh of his flesh and bone of his bone; that if his bones be sound, and not broken, our bones shall quickly withal recover soundness. And yet a greater joy to be heard of than this, for then indeed we shall hear of our greatest joy, when we shall hear this voice, Arise, thou that sleepest, and stand up, and God shall give

---

[1] Luke ii. 10, 11: "Behold, I bring you good tidings of great joy, which shall be to all people. For unto you is born this day in the city of David a Saviour, which is Christ the Lord." [2] John xix. 36; Ps. xxxiv. 20.

thee light;[1] for at the hearing of this voice, all bones, though broken into a thousand pieces, though burnt, or beaten to dust and ashes, shall all come together and be knit together, and shall be covered again with this very flesh;[2] and in this flesh I shall see my Redeemer.[3] And now, O my soul, thou mayest comfort thyself in hope that, though thy bones be broken now, yet a time will come when they shall rejoice, and should never indeed rejoice if they were not now broken; for this is a world for breaking of bones; but we look for a new heaven and a new earth,[4] when for their breaking now they shall have beauty for ashes, and a garment of gladness for the spirit of heaviness.[5]

But, O merciful God, put me not off so long for my joy; my broken bones will be in a worse case than Lazarus's body was after four days' burying,[6] if thou let me lie so long in the grave of thy displeasure. My case requires a present remedy, and a remedy may be applied in the turning of a hand, at least, with the turning of a face. Only turn away thy face from my sins[7] [**ver. 9**], and my broken bones will quickly rejoice; for to turn away thy face from my sins is to turn away thine anger for my sins; and to turn away thine anger is to receive me into grace; and if of this I might be once assured, it would make my broken bones more nimble to leap for joy than Abraham was to see thy day;[8] for as it was the apprehension of thine anger that broke my bones, so nothing can set them together, and put them in joint again, until I be secured of thy grace and favour.

But am I well advised in praying God to turn away his face from my sins? for am I not so wholly overspread with sin, that if he turn away his face from my sin, he must needs turn it away from me too; and then in what horror of darkness should I be left? But is it not that thy wisdom, O God, is so transcendent that thou canst easily abstract the sinner from the sin; and then the more thou turnest thy

---

[1] Eph. v. 14: "Awake, thou that sleepest, and arise from the dead, and Christ shall give thee light." [2] Cf. Ezek. xxxvii. 1—10, the vision of dry bones. [3] Job xix. 26: "In my flesh shall I see God." [4] 2 Pet. iii. 13. [5] Isa. lxi. 3: "To give them beauty for ashes, the oil of joy for mourning, the garment of praise for the spirit of heaviness." [6] John xi. 39. [7] Ps. li. 9: "Hide thy face from my sins, and blot out all mine iniquities." (A.V.) [8] John viii. 56.

face from my sin, the more thou wilt turn thy face upon me, and the more I shall enjoy the light of thy countenance?[1] If thou shouldst not turn away thy face from my sin, but stand looking upon it, alas, O God, it would be a worse sight than that which Ham saw in his father's nakedness; and a good son turned away his face from that,[2] and canst thou be a good Father, and not turn away thy face from this? God forbid, thou shouldst ever say to me, as thou didst once to our first parent, Adam, Where art thou?[3] a question that was never asked but when it was followed with a curse. For why shouldst thou ask where I am, but that thou canst not see where I am? and how can it be thou shouldst not see where I am, but that thou canst not see me for sin? Use then, O God, the transcendency of thy wisdom, abstract me from my sin, and make my sin and me two several objects, that, turning thy face from my sin, thou mayest turn it upon me, and not need to ask me where I am, but mayest see me where I am, and by seeing me make me enjoy the light of thy countenance.

But is my sin so pleasing a prospect that I should need to fear lest God should stand looking upon it? Indeed, after his first creation, he looked upon all his creatures, and saw them all exceeding good,[4] and this was a prospect worth his looking on. But my sins, O God, are none of thy creatures; there is no goodness at all to be seen in them; therefore, look not upon my sins, but upon my repentance, and in this thou shalt find *veteris vestigia formæ* [some traces of the pristine beauty], that thou needst not to alter thy style, but say still, It is exceeding good. But seeing, if thou turn away thy face from my sin, thou must needs turn it upon something else, upon what is it indeed I would have thee to turn it? Upon me? No. Upon my repentance? Neither. But though not upon my sins, yet upon him that hath taken my sins upon him, that as in him thou art well pleased,[5] so through him thou mayest be well pleased with me, and with my repentance.

But what safety is it to me that God turn away his face if

---

[1] Ps. iv. 6.   [2] Gen. ix. 22, 23.   [3] Gen. iii. 9.   [4] Gen. i. 31.   [5] Matt. iii. 17.

his ears stand open? for my sins are crying sins, and it may be as hurtful to me that God hear their cry as see their foulness. For what brought Cain to all his misery but that God heard the cry of his sin?[1] But know, O my soul, that God consists not of parts, though our weak capacities express him so; and if we express him by parts, know also there is an absolute and sweet harmony between them in God, that if his face be turned away from seeing the foulness of our sins, his ears shall never stand open to let in their crying.

But what am I the better that thou turn away thy face from my sin, if my sin continue and remain upon me still? For is it not the bold nature of sin to be always pressing into thy sight, and as it were forcing thee to see it, whether thou wilt or no? Oh, therefore, not only turn away thy face from my sins, but blot my sins out, that as by turning away thy face thou mayest not see my sins, so by blotting them out I may have no sins to be seen. But if God turn away his face from my sins, how shall he see to blot them out? Not, therefore, *faciem cognitionis*, but *faciem indignationis*,— not his face with which he sees all things, but his face with which he frowns upon evil things.

But are not my sins themselves blots? and how can blots be blotted out? They are blots indeed upon my soul, but they are fair characters[2] in God's book; and there is a relation between God's book and my soul, that if they be blotted out in his book, they shall never be legible in my soul.

But, O gracious God, I dare not trust to this neither; for though by blotting them out they may be made not legible, yet the very blotting them out will be a mark of remembrance that they were once there; and is it not a fearful thing to think thou shouldst but once remember them? Oh, therefore, not only blot my sins out, but *create in me a clean heart*[3] [**ver. 10**], that as by blotting them out they may be made not legible, so by creating in me a clean heart there may be no

---

[1] Gen. iv. 10.   [2] They are clearly expressed, distinctly written down.   [3] Ps. li. 10: "Create in me a clean heart, O God, and renew a right spirit within me." (A.V.)

mark of remembrance that ever they were written. Indeed, this blotting out of sins is but an ablative case [1] in the work of sanctification; the dative is of much more use, for this dative [2] is the giving me a new heart; and seeing the heart is the beginning of life, by having a new heart I shall begin a new life, and the sins of my old heart shall be no more remembered.

O great God, into how many several forms of assistance do we miserable sinners diversify thy glorious majesty? We made thee first our Launderer,[3] to wash us; then our Physician, to purge us; and now our Creator, to new make us;[4] and indeed there was no staying till we came hither. Our dove can find no rest for the sole of her foot till she return into this ark again;[5] for if my sin were only a foulness, it might be helped with washing; or if only a staining, it might be helped with purging; but seeing it is a total and absolute corruption, now nothing can help it but a new creation.

But how should David come to be so foul? Was it by conversing with Bathsheba?[6] But what foulness could he take from her, who came but then newly out of her bath?[7] O my soul, it is not a bath of milk and roses that can make a cleanness in God's sight. God hath strange eyes; he can see foulness in Bathsheba, though coming out of a neat[8] bath; and can see cleanness in Jeremiah, though coming out of a dirty dungeon;[9] he can see foulness upon Dives, for all his deliciousness and daintiness; and can see cleanness upon Lazarus, for all his lying amongst the dogs.[10] This David knew well, and therefore all his suit is still for cleanness: Wash me, and cleanse me from my sins; purge me with hyssop, and I shall be clean; create in me a clean heart, O God.[11] All for cleanness still; for he knew if he could get cleanness he should have a beauty which the stars want, for the stars are not clean in God's sight;[12] he knew that by having a clean heart, he should not only be fit for God to see, but fit to see God; as Christ said, Blessed are the

---

[1] A case of removal, of taking away. [2] A case of giving. [3] Masc. form of laundress. [4] Ps. li. 2, 7, 10. [5] Gen. viii. 9. [6] See title of this Psalm. [7] 2 Sam. xi. 2, 4. [8] Clean. [9] Jer. xxxviii. 6. [10] Luke xvi. 19, etc. [11] Ps. li. 2, 7, 10. [12] Job xv. 15: "The heavens are not clean in his sight."

clean of heart, for they shall see God.¹ And then, if to be seen of God be the greatest glory, and to see God the greatest happiness, O how glorious and happy must a clean heart needs be that is made capable to enjoy them both!

Oh, therefore, create in me a clean heart, O God, and renew a right spirit within me; for thou hast not so finished thy work of creation but that thou retainest thy power of creating still; and wherein canst thou better employ that power than in creating of clean hearts? It was a work of infinite glory to be the Creator of heaven and earth, yet to be the Creator of clean hearts is of all thy works of glory the most glorious work. And, indeed, were it not better for me, and more ease for God, to create in me a clean heart once for all than to be so troubled with continual purgings and washings, as now he is, as now I am? for alas, O Lord, thou mayest sooner purge my heart out of my body than purge sin out of my heart, but that it will always be returning to its vomit,² and I shall break thy rest continually with importuning thee to wash me.

But why do I pray to God for a clean heart, and not as well for clean eyes and clean hands, seeing these also have their share in foulness as well as that? But is it not that these are but the emissaries of the heart, and do all they do by the heart's direction; that if the heart be clean, these also will be clean of course; mine eyes will be clean, and never look more after any more Bathshebas; my hands will be clean, and never be more imbrued in the blood of any Uriahs.³

But did not God create in me a clean heart once already? And yet how foul is it grown now? And what hope is there if he create in me a new clean heart, but that it will grow as foul as this I now have? But can it properly be said that God did ever create in me a clean heart before? He *made* me one indeed, but he *created* me none; he only created heaven and earth, as it is said, In the beginning God created heaven and earth,⁴ and of that earth he made me a body,⁵

---

¹ Matt. v. 8: "Blessed *are* the pure in heart," etc.   ² 2 Pet. ii. 22.   ³ 2 Sam. xi. 2, 14—17.   ⁴ Gen. i. 1.   ⁵ Gen. i. 26: "Let us make man." Gen. ii. 7: "The LORD God formed man *of* the dust of the ground," but see Gen. i. 27: "So God created man."

and in that body a heart; so I had a made heart before, but not a created heart till now; for made is of matter pre-existent, but created is of nothing: although therefore my made heart, being made of dust, hath always been apt to gather dust, yet my created heart, as made of nothing, will have nothing in it from whence to gather foulness. But, O my soul, trust not to this; for though there should be no foulness in the heart itself, yet the stink of the prison in which it lies will be always cause enough to breed infection, unless thou canst get some such sovereign perfume that may keep [from harming us] our ill airs and keep the place sweet. Oh, therefore, not only create in me a clean heart, but renew a right spirit within me; for this right spirit makes a better perfume than that of Tobias's fish,[1] to keep all unclean spirits from coming near the heart. As therefore Moses described the genesis of man by saying that God first made him a body, and then breathed a soul into him,[2] so David describes here the *palingenesis* [regeneration or new creation] of man by saying, Create in me a clean heart, and renew a right spirit within me; that if Nicodemus had well understood this Psalm of David, he needed not to have made such a wonder at Christ's speech, when he said, Except a man be born again, he cannot enter into the kingdom of heaven;[3] for what is it to be regenerate and born again but to have a clean heart created, and a right spirit renewed in us? If only a clean heart be created, and not withal a right spirit renewed within me, this will be but *vehiculum sine auriga* [a chariot with no driver]; and I shall presently fall into the mire of sin again, and grow as foul as ever I was before; but if thou vouchsafe to add a right spirit to my clean heart, this will keep me right in the paths of righteousness; and then, as I now praise thee for making me clean, so shall I praise thee as much, or rather much more, for keeping me clean.

Thou, O God, that art the Maker, art also the Renewer of all things, yet I ask thee for renewing of nothing in me, but only a right spirit: my years are waxed old, and vanished away

---

[1] Tobit vi. and viii.   [2] Gen. ii. 7.   [3] John iii. 3: "Except a man be born again, he cannot see the kingdom of God;" and ver. 5: "Except a man be born of water and *of* the Spirit, he cannot enter into the kingdom of God."

as a smoke,[1] yet I require thee not to renew them; my strength is dried up like a potsherd,[2] and my moisture is turned into the drought of summer,[3] yet I require thee not to renew them; all my worldly friends are either taken from me or gone from me, yet I require thee not to renew them; all that I require thee to renew to me is only a right spirit, for so long as this right spirit remained with me and was my guide, I walked before thee in all uprightness; I durst then say, Search me, O God, and try me; examine my heart and my reins;[4] but as soon as this spirit grew to decay and waxed faint within me, I presently begun to falter in my steps; my iniquities multiplied so fast that they quickly grew to be more than the hairs of my head;[5] everything was a temptation unto me, and every temptation prevailed against me; but now, O God, renew a right spirit within me, and this right spirit will set all right that is amiss in me, because it is a right spirit; will renew and quicken all that is dead and dull within me, because it is all spirit.

But what more good will a right spirit do when it is renewed, than it did before, when it was first given? If it prospered not at the first planting, what assurance of prospering at the second? But is it not that a right spirit in a created heart may stand firm, though in a made heart it gave ground and failed? and specially when it is a right spirit renewed, seeing renovation is always with addition of strength, and no part of a house is commonly so strong as that part is which is newly repaired. *Secundæ cogitationes* are *sapientiores*, and *secundi conatus* are *fortiores* [Second thoughts are wiser and second efforts stronger]. Though once going about Jericho did the walls no hurt, yet the going about them again and again made them fall to the ground;[6] though one cock crowing wrought nothing upon Peter, yet the second time's crowing made him weep bitterly.[7] Oh, then, renew in me a right spirit, O God, and the walls of my sinful Jericho will fall to the ground, the stupor of my dull brains will resolve into tears.

---

[1] Ps. cii. 3: "For my days are consumed like smoke." [2] Ps. xxii. 15. [3] Ps. xxxii. 4. [4] Ps. cxxxix. 23: "Search me, O God, and know my heart: try me, and know my thoughts." [5] Ps. xl. 12: "Mine iniquities . . . are more than the hairs of my head." [6] Josh. vi. 12—20. [7] Mark xiv. 30, 68, 72.

When sin seeks to enter, and to get entertainment with us, it makes us believe we shall be like gods;[1] but when it is once entered, and hath gotten possession, it leaves us to find we are not so much as fit for God's company; and it seems as though we were put to our choice here, whether we will have sin's company or God's, for both we cannot have: if entertain sin, then we must take our leave of God; if enjoy God's presence, then we must give no entertainment to sin: a hard choice to flesh and blood, but a right spirit resolves it presently. Cast me not off from thy presence, O God [2] [**ver. 11**]; let me enjoy that; and as for sin, I utterly renounce it, though it should present itself to me in greater pomp than Solomon clothed in all his royalty.[3] I had rather live one day in thy courts,[4] to enjoy thy presence, than to live accounted the son of Pharaoh's daughter,[5] and Methuselah's age,[6] in all the pleasures of the world. Do we see how the presence of the sun cheers up the air, makes glad the earth, and enlightens the whole world, and can we not see the wonderful effects of comfort which are wrought in the soul by the presence of God, in comparison of whom the sun is not so much as a mote in the sun? If it be thy pleasure, O God, to withdraw thy presence from me, to make me sensible of my weakness, yet cast me not off from thy presence in displeasure, to make me despair of thy love. If thou wilt needs put a veil upon thy face, to keep mine eyes from seeing thee, yet let it be but as the veil upon Moses' face, to keep mine eyes from dazzling.[7] It is potion bitter enough to be deprived of thy presence, though done in never so fair a manner; but to be cast out of thy presence, as done in anger, what is this but to give me gall and wormwood to drink? If I needs must die, let it be on the top of Nebo, where I may see the land of Canaan before me,[8] for there thy presence is to comfort me; but let it not be in the valley, where there is no representation of thy glorious presence to give me comfort. My sin, O God, I know is

---

[1] Gen. iii. 5. [2] Ps. li. 11: "Cast me not away from thy presence, and take not thy holy spirit from me." (A.V.) [3] Matt. vi. 29: "Solomon in all his glory." [4] Ps. lxxxiv. 10. [5] Heb. xi. 24. [6] Gen. v. 27. [7] Exod. xxxiv. 30, 33. [8] Deut. xxxiv. 1—5.

such that may justly make me to fly from thy presence, as it once made Adam, when he hid himself from thee;[1] yet in this case I may hope thou wilt look after me, as thou didst then vouchsafe to look after him; but if thou cast me out of thy presence, and that it be done by thine own hand, alas, O Lord! what hope is there left me of ever coming into thy presence again? As long as I am in thy presence, there is hope; I may entreat, and thou art apt to be entreated; I may fall down and humble myself, and thou givest grace to the humble;[2] but if it should once come to this, that I were cast out of thy presence, alas, O God! thou wouldst then be quite out of sight, clean out of hearing, that no entreaty could be heard, no humbling be seen, either to give me the comfort of hope, or to put me in hope of any comfort. If thou, O God, shouldst cast me off from thy presence, whom could I hope to have present with me? The angels would be my guardians no longer, for they would soon take notice of thy displeasure, and would never regard [one] whom thou rejectest. The saints would be my associates no longer, for if they found me not in thy presence they would perfectly know I was none of their society, and their communion extends no further. And what company then could I hope to have? Cain, perhaps, and Ham, the damned crew, miserable comforters,[3] or rather no comforters, but augmenters of my misery. But yet, O God, if my sins unexpressible have made thee inexorable, and that thou wilt needs cast me off from thy presence, at least take not thy Holy Spirit from me; for what were this but to put me out of thy service, and then to take away thy livery too? Yet as long as I have thy livery on, it keeps me in credit, it gives me countenance, it leaves me hope I may be entertained again; as long as thy Holy Spirit stays with me, I have one to comfort me, one to put me in hope I may be received into favour again; in no worse case than Pharaoh's butler was, who, in disgrace for a time, was afterwards restored to his former place;[4] but if thou take thy livery from me, if thou take thy Holy Spirit from me, alas, O Lord! I am then

---

[1] Gen. iii. 8.   [2] Jas. iv. 6.   [3] Job xvi. 2.   [4] Gen. xl. 13.

utterly undone; none left to comfort me; none to speak for me; in as ill a case as Pharaoh's baker,—nothing left me to hope in but a dream, and that dream nothing but of white baskets, out of which the birds shall eat, but nothing that is good for me to taste.[1] If thy Holy Spirit should of himself depart from me, it would be a parting exceeding grievous unto me; but for thee, O God, to take him from me, where the manner of losing is as much as the loss, what grief can be spoken of so unspeakable?

But having said, Cast me not off from thy presence, it may seem superfluous to say, Take not thy Holy Spirit from me; seeing this of necessity follows upon that; for how can God's Holy Spirit be but where he is himself? and how can it tarry with me, if I tarry not with him? They both indeed grow upon one tree, yet are several fruits. God's presence brings with it a passive influence, his Holy Spirit an active; although therefore, O God, thou bar me of thy presence, and leave me inglorious,[2] yet take not away thy Holy Spirit from me, to leave me profane. Thy Holy Spirit is the Sanctifier,[3] and wilt thou leave me to impiety and profaneness? Thy Holy Spirit is the Director,[4] and wilt thou leave me without a guide in the dangerous passages of this wicked world? Thy Holy Spirit is the Comforter, and wilt thou leave me disconsolate[5] in my manifold miseries? If thou take thy Holy Spirit from me, what spirit will be left me but a spirit of error, a spirit of uncleanness, a spirit of despair? and canst thou for pity leave me a prey to such outrageous spirits? O Lord, though my sins be as great as Cain's, yet suffer me not to despair like Cain;[6] though my sins be greater than Saul's, yet suffer me not to distrust thee like Saul;[7] but as it is a benefit, so let it be a pledge of thy presence, and of thy Holy Spirit; that I can pray unto thee for thy presence, and for the continuance of thy Holy Spirit. When I remember the sweet comforts I have sometimes found in the motions of thy Holy Spirit, and when I think

---

[1] Gen. xl. 16—19. [2] 1 Sam. iv. 22: "The glory is departed from Israel: for the ark of God is taken." [3] 1 Pet. i. 2: "Through sanctification of the Spirit." [4] Rom. viii. 14: "Led by the Spirit." [5] John xiv. 16—18. [6] Gen. iv. 13. [7] 1 Sam. xxviii. 15.

of the joy I have conceived of thy salvation, oh, how my heart seems to leap within me, and how am I ravished with ecstasies of delight? And now to think this comfort should be taken from me, this joy should be bereft me,—oh, what torment, what death, what hell can be so grievous!

But how can God cast me off from his presence, though he would? Is not God everywhere? and am not I somewhere? and must I not, then, needs be where he is, and in his presence? God indeed hath a presence of being, and this is everywhere; and he hath a presence of power, and this is everywhere; but he hath a presence of grace and favour, and this is not everywhere. His presence of power is as well in the ant as in the elephant; yet it maketh not the ant an elephant; and therefore this is not the presence that I desire. His presence of being is as well in hell as in heaven;[1] yet it makes not the hell a heaven; and therefore neither is this the presence that I desire: but his presence of grace and favour is not as well in the wicked as in the penitent; for if it were, it would make the wicked penitent; and therefore this is the presence which I so much long to keep, which I so much fear to lose.

But why should I fear lest God should cast me off from his presence? Is not his delight amongst the children of men?[2] and am not I one of that generation? And why should I fear lest he should take his Holy Spirit from me? Was it not he that gave it me at first? and is he one that will give a thing and then take it away again? Yet my sins make me that I cannot but fear; for why should he not cast me out of his sight, who have wrought so much wickedness in his sight? why should he let his Holy Spirit stay there, where it is so much grieved? for what do my grievous sins but grieve it? Oh, vile sin, of what cause thou art the effect, I know not; but this I know, thou art the cause of most vile effects, for thou only art the cause that God is like to cast me off from his presence; thou only the cause that God is like to take his Holy Spirit from me; and, seeing in God's presence there is fulness of joy for evermore, alas, in being cast out

---

[1] Ps. cxxxix. 8. [2] Prov. viii. 31.

of his presence, what is left me but the fulness of misery for evermore!

But seeing thou hast not cast me off from thy presence, but only removed thy presence from me, because thy pure nature could not endure to stay in a polluted heart; yet now that I am new made, and that thou hast created a clean heart within me,—now thou mayest return, and restore to me the comfort of thy presence, the joy of thy salvation; and by this thou shalt show thou didst not take it away to keep it away, but to make it more precious in restoring; thou shalt show thou didst not leave me to forsake me, but to make thyself more welcome in returning. But though some things are of such condition that we find their goodness more by wanting than by enjoying, as sickness makes us more sensible of health, yet this needed not in the comfort of thy presence, seeing of this there can be no satiety, and we can never so well learn to desire thee by wanting thee as we are taught to embrace thee by enjoying thee.

Although the suits I make to thee, O God, be many, yet they are all so subordinate to one another, that if thou deniest me one, it were as good for me thou shouldst deny them all; for what good will it do me to have a clean heart created in me, and thy blessed presence removed from me? what good to have a right spirit renewed, and thy Holy Spirit to be taken away, as if thou shouldst supply me with props, and take away foundations? The fear of this, lest thou shouldst cast me out of thy presence, and take thy Holy Spirit from me, hath so deeply wrought upon me, and brought me so low, that I find no physic now so necessary for me as a restorative. Oh, therefore, Restore to me the joy of thy salvation[1] [**ver. 12**]; for this restorative exceeds not only all the simples of nature, but all the compounds of art, for what alchermes,[2] what gellies,[3] what *aurum potabile* [drink-

---

[1] Ps. li. 12: "Restore unto me the joy of thy salvation; and uphold me *with thy free spirit.*" (A.V.) [2] Or alkermes, "a confection made of certain red or scarlet grains, called kermes." (Bailey's Dict.) This kermes (akin to the cochineal insect) is defined as "the grain of the scarlet oak." (Bailey). [3] Or jellies, "liquor of meat, etc., boiled to a thick consistence." (Bailey's Dict.)

able gold],[1] can be comparable to this restorative, the joy of thy salvation? But had not this been a fitter suit for Nebuchadnezzar, from whom God took away at once his sense, his reason, and his kingdom,[2] than for David, from whom God never took anything that we know of, but only his child begotten in adultery?[3] Yet David will hardly be drawn to think so, for hear the moan he makes: Alas, O Lord! I live now, as it were, cast out of thy presence, which is more to me than for Nebuchadnezzar to be cast out of his kingdom. I feed now upon the bread of sorrow, which is more to me than for Nebuchadnezzar to feed upon the grass of the earth; I sit now as a sparrow upon the housetop,[4] desolate and disconsolate, which is more to me than for Nebuchadnezzar to have no companions but the beasts of the field; and yet, O Lord, only restore to me the joy of thy salvation, and it shall be more to me than for Nebuchadnezzar to be restored to his sense, his reason, his kingdom again. This joy is to me as Isaac was to Abraham,[5] the whole comfort of my life; and thou restoredst him to his father in great compassion, and wilt thou have no compassion on me, and not restore my Isaac to me again? O merciful God, take away my goods, take away my health, take away my life, but take not away this joy from me, unless thou mean to restore it again; for without this joy my goods will do me no good, I shall be sick of my health, I shall be weary of my life; all joy without this joy is but a shadow of joy—no solidness, no substance in it. Other joys I can want,[6] and yet want[7] no joy; but how can I want the joy of thy salvation but I must needs fall into the hell of my own perdition?

Indeed, all these graces, and specially these four, a right spirit, and God's presence, his Holy Spirit, and the joy of his salvation, are all, I may say, of a covey like partridges, that always keep together; or if at any time parted by violence, they never leave calling after one another till they meet

---

[1] Gold make liquid so as to be drinkable; or rather a rich cordial liquor with pieces of leaf-gold in it. (Bailey's Dict.) [2] Dan. iv. 31—33. [3] 2 Sam. xii. 15—19.
[4] Ps. cii. 7: "I watch, and am as a sparrow alone upon the housetop." [5] Gen. xxii. 11—13. [6] Be without. [7] Lack, need.

again. And thus a right spirit calls after God's presence, his presence after his Holy Spirit, his Holy Spirit after the joy of his salvation, and the joy of his salvation calls after them all. O then, Restore to me the joy of thy salvation, that this covey of thy graces may be kept together, and that the mournful voice of calling after one another may no more be heard to disquiet my soul.

But how can God restore that which he took not away? For can I charge God with the taking away the joy of his salvation from me? O gracious God, I charge not thee with taking it, but myself with losing it; and such is the miserable condition of us poor wretches, that if thou shouldst restore no more to us than what thou takest from us, we should quickly be at a fault in our estates, and our ruin would be as sudden as inevitable.

But why am I so earnest for restoring? for what good will restoring do me if I cannot keep it when I have it? and how shall I more keep it, being restored, than I kept it before being enjoyed? And if I so enjoy it as still [to] fear to lose it, what joy can there be in such enjoying? O therefore, not restore it only, but establish me with thy free Spirit, that as by thy restoring I may enjoy it entirely, so by thy establishing I may enjoy it securely. Indeed, if thou shouldst only restore it, and then leave it for me to keep, I should presently run a hazard of losing it again; but when thou restorest it, and then confirmest it, and that with the seal of thy free Spirit,[1] this gives me an indefeasible[2] estate, and absolutely frees me from fear of losing it any more for ever. Alas, my soul, what qualms have these been? what floatings between fear and hope? All the comfort is that as hope sets out first, and gets the start of fear, so it keeps the field last, and gets the goal from fear. For hope, setting out by God's renewing a right spirit, and then disturbed by fear lest he should take away his Holy Spirit, gets the victory at last by being established with God's free Spirit; for this establishing fixeth our floating, and frees us from having these qualms of

---

[1] Eph. i. 13, 14: "Ye were sealed with that holy Spirit of promise, which is the earnest of our inheritance," etc. [2] That cannot be defeated or made void (Bailey's Dict.)

fear and hope any more. Not that we can ever be free where they are, but that they should be where we are; not fear, because in a haven; not hope, because in possession.

But what mystery is it that David intends here by his triplicity of spirits—a right spirit, a holy spirit, a free and principal[1] spirit? Are they not all one Holy Ghost, but divers operations,—called, therefore, the right Spirit, because it directeth us; the holy Spirit, because it sanctifieth us; the free and principal Spirit, because it governs us? And thus understood, we may see from whence the collect in our Liturgy was gathered, which saith, Direct, sanctify, and govern us in the ways of thy laws, and in the works of thy commandments.[2] Or is it that he makes three suits for three spirits, as intending[3] to every person in the Deity; one intimating the second person by the right Spirit, as being the way and the truth;[4] the third person by the Holy Spirit, as being the author of sanctification;[5] the first person by the free and principal Spirit, it being he that must say, *Fiat* [let there be[6]], to all that is done? And thus understood, we may see from whence is framed that versicle in our Litany which saith, "O holy, blessed, and glorious Trinity, three Persons and one God, have mercy upon us miserable sinners."

And now is David *montepotitus* [one who has scaled a mountain], gotten up, I may say, to the top of Mount Gerizim,[7] after many wearisome and painful steps. He was indeed so oppressed with the burden, and so fettered with the chain of his sins, that he seemed as a man distracted, not knowing in the world what course to take; yet not willing to be wanting to himself, he tries all the ways and useth all the means he can possibly devise or think of. First, he prays God to wash him from his sins; and lest washing should not be sufficient, he prays next to be purged from his sins; but not trusting to these outward means, he thinks upon a new course, and prays to have

---

[1] The Vulgate has "principali spiritu," with thy principal or governing spirit.
[2] After the Offertory in the "Order of the Administration of the Lord's Supper or Holy Communion." [3] Directing attention. [4] John xiv. 6: "I am the way, the truth, and the life." [5] 1 Pet. i. 2: "Through sanctification of the Spirit."
[6] Gen. i. 3, 6, 14. [7] The mountain of blessings, see Deut. xi. 9.

his sins blotted out, as much as to have God's debt-book crossed; yet not satisfied with this neither, he then flies to inward means, and prays not only to have a clean heart created, but a right spirit renewed in him, that so he may be *purus corpore et spiritu* [pure in body and spirit]; and now one would think he were certainly past all danger yet even here he falls into the most dismal frights that ever seized upon a perplexed soul, for he fears lest God should cast him off from his presence, and lest he should take his Holy Spirit from him,—most dismal frights indeed; yet recovering his spirits, he bethinks himself at last of a way that either will serve to make him a free man, or he must never look to be; and that is, to be established with God's free Spirit, and this indeed strikes the stroke, and therefore this he makes his *murus aheneus* [wall of brass], for being now established with God's free Spirit, he finds himself so free, that he thinks himself able to set up a free school, and is confident to say, *Then will I teach thy ways to the wicked, and sinners shall be converted unto thee*[1] [**ver. 13**]. Then if thou say unto me, *Et tu conversus, converte fratres* [And thou, when thou art converted, convert thy brethren],[2] I shall do it, both boldly and effectually: boldly, for I shall teach thy ways to the wicked, who are but unruly scholars; and effectually, for sinners shall be converted unto thee, which is the end of all schooling. And then, if the angels give a *plaudite* [a clapping of hands] to their conversion, I doubt not, O God, but thou also wilt graciously accept the humble service of the converter, and even thyself shalt receive a benefit in thy glory, by the benefit which I receive by thy pardon; for as there have been many scandalled[3] by my sin, so there shall be many reclaimed by my repentance; and they who loved thee not for thy justice, shall fear thee for thy mercy; and they who feared thee not for thy mercy, shall love thee for thy justice, and thy name shall be great amongst all nations.[4] O happy conversion

---

[1] Ps. li. 13: "*Then* will I teach transgressors thy ways; and sinners shall be converted unto thee." (A.V.) [2] Luke xxii. 32: "When thou art converted, strengthen thy brethren." [3] Scandalized, caused to stumble. [4] Jer. xxxiii. 9: "A name of joy, a praise and an honour before all the nations of the earth."

that is not barren, and ends in itself, which was a curse in Israel; but, as a fruitful mother, continues a race of conversions, and shall therefore make the converter shine in heaven, as a star of the greater magnitude.[1]

But am I a fit man to teach thy ways to the wicked, who have walked all my life long in the ways of wickedness? Am I likely to be a means for converting of sinners, who have hitherto been occasion of perverting the godly? Thou, O God, that tookest Amos from among the herdmen of Tekoa,[2] to make him a prophet, thou also canst take me from among the wicked of the world, to make me a converter of sinners. I take not upon me to teach the godly, who may better teach me; I teach only the wicked. None but sinners are for my school; I am not a shepherd to tend the fold, but to fetch in strayers. The title of my profession is *dux conversorum*, a guide of converts: all my doctrine is only repentance; and if any such be that need no repenting, they need not my teaching, nor belong to my school. But if any man think repentance a lesson so easy that he can take it out and learn it without a teacher, let him but hear the lesson read which I have learned, and [which] he must if he will be a convert. Let him see my eyes swollen with the floods of my tears, and so must his be; let him see me lie grovelling under sackcloth and ashes, and so must he do; let him see my knees brawned with kneeling at prayer, and so must his be; let him see me go fasting with bread and water, and so must he do; let him see my back gored with stripes of contrition, and so must his be; let him see my breast torn with sighings and groanings, and so must he do; and if all this be not enough to make a hard lesson, let him see my heart broken and shivered with sorrow, and so must his be. And now let flesh and blood tell me if this be a lesson to be learned without a teacher.

But if repentance be so hard a lesson to learn, how can David be so confident of his teaching to say that

---

[1] Dan. xii. 3: "They that be wise shall shine as the brightness of the firmament; and they that turn many to righteousness as the stars for ever and ever." [2] Amos i. 1.

sinners shall be converted by it? Indeed, when kings become schoolmasters, no marvel if sinners become converts; for who knows not the force of *regis ad exemplum* [according to the king's example]? But is David then the only phœnix[1] in this kind? Have we not amongst us at this day,—and long may we have a king like David, who though he teach not the same lesson that David did (for his lesson was only repentance), yet his whole life is a picture of piety and uprightness,—a lesson so much better than David's, as to be in the first form of virtue is far more worthy than to be but in the second?

But oh, the unquiet state of a guilty conscience! David was much troubled at first about procuring his cleanness, and now he seems as much troubled about expressing his foulness. Is it the *malus genius* [evil nature] of sin, that is never without fear, and therefore creeps into all corners? or is it the *bonus genius* [good nature] of repentance, that is never without care, and therefore searcheth all corners? David had asked God forgiveness for his iniquity, his sin, his offences, his transgressions—corners enough to meet with any sin of what kind soever; but is it enough to confess our sins and to ask forgiveness in general terms, and never to make mention of any sin in particular? Indeed, where sins be infinite, it were an infinite labour to mention them all, and with all our labour could never be done; but yet, where there are eminent sins—sins, like Saul, higher than their fellows by head and shoulders[2]—not to mention such sins were a kind of concealing them, as if we meant to hide them in the throng, that they might pass unperceived; and there must be no concealing if we look for cancelling. Behold, then, O God, an eminent sin—a sin indeed like Saul, so high above his fellows that I dare not say what it is without saying, *Deliver me* first; *Deliver me from blood-guiltiness, O God, thou God of my salvation*[3] [**ver. 14**]. And blame me not for

---

[1] "A bird in Arabia, about the bigness of an eagle, which is reported to live 600 years; and that there is but one of them in the world at a time; and that she, having lived that time, builds her a nest of combustible spices, which being set on fire by the sun, she fans it with her wings, and burns herself in it; and that a worm rises out of her ashes, which comes to be a new phœnix." (Bailey's Dict.) [2] 1 Sam. ix. 2. [3] Ps. li. 14: "Deliver me from bloodguiltiness, O God, thou God of my salvation; *and* my tongue shall sing aloud of thy righteousness."

doubling the name of God here, seeing it is a deliverance that requires a double proportion of God's assistance; for though every sin may be said a sin of blood, as whereof the wages is death,[1] yet this actual shedding of blood is a sin of the most scarlet die, and stands in need of the greatest measure of God's free Spirit to free it.

But what need David pray God to deliver him from blood-guiltiness? for what blood had he shed? Much, no doubt, in war; but that was lawful, and left no guiltiness, and therefore needed no deliverance. But what blood did he shed unlawfully? No more did Ahab, no more did Jezebel, yet as guilty of blood as if they had shed it.[2] When magistrates command a thing to be done, they do it; when a malicious person imprecates a mischief to be wrought, he works it; when a man plots a villany to be acted, he acts it; and in all these ways, though David actually shed no blood, yet he was as guilty of blood as if he had shed it. *Per alium* [through another] here is as much as *per se* [by oneself]; and therefore David knew he had cause enough to say, Deliver me from blood-guiltiness, O God.

But is there any hope that this sin of blood may ever be remitted, seeing God hath spoken it peremptorily, He that sheddeth man's blood, by man shall his blood be shed? and can I look that God will break his word to do me a pleasure? But is it not that God's threatening is ever with condition? For was it not so in Nineveh? Forty days, and Nineveh shall be destroyed.[3] Yet forty days came, and Nineveh was not destroyed.[4] Was it not so to Hezekiah? Set thine house in order, for thou shalt die of this sickness. Yet Hezekiah died not of that sickness, but lived fifteen years after.[5] I know, indeed, that the condition of God's will there, though not expressed, was yet intended. Unless they repented; but what may be the condition of his will here? No doubt repentance too, but with this codicil annexed: His blood shall be shed unless he can find some other that will shed his blood for him. And, alas, if this be the condition, what am I the nearer? For where can I find out any that

---

[1] Rom. vi. 23.   [2] 1 Kings xxi. 1—14.   [3] Jonah iii. 4: "Yet forty days and, Nineveh shall be overthrown."   [4] Jonah iii. 10.   [5] 2 Kings xx. 1—7.

will shed his blood for me? and if I could find one willing, where can I find one able? An eye for an eye, a tooth for a tooth,[1] and yet a man may live; but blood for blood, and who can live, unless he be a God? An angel cannot do it, for he hath no blood to shed; a man cannot do it, for he cannot lay down his life and take it up again; thou only canst do it, who art both God and man, thou God of my salvation; for thou art the Lamb that was slain, and is alive,[2] and I know that my Redeemer liveth.[3] And wilt thou shed thy blood for me, and not deliver me from blood? Wilt thou pay a ransom for me, and let me be a captive still? Wilt thou pay so dearly for a thing, and not take it when thou hast done? Oh deliver me from blood-guiltiness, O God, and my tongue shall sing aloud of thy righteousness.

But why should David pray to be delivered from bloods, as the words indeed are? For seeing he shed but the blood of Uriah only, the singular number might well enough have served. Is it that the plotting of Uriah's death drew with it the deaths of many others,[4] and so just cause of praying to be delivered from bloods? Or is it that the several respects of relation in Uriah made his blood as so many several bloods in God's account? One blood as of the husband of Bathsheba; another as of David's own subject; another as of an innocent person; another as of a faithful servant; another as of a silly lamb, that carried letters of his own death;[5] and (which is most of all) another as of one that was venturing his life for David. But if these several respects make so many several bloods, and every blood must have a deliverance, where shall we find a deliverer of so many respects to make so many bloods to serve for deliverance? Indeed, we may look all the world over and find none such to be found, but only thou, O God, who art the God of my salvation; for in thee alone may all the like respects be found. To answer the blood of the husband of Bathsheba, here is the blood of the husband of the Church;[6] to answer the blood of King David's subject, here is the

---

[1] Ex. xxi. 24. [2] Rev. v. 6, i. 18. [3] Job xix. 25. [4] 2 Sam. xi. 17: "There fell *some* of the people of the servants of David; and Uriah the Hittite died also." [5] 2 Sam. xi. 14, 15. [6] 2 Cor. xi. 2.

blood of the King of Heaven's subject; to answer the blood of an innocent person, here is the blood of him who only could say, Which of you could reprove me for sin?[1] to answer the blood of a faithful servant, here is the blood of him who was in the house of God more faithful than his most faithful servant Moses;[2] to answer the blood of a silly lamb, that carried letters of his own death, here is the blood of him who carried our flesh of purpose to suffer death;[3] and that (which is most of all) to answer the blood of him that was then venturing his life for David, here is the blood of him that was then shedding his blood for them that shed his blood. But seeing, by this account, we find six several bloods in Uriah's shed by David, where find we six several bloods in Christ shed by him? Indeed, just six, and no more nor less; one blood which he sweat in the garden;[4] another which he shed with the stripes of the whips;[5] another drawn from him with the pricks of the thorns;[6] another which he shed on the cross with the nails in his feet; another with the nails in his hands;[7] and the sixth which he shed out of his side with the point of the spear.[8] And now that we have bloods enough to serve for deliverance, how shall we be able to apply them? Is it not that they are all re-collected, and put into that cup of which he said, Drink ye all of this?[9] For the blood of this cup is that which washeth away our sins; that which purgeth us with hyssop; that which renews a right Spirit within us; that which restores to us the joy of his salvation; that which establisheth us with his free Spirit; and, lastly, that which delivers us from bloods, that David had great cause to say, and we no less than he, Deliver me from bloods and blood-guiltiness, O God, thou God of my salvation, and my tongue shall sing aloud of thy righteousness.

And now we may conceive a match, as it were, to be tried here between Blood and Repentance, which of them shall cry loudest and be soonest heard of God. Blood cries for vengeance,[10] and God is the God of vengeance;[11] Repentance

---

[1] John viii. 46: "Which of you convinceth me of sin?" [2] Heb. iii. 2, 5. [3] Heb. ii. 9. [4] Luke xxii. 44. [5] Matt. xxvii. 26. [6] Matt. xxvii. 29. [7] John xx. 25. [8] John xix. 34. [9] Matt. xxvi. 27: "Drink ye all of it." [10] Gen. iv. 10. [11] Rom. xii. 19.

cries for mercy, and God is the God of mercy;[1] and so they seem both upon equal terms yet; but if we mark the order of God's titles, we shall find his mercy to take [precedence] of his justice: *Misericordia superexaltat judicium* [mercy exalteth judgment],[2] and therefore Repentance which cries for mercy shall be heard before Blood which cries for justice. But if Repentance cannot get it with crying, she will at least with singing, for she never sung till now; and now she sings, My tongue shall sing aloud of thy righteousness,[3] where blood only cries but cannot sing; and seeing singing makes better music in God's ears than crying, Repentance shall be heard when Blood shall be put to silence. But how loud will the singing be, when not only Repentance sings, but Joy also, which is a loud singer, shall join in concert and sing with her; and if ever Joy sung, it will sing now, for what greater joy than for a bondman to be set at liberty? for a man condemned for blood, to be delivered from blood? And if no joy can be greater than this, then certainly no singing can be louder than that; but what this song is that Repentance and Joy join in comfort to sing—seeing the sweet singer of Israel[4] hath not vouchsafed to deliver himself—it is not for any man now living to deliver it; only we may conceive that Repentance's part is *de profundis* [out of the depths],[5] and that Joy's part is *in excelsis* [in the highest],[6] Repentance sings the Hosanna,[7] and Joy the Alleluia.[8]

But may we not wonder at David how he dares speak thus to God: Deliver me from blood, and my tongue shall sing of thy righteousness? as though he thought he might commit a wilful murder, and then have his pardon of God for a song; and what should his song be of?—of God's righteousness. But what righteousness is in this, to suffer a righteous person to be murdered, and then to set the murderer free? As much righteousness as this we may find in a Jew, who cried, Crucify Christ, and deliver Barabbas.[9] But, O my soul, forbear such thoughts, or rather tremble at such blasphemies; remember first, that this song is not for

---

[1] Ps. cxvi. 5: "Our God is merciful." [2] Vulg. "Superexaltat autem misericordia judicio"—"And mercy rejoiceth against judgment," Jas. ii. 13. [3] Ps. li. 14. [4] 2 Sam. xxiii. 1: "The sweet psalmist of Israel." [5] Ps. cxxx. 1. [6] Luke ii. 14. [7] Matt. xxi. 9, 15. [8] Rev. xix. 1, 3, 4, 6. [9] Matt. xxvii. 21, 22.

getting of pardon, but for giving of thanks; and what thanks so acceptable as that which is cheerfully spoken, and what spoken so cheerfully as that which is sung? And then consider what God's righteousness is. He saith himself, his ways are not as our ways,[1] and may not we as well say, his righteousness is not as our righteousness? Our righteousness is blood for blood, but God's righteousness may be a song for a murder. But then consider withal, what this song is, and how hard a thing it is to sing of God's righteousness; the angels have enough to do to sing it; it is their Alleluia; and seeing the singing this Alleluia is the chiefest service of an angel, what deserves he less than an angel's place that can sing of God's righteousness? And that we may see how transcendent a matter it is to do it, behold David here, a man far abler than any of us, yet finds himself not able so much as to open his lips towards it, but is fain to call to God for help: *O Lord, open thou my lips; and my mouth shall shew forth thy praise* [**ver. 15**]. Open them indeed, to bid Joab number the people,[2] and to entice Bathsheba to folly, I can; but to open them to sing of thy righteousness, and to show forth thy praise, I am utterly unable, unless thou vouchsafe to open them for me. Oh then, open thou my lips, O God, for else I shall be forced to break off abruptly, and after so many great favours received be fain to go my ways without so much as saying, I thank you. But it shall never be said of David that he is so unmannerly, so ungrateful. If thou but please to open my lips, for then, as I have sung this penitential Psalm for myself, so I will sing an encomiastical hymn [3] for thee, and this fiftieth Psalm,* as well as the fiftieth year, shall have its jubilee.[4] If thou open not my lips, neither Repentance will cry, nor Joy will sing, but both will be as dumb as the devil in the gospel;[5] but if thou open my lips, my mouth will turn organist, and I shall strive with the angels in singing their Alleluia. If I only open my lips, they will quickly

---

[1] Isa. lv. 8. [2] 2 Sam. xxiv. 1. [3] Hymn of praise. [4] Lev. xxv. 9. [5] Mark ix. 25: "*Thou* dumb and deaf spirit," etc.

* So reckoned by many of the ancients. [Author's note. This is done by the Septuagint, which joins in one Psalms ix. and x., and thus makes this Psalm l. instead of Psalm li.]

shut again, and there will not be a praise that is worthy of thee; but if thou open them, thou openest and no man shutteth,[1] and then I shall show forth thy praise to all generations. Thy praise, but for what? for thy washing and purging me, for thy creating in me a clean heart, and renewing a right spirit within me; for thy restoring to me the joy of thy salvation, and for establishing me with thy free spirit; that we may know it is no ordinary opening of lips that will serve, seeing it is not a single praise, but a whole troop of praises, that must come forth at once: I must praise thee for thy humility, that disdainest not to make me clean; I must praise thee for thy bounty, that deniest not to make me new; I must praise thee for thy patience, that attendest my repentance; I must praise thee for thy graciousness, that acceptest my repentance; and before all these, I must praise thee for thy mercy, that art willing; I must praise thee for thy power, that art able; I must praise thee for thy justice, that knowest why; I must praise thee for thy wisdom, that knowest how to forgive me my sins, and to deliver me from blood; but above all these I must praise thee for thy glory, that having made the sands of the sea, the stars of heaven, so innumerable, yet all of them put together are not counters enough to sum up thy praises.

And now I was thinking, what were fit to offer to God for all his loving-kindnesses he hath showed me;[2] and I thought upon sacrifices[3] [**ver. 16**], for they have sometimes been pleasing to him, and he hath oftentimes smelt a sweet odour from them;[4] but I considered that sacrifices were but shadows of things to come, and are not now in that grace they have been; for old things are past, and new are now come;[5] the shadows are gone, the substances are come in place; the bullocks that are to be sacrificed now, are our hearts; it were easier for me to give him bullocks for sacrifice than to give him my heart; but why should I offer him that he cares not for? my heart, I know, he cares for;

---

[1] Rev. iii. 7.   [2] Ps. cxvi. 12: "What shall I render unto the LORD *for* all his benefits toward me?"   [3] Ps. li. 16: "For thou desirest not sacrifice; else would I give *it*: thou delightest not in burnt offering."   [4] Gen. viii. 21: Exod. xxix. 18.
[5] Rev. xxi. 4, 5: "The former things are passed away. .... Behold, I make all things new."

and if it be broken, and offered up by penitence and contrition, it is the only sacrifice that now he delights in[1] [ver. 17].

But can we think God to be so indifferent that he will accept of a broken heart? Is a thing that is broken good for anything? Can we drink in a broken glass, or can we lean upon a broken staff? But though other things may be the worse for breaking, yet a heart is never at the best till it be broken; for till it be broken we cannot see what is in it; till it be broken, it cannot send forth its sweetest odour;[2] and therefore, though God love a whole heart in affection, yet he loves a broken heart in sacrifice. And no marvel, indeed, seeing it is even he himself that breaks it; for as nothing but goat's blood can break the adamant,[3] so nothing but the blood of our scapegoat, Christ Jesus, is able to break our adamantine hearts. Accept therefore, O God, my broken heart, which I offer thee with a whole heart, seeing thou canst neither except against it for being whole which is broken in sacrifice, nor except against it for being broken which is whole in affection.

But is not this to make God a cruel God, to make him delight in broken hearts, as though he took no joy but in our sorrowing, no pleasure but in our tormenting? It is true, indeed, God delights to be merciful; but yet he delights not to be merciful unjustly; and justly he cannot be merciful but where he finds repentance. And seeing repentance can never be without sorrowing, and such sorrow as even breaks the heart with sorrow, this makes the broken heart a pleasing sacrifice to God; because, as a just man's prayer ties up his hand, as it were, from doing of justice, so a sinner's repentance sets him at liberty for showing of mercy.

And now that I have prayed, and offered sacrifice for myself, shall I forget my mother Zion? For is not Zion the common mother of us all?[4] Shall I forget the glorious city Jerusalem, whereof I am a member and a citizen? Can I prosper if my Zion suffer? Can I be safe if Jerusalem be in

---

[1] Ps. li. 17: "The sacrifices of God *are* a broken spirit; a broken and a contrite heart, O God, thou wilt not despise."   [2] Mark xiv. 3.   [3] Diamond.   [4] Gal. iv. 26.

danger? O then, *Do good, O God, in thy good pleasure to Zion: build thou the walls of Jerusalem* [**ver. 18**]. But shall I put God to so mean a work to be a builder of walls? O glorious God! what fitter work for thy almighty power? For what is it to build the walls of Jerusalem but to defend Jerusalem from her enemies? And what arm of defence hath Jerusalem to trust to against the host of her enemies but thine only, O Lord, who art the Lord of Hosts? Thou hast indeed laid a sure foundation in Jerusalem;[1] but what is a foundation if there be no walls reared? A foundation is to build upon, and to what purpose if it be not built upon? and who is able to build upon it but thou, O God, the great builder of the world, who with thy only word didst build the world? What is a vineyard if it have no hedges to fence it? No more is Jerusalem, if it have no walls to defend it; for is it not subject to all sudden surprises? lies it not open to all hostile invasions? And so we should lose the end of Zion in the midst of Zion. For what is Zion but a sanctuary for sacrifices? and how can we offer thee the sacrifice of thanksgiving for our safety if we cannot offer our sacrifices in safety, and what safety if there be no walls to defend us? Oh, therefore, build thou the walls of Jerusalem, and then, as in thy good pleasure, thou hast done a pleasure to Zion, so thou shalt smell a sweet odour, and take pleasure in Zion; for we shall offer thee *the sacrifices of righteousness, with burnt offering*[2] [**ver. 19**], the offering of a true though imperfect righteousness, in the Jerusalem here below; and with *whole burnt offering*, the offering of a perfect righteousness, in the Jerusalem that is above; and we shall offer *bullocks upon thine altar*, sing our Alleluias upon that altar under which the saints lie now and sing their dirges; their dirge of How long, O Lord, holy and true,[3] shall be changed into songs of eternal jubilee; angels and men, Christ himself, and his members, shall all cast down their crowns before thee, that thou only mayest be All in all,[4] and that thine may be the

---

[1] Isa. xxviii. 16.   [2] Ps. li. 19: "Then shalt thou be pleased with the sacrifice of righteousness, with burnt offering and whole burnt offering; then shall they offer bullocks upon thine altar."   [3] Rev. vi. 10.   [4] 1 Cor. xv. 28.

kingdom, the power, and the glory, for ever and ever, Amen.[1]

And now that we have heard the penitent David make his confession, and say his orisons; seen him make his oblations, and offer his sacrifices to God, it may not be unfit to draw an observation or two from the manner of his liturgy; and first, that this whole Psalm hath in it throughout *bimembres sententias*, verses consisting of two parts, whereof the latter is ever an augmentation of the former, as when he saith, Wash me from mine iniquity; it follows, and cleanse me from my sins, which is more than washing, and so an augmentation. When he saith, I know mine iniquity, it follows, and my sin is ever before me, which is more than knowing his sin, and so an augmentation. When he saith, Against thee only have I sinned, it follows, I have done this evil in thy sight, which is more than sinning against him, and so an augmentation. When he saith, I was born in iniquity, it follows, and in sin hath my mother conceived me, which is more than to be born in sin, and so still an augmentation; as likewise in all the rest, if we run them over, which shows the great haste that David makes in his journey of repentance; and therefore takes two paces at one stride, and climbs, as it were, two stairs at one step.

A second observation may be, that almost all the Psalm through, but most apparently in the middle verses, one deprecates the evil, and the next following obsecrates[2] the good. One expresseth a detestation of his sins, and the next following an application of God's mercies, like a gardener that with one hand plucks up weeds and with the other plants sweet flowers. For in saying, Purge me from my sins, he deprecates the evil, and plucks up weeds; and in the next following, Make me to hear of joy and gladness, he obsecrates the good, and plants sweet flowers. In saying, Turn away thy face from my sins, he deprecates the evil, and plucks up weeds; and in the next following, Create in me a clean heart, he obsecrates the good, and plants sweet flowers. In saying, Cast me not off from thy

---

[1] Matt. vi. 13.   [2] Earnestly entreats.

presence, he deprecates the evil, and plucks up weeds; and in saying, Restore to me the joy of thy salvation, he obsecrates the good, and plants sweet flowers. And by this he seems, as it were, to besiege God round with his petitions, and to hold him fast with both hands as Jacob did the angel,[1] that he may leave him no way to escape, and be sure not to let him go without a blessing.

Another observation may be this, that in all this Psalm David arrogateth nothing to himself but sin and misery, lying wholly at God's mercy for the remission of his sins; and so far from any ability to satisfy for himself, that he acknowledgeth in himself an utter disability but to speak a good word, or but to think a good thought; and indeed we may truly say that all the spirits in the arteries, all the blood in the veins of this Psalm, are but blasts and drops of the anthem[2] in Christ's prayer: For thine is the kingdom, the power, and the glory, for ever and ever, Amen.

---

[1] Gen. xxxii. 26.   [2] Doxology.

www.ingramcontent.com/pod-product-compliance
Lightning Source LLC
Chambersburg PA
CBHW021344230426
43666CB00006B/408